The British Horse Society  Career Pathways

Complete Equestrian
Volume 3
Your companion for horse care, welfare, training, riding and coaching

KENILWORTH PRESS

Copyright © 2017, 2024 The British Horse Society

First published in the UK as Complete Horsemanship Volume 3,
in 2017 by Kenilworth Press, an imprint of Quiller Publishing Ltd

Reprinted 2019

British Library Cataloguing-in-Publication Data
A catalogue record for this book is available from the British Library

ISBN 978 1 910016 54 1 (paperback)
ISBN 978 1 910016 55 8 (e-book)

The right of The British Horse Society to be identified as the author of this work has been asserted in accordance with the Copyright, Design and Patent Act 1988.

The information in this book is true and complete to the best of our knowledge. All recommendations are made without any guarantee on the part of the Publisher, who also disclaims any liability incurred in connection with the use of this data or specific details.

All rights reserved. No part of this book may be reproduced or transmitted in any form or by any means, electronic or mechanical including photocopying, recording or by any information storage and retrieval system, without permission from the Publisher in writing.

Design by Becky Bowyer

Printed in China

Kenilworth Press
An imprint of Quiller Publishing Ltd
The Hill, Merrywalks, Stroud GL5 4EP
Tel: 01453 847800
Email: info@quillerbooks.com
Website: www.quillerpublishing.com

Complete Equestrian
Volume 3
Your companion for horse care, welfare, training, riding and coaching

Contents

ACKNOWLEDGEMENTS 6

INTRODUCTION 7

SECTION 1 HORSE CARE AND STABLE MANAGEMENT 11

    Chapter 1   Yard Management 13

    Chapter 2   Handling Difficult Behaviour 27

    Chapter 3   Horse Anatomy and Physiology 41

    Chapter 4   Conformation, the Foot and Shoeing 57

    Chapter 5   Common Health Conditions 87

    Chapter 6   Feeding 127

    Chapter 7   Fitness Training 153

    Chapter 8   Travelling Horses 169

    Chapter 9   Grassland Management 181

    Chapter 10 Tack and Equipment 189

    Chapter 11 Lungeing 215

SECTION 2 RIDING 225

    Chapter 12 Flatwork and Jumping 227

SECTION 3 COACHING 267

    Chapter 13 Towards More Advanced Coaching 269

WHAT'S NEXT? 319

Acknowledgements

The British Horse Society acknowledges with thanks permission to use the following images within this book, all of which are copyright of the individuals and organisation who kindly supplied them.

Chapter 3

Images courtesy of *Gillian Higgins*

Chapter 5

Images of symptoms of strangles; images of ringworm infecting human and horses. A horse with sweet itch. Lymphangitis in a hind leg. Courtesy of *Derek Knottenbelt*.
A pony showing a laminitic stance; pony with a distinctive thick, curly coat associated with Cushings. Courtesy of *Animal Health Trust*.

Chapter 6

A hay steamer. Courtesy of *Haygain*.
Alfalfa pellets. Courtesy of *Baileys Horse Feeds*.
Dengie's condition/fat scoring chart. Courtesy of *Dengie Horse Feeds*.
Spillers Feeds.

Chapter 7

Dr David Marlin provided assistance with this text.
Picture of canter work in a field courtesy of *iesportsmedia.com*.

Chapter 8

Areas to check on a horsebox or trailer before travelling. Courtesy of *Ifor Williams Trailers Ltd*.
A loading ramp. Courtesy of *Emma Bearman Photography*.

Chapter 9

Paddock sweeper. Courtesy of *Gurney Reeve & Co Ltd* manufacturer of Suton Sweepers.

Chapter 10

Picture of Taper Gauge. Courtesy of *International Society for Equitation Science* (ISES).

A saddle tree. Courtesy of *Nikki Newcomb SMS QSF, Bliss of London*.
Series of photographs of saddle cloths, numnahs and pads and individual photographs of cross-country boots and overreach boots. Courtesy of *Horse Health*.
Double bridle. Courtesy of *The Society of Master Saddlers*.

The British Horse Society also acknowledges with thanks the assistance of the following riding centres and their staff in the production of photographs for this book: *Wellington, Lyne House Livery, Pittern Hill Stables, Millfield, Brampton, Huntley, Summerfield Stables,* and *Warwickshire College*. Pictures throughout this publication supplied by *Tara Taylor, Jon Stroud Media* and *CHS Photography*.

Introduction

Introduction

Welcome to the *Complete Equestrian Volume 3* from The British Horse Society (BHS).

Within our third in a series of *Complete Equestrian* (previously *Complete Horsemanship*) books we provide a thorough insight to horse care and stable management, from understanding horse anatomy and physiology to introducing yard management. We discuss how to continue developing your flatwork and how to further improve your jumping technique, as well as an introduction to jumping cross-country obstacles. We also build further on the basics of lungeing a horse and coaching a rider.

What sets the BHS Career Pathways and our *Complete Equestrian* books apart from other education providers and books is our mission to put the welfare of the horse at the heart of everything that we do. We believe care and management are something that everyone who is passionate about horses should seek to learn. Our BHS 'Stages' qualifications encompasses horse care, welfare and management along with riding, training and coaching skills in order to create the complete equestrian coach. Our goal is to provide the knowledge that will help you work in harmony with a happy, healthy horse who is able to perform at the peak of their ability.

In Volume 3 you will find chapters on:

- Yard management.
- Reasons for and how to handle difficult horse behaviour.
- Horse anatomy and physiology — a deeper understanding.
- Assessing horse conformation and foot balance and the use of different types of shoes.
- Identifying, treating and preventing common health conditions.
- How nutritional intake can be affected by different types of work.
- How to develop a fitness programme.
- Care, and legal requirements, when travelling a horse.
- Effective grassland management.
- Selecting and assessing the fit of tack for dressage and jumping.
- Lungeing a horse to maintain training.
- Further developing flatwork to include lateral work.

- Developing jumping skills and introducing cross-country.

- Coaching — progressing the rider beyond the basics.

Beginning in 1947, the BHS pioneered the creation of a comprehensive system of equestrian education for the welfare of the horse. During the intervening years, we have continued to develop the BHS system with expertise from world-class professionals in equine science and equitation.

Today, the BHS education system is one of the best and most widely-respected in the world. The *Complete Equestrian* books support anyone wishing to enhance their knowledge, or to study qualifications in equine. There are a number of bespoke professional career pathways available, depending on your long-term goal. Whether it's becoming a successful groom or a stable manager, a professional rider or a specialist coach, there's a pathway to choose from.

Equestrian qualifications show potential employers of the skills you have accrued for a career with horses. BHS qualifications are internationally recognised, with some of the best coaches, riders and grooms coming through the Pathway, including BHS Fellow Yogi Breisner.

The BHS gives each individual the opportunity to gain qualifications and awards in their chosen profession. The qualifications have been specially developed through extensive consultation with the equine industry to incorporate the latest research and thinking, with current practices and friendly assessment methods.

Chapter 1
Yard Management

General responsibilities
Adherence to legal requirements
Employment rights
Summary

Yard Management

As your training progresses you may find you are given more responsibility for organising the general running of the yard under the guidance and support of a yard manager or senior supervisor. Your responsibilities are likely to be many and varied, depending on the type of yard and how the yard is run, and they may increase as you become more experienced. Some of the areas you might be given responsibility for at various levels are outlined in this chapter.

General responsibilities

Horse welfare

The welfare of the horse should be at the heart of everything you do. The Animal Welfare Act (England and Wales), Welfare of Animals Act (Northern Ireland) and Animal Health and Welfare (Scotland) Act states that it is the duty of the person responsible for an animal to ensure that the needs of the animal are met to the extent required by good practice. These needs include:

- Need for a suitable environment.
- Need for a suitable diet.
- Need to be able to exhibit normal behaviour patterns.
- Any need the animal has to be housed with, or apart from other animals.
- Need to be protected from pain, suffering, injury and disease.

As part of your daily duties you are responsible for ensuring all horses in your care have all their needs met.

Monitoring stock levels

The amount of storage available will dictate how much feed and bedding can be kept on a yard. For yards with limited space, restocking might have to be done weekly, whereas for yards with ample storage restocking may happen every few months. It is useful to have an understanding of approximately how long the stock you have should last, so more can be ordered in plenty of time.

A rough estimation can also help you work out if you are going through stock too quickly and if you need to investigate why it is happening.

The time of year and weather conditions will have an effect on how much feed and bedding are used. If the horses live out in the summer less will be used, therefore you need to beware of over-ordering feed that may spoil before you can use it. When new stock such as feed is ordered any existing stock should be checked for the use-by date and stored so that the bags with the shortest date are used first.

Facility maintenance

This is an ongoing job and is essential in order to keep the facilities in good repair and prolong their lifespan. It also helps to keep the yard safe, clean and tidy and create a professional image.

Create a rota of jobs that will need doing daily, weekly, monthly and yearly along with the routine tasks of running a yard, to help keep track of what needs doing and when. Some examples might include:

> *Daily*: sweeping out the feed room and tack room, harrowing the school, removing droppings from fields.
>
> *Weekly*: weeding, cleaning out the drains.
>
> *Monthly*: cleaning windows, de-cobwebbing stables.
>
> *Yearly*: painting, washing and disinfecting stables.

Depending on the size of the yard and the tools available to you, some of these tasks may be done more or less regularly. As well as planned maintenance there will be running repairs, such

It is useful to create a rota of jobs that need doing, such as harrowing the school; this may be a daily job if the arena is in regular use.

as broken fence posts, which should be dealt with promptly to prevent them becoming a more serious problem.

Supervising junior team members

No matter what your role in the business you should always endeavour to set a good example by following best practice procedures and working to a high standard. Take pride in every aspect of the job, from how you dress to your conduct around clients and staff. **This also includes the use of social media; remember everyone has access to this so be careful what you post and how it may be perceived by the wider public.**

A large part of working on a yard involves working together as a team, often with people who have a wide range in age and experience. For the team to run efficiently, roles and responsibilities should be discussed and clearly defined so that everyone understands what is expected of them. Rules of the yard and health and safety procedures should be made clear and followed by all members of staff at all times.

Get to know your team and find out about their motivation and aspirations for their careers to help identify potential training opportunities and ensure that all team members receive adequate support.

The smooth running of a yard relies on good communication between all team members. All instructions need to be clear and contain enough information to allow the task to be carried out successfully. Equally important is the ability to listen to feedback or concerns from other

As part of your role you may be required to deliver training to junior staff members.

team members. Regular team meetings and one-to-one sessions are a good way of creating an opportunity for staff to raise any potential issues or concerns.

It can be difficult to deal with a member of staff whose work is not up to standard. In the first instance, try to find out why the work is falling short of what is expected. There may be a lack of understanding of what is required, or perhaps they are lacking in confidence when it comes to working with a particular horse. It might be that a bit of extra support or training is required to prevent an issue from happening again. If you are concerned about a particular member of staff, seek support and guidance from your manager.

An essential skill of being a good supervisor is organisation. You need to ensure that everyone knows what they are doing and when. This could take the form of creating a daily list and allocating tasks amongst staff according to their experience, to ensure that they are carried out safely and efficiently. When allocating tasks, consider each person's level of fitness as well as their experience — remember it will take a person new to mucking out longer to complete a stable than a more experienced member of staff.

Adherence to legal requirements

The yard manager should be aware of all the legal requirements associated with the running of the yard, including employment law, and responsible for seeing that they are adhered to but you should develop an awareness of these issues, in your own interests and those of other staff and clients.

Equity, Diversity and Inclusion

The Equality Act 2010 legally protects people from discrimination in the workplace and also in wider society.

The Act covers nine protected characteristics:

- Age
- Disability
- Sex
- Sexual orientation
- Gender reassignment
- Race

- Religion or belief
- Marriage or civil partnership
- Pregnancy or maternity

If you feel you have been discriminated against or have witnessed discrimination speak to a senior member of staff. If you don't feel you can talk to your employer there are organisations you can contact for advice such as Citizens Advice or the Equality Advisory Support Service.

> **Equality** this means the fair treatment of everyone and creating equal possible outcomes for all.
>
> **Equity** recognises that each person has different circumstances and allocates the exact resources and opportunities needed to reach an equal outcome.
>
> **Diversity** is the mix of people.
>
> **Inclusion** can be described as the culture in which people can come to work and feel comfortable and confident to be themselves. An inclusive environment is one where everyone feels valued.
>
> **Discrimination** is treating someone unfairly because of who they are.

Health and safety policy

The Health and Safety at Work Act (1974) is the main piece of legislation you need to be aware of. It details the basic general duties that all employers and employees must follow. If there are five or more staff members it is a legal requirement to have a written Health and Safety Policy. However, although not actual employees, the number of volunteers in any workplace will also need to be included — for example two volunteers each helping for 2½ days a week would equate to one full-time employee.

The policy is designed to inform people about how to deal with health and safety issues that affect what you do and how you carry out your work. It is there to show the business's commitment to health and safety and to identify who has what responsibilities within your business. Most policies are split into three sections:

- The statement of general policy on health and safety at work sets out the business's commitment to managing health and safety effectively, and what it wants to achieve.

- The responsibility section sets out who is responsible for specific actions.

- The arrangements section contains the detail of what the business is going to do in practice to achieve the aims set out in its statement of health and safety policy.

A Health and Safety Policy doesn't have to be complicated or lengthy. There are templates and guidance available online to help you get started.

Health and safety and risk assessment

Both employers and employees have a responsibility towards health and safety in the workplace.

A big part of this for employers/supervisors is to carry out a risk assessment of all areas accessed by staff and visitors and activities that take place, and put in place relevant controls to help mitigate the risk. All staff must receive training and instruction in how to carry out tasks safely and how to follow the controls put in place, such as wearing PPE (Personal Protective Equipment).

All activities carried out, from mucking out to riding, will need to be risk-assessed. There is no set way of carrying out a risk assessment but it should include:

- The activity to be undertaken, for example, disinfecting stables.

- Identifying the potential hazard, for example chemicals.

- Who may be harmed by the activity, which could include employees, clients, or visitors.

- Evaluating the likelihood of an accident happening and the severity of the injury or damage, for example, spillage, inhalation of fumes.

- Identifying controls to put in place to minimise the risk, this could include steps such as wearing gloves and a face mask or roping off the area to keep people away.

- Recording your findings on the risk assessment.

- Reviewing regularly and updating if required.

There are several formulae that can be applied to evaluate the likelihood of an accident occurring and the potential severity of an injury. One is a scale of 1–3 and the other is on a scale of 1–5. Both methods will identify areas of high and low risk so preventative measures can be put in place to reduce or eliminate the risk.

There should be a risk assessment for all activities on the yard. Based on the risk assessment the yard will have a policy, for example, on the PPE that should be worn for turning out, and how many horses can be led by one person at a time.

Risk assessments should be available for anyone who asks to see them and should be reviewed and updated yearly with the date and/or version clearly displayed on each one.

Working with horses is a high-risk occupation and unfortunately, even with risk assessments in place, accidents and incidents do occur. If there is an accident, resulting in an injury, it is important that you follow the correct procedure and report it to the relevant authorities if necessary.

The Reporting of Injuries, Diseases or Dangerous Occurrences Regulations (RIDDOR)

These are the regulations that require employers to report and keep records of:

- Work-related accidents that cause death.

- Work-related accidents that cause certain serious injuries (reportable injuries).

- Diagnosed cases of industrial diseases.

- Certain dangerous occurrences (incidents with the potential to cause harm).

However, not all accidents need to be reported; this is only required when the accident is work-related and it results in an injury of a type that is reportable (details of which types of accidents are reportable can be found on the HSE website, www.hse.gov.org).

Types of reportable injury include:

- Deaths if these arise from a work-related accident.

- Specified injuries to workers:

    » Fractures other than to fingers, thumbs or toes.

    » Amputations.

    » Any injury leading to permanent loss or reduction of sight.

    » Any crush injury to the head or torso causing damage to the brain or internal organs.

    » Serious burns which cover more than ten per cent of the body or cause significant damage to the eyes, respiratory system or other vital organs.

    » Any scalping requiring hospital treatment.

    » Any loss of consciousness caused by head injury or asphyxia.

    » Any other injury arising from working in an enclosed space which leads to hypothermia or heat-induced illness that requires resuscitation or admittance to hospital for more than 24 hours.

- Over seven-day injuries to workers; where an employee is away from work or unable to perform their normal work duties for more than seven consecutive days.

You must keep a record of any accident, occupational disease or dangerous occurrence that requires reporting, or any other occupational incident that causes a worker to be away from work for more than three days. This can be recorded in the accident book.

Should you need to report an accident to RIDDOR it can be done online through the HSE website.

First aid provision

Health and Safety (First Aid) Regulations state that employers are required to have adequate provision for first aid in the workplace. It is advisable to have a number of trained first aiders who can be called upon in the event of an accident, and all staff should receive training on what to do in the event of an accident. Ideally all coaches should have an up-to-date first aid certificate and all accidents and incidents, no matter how minor, should be recorded.

Safeguarding

Any business that involves activities with children (under 18) or adults at risk is required to have measures in place to keep people safe. This includes protection from abuse or harm from things like bullying, neglect, or physical, emotional, or sexual abuse. There should be someone on every yard trained in safeguarding to whom you can report concerns.

Anyone who is working with children is required to have a criminal record check. The minimum age at which one can be applied is 16 years. There is usually a fee to pay and they can be applied for from:

1. The Disclosure and Barring Service (England and Wales).
2. Disclosure Scotland.
3. Access NI (Northern Ireland).
4. Garda Vetting (Republic of Ireland).

Fire regulations

Each part of the UK and Ireland has its own fire regulations, so make sure you are familiar with those relevant to you. In general, to comply with all fire regulations a preventative fire risk assessment of the premises should be carried out by a responsible person. The responsible

Each yard should have a fire risk assessment, and a specified fire procedure.

person has a duty to recommend and provide the general fire precautions to be taken in order to reduce the risk of fire. The risk assessment is undertaken in the same way as a normal risk assessment, but focusing on fire.

All means of escape (MoE) should be clearly marked and kept clear at all times, and all staff should be trained in what to do in the event of a fire. There should be clear fire procedure instructions placed around the yard, and the assembly points should be clearly marked.

Control of hazardous substances

Every potentially harmful substance used on a yard, such as veterinary medicines, cleaning materials, petrol, hoof oil, fly repellent, pest control chemicals, paint, fencing treatments should be recorded under the Control of Substances Hazardous to Health (COSHH) regulations. Hazard or data sheets should be available for each substance. These are usually available from the supplier, and give details on:

- The chemicals present.

- How someone might be exposed to them, for example, inhalation, absorption through the skin.

- Information on how the product should be handled, for example, anyone handling the product must wear gloves.

- How it should be stored, for example, locked in a container.

- Emergency measures to take in case of an accident.

Any substance that may cause harm should be stored safely in a locked cupboard or suitable container and the COSHH sheets should be kept with these substances. Staff should receive relevant training in how to use the products and be provided with any relevant PPE such as gloves or eye protection.

Data protection

Data Protection is an important element of working with clients, contractors and employees. The Data Protection Act controls how Personal Data is used by businesses or individuals acting in a professional capacity. You must be aware of the requirements and act appropriately. You must recognise whenever you collect/hold/use Personal Data and ensure that it is:

- Only the very minimum information that you need to carry out your service

- Accurate and up to date

- Accessible by the individual

- Kept safe and secure

- Kept for no longer than is necessary

- Only used for the purpose it was collected

- Handled according to the appropriate data protection regulations

The BHS has guidance and templates available for you to use to ensure you are compliant.

Employment rights

You should be aware of your employment rights, including contract of employment, National Minimum Wage or National Living Wage and hours of work regulations. If you have any queries, or junior staff members come to you with queries, the details below provide some useful points of contact:

The UK Government's website provides current information in relation to Government services, including employment rights and state benefits, www.direct.gov.uk.

Citizens Advice is an independent charity in the UK that gives free, confidential information and advice to help people with legal, consumer and other problems, www.citizensadvice.org.uk.

The Advisory, Conciliation and Arbitration Service (ACAS) provides information and advice for employers and employees on all aspects of workplace relations and employment law, www.acas.org.uk.

The Equality Advisory Support Service provides advice and assistance to individuals on issues relating to equality and human rights, www.equalityadvisoryservice.com.

The British Grooms Association is a professional body for people who work with horses. It is a social enterprise and is non-profit making. It brings together all who work hands on with horses offering support, dedicated career advice and promotes professionalism and good practice, www.britishgrooms.org.uk.

Summary

- At the core of everything you do you should consider each horse's welfare.

- The types of tasks you may be responsible for include ensuring the welfare of the horses and ponies, monitoring stock levels, facility maintenance and supervising junior team members.

- There are several areas of legislation you should be aware of. These include health and safety including risk assessments, RIDDOR, first aid provision, fire regulations, COSHH, safeguarding, equity, diversity and inclusion and data protection.

TRAINING TIPS

1. Read through your yard's health and safety policy and risk assessment so you are familiar with how these are produced and adhered to, and the types of activities that have been mentioned.

2. If you have the opportunity to attend a first aid course this is highly valuable, even if you are not the yard's designated first aider.

3. Similarly, attending a safeguarding course will provide you with useful information that you can be aware of when working with children (under 18s) and vulnerable adults.

4. For more information about safeguarding visit the BHS website.

Chapter 2
Handling Difficult Behaviour

Horses displaying stereotypical behaviour

Horses who are difficult to handle

Undesirable ridden behaviour

Summary

Handling Difficult Behaviour

To begin to understand some of the causes of undesirable behaviour in horses, we need to appreciate the difference between modern methods of keeping horses and the horse's natural environment. Before horses were domesticated by humans, they lived in herds for security from predators and roamed to find forage to eat, moving in search of new pasture when the area they were on was spent.

Faced with predators, the horse used flight as a defence. If outmanoeuvred by these predators, horses could resort for survival to fight options of rearing, spinning, kicking back, bucking and biting. We regard these actions as undesirable behaviour in our modern horses but it is easy to understand how and why a horse may revert to these behaviours if they feel frightened or threatened.

As horses are herd or group animals, they may become distressed if they are asked to live or work on their own. This helps us to understand behaviour such as napping when a ridden horse is asked to leave a group of others. Therefore, in training, horses need to be taught to behave in some ways that go against their natural instincts.

In particular, stabling a horse for long periods without access to grazing which may cause stress and anxiety and cause undesirable behaviour. This isolated and restricted environment works against the horse's instincts in two ways: it deprives them of companionship and their natural inclination to roam. Also, unless they have more or less ad lib access to forage, it will be unnatural for them as a trickle-feeder, thereby upsetting their natural digestive processes and causing further physical and mental stress.

Access to regular turnout is ideal for both the horse's psychological and physiological well-being.

In these circumstances it is easy to appreciate how undesirable behaviour may develop; this can include stereotypical behaviours such as box-walking, crib-biting, wind-sucking and weaving, as well as aggressive behaviour. These behaviours are described in detail in *Complete Equestrian Volume 2*.

Horses displaying stereotypical behaviour

Stereotypical behaviour can be defined as 'a repetitive pattern of behaviour with no obvious goal or function'. Stereotypical behaviour is rarely seen in animals in the wild and is only displayed by domesticated animals and wild animals in captivity. It often occurs as a result of an animal's living environment not meeting their psychological needs.

For some stereotypical behaviours there are products available on the market which provide a short-term solution. These include collars for wind-sucking and crib-biting and anti-weave grilles to prevent weaving. However, these products do not address the root cause of the horse's anxiety and can actually cause or exacerbate stress. Horses who display stereotypical behaviour should not be isolated from other horses. The best solution is to increase turnout and allow access to ad lib forage.

Carefully introducing enrichment activities can reduce stress and anxiety for some horses. However some horses may find enrichment activities overwhelming which can increase their levels of stress therefore all enrichment activities should be introduced gradually and the horse's response monitored carefully.

Turnout provides exercise for the horse, including an opportunity to let off steam if they feel the need to do so and display natural behaviours which is important for a horse's physical and mental well-being. Horses who are deprived of sufficient exercise or turnout may be more lively or bolshy when ridden and handled and, in more severe cases, they may show aggressive behaviour. As well as considering access to turnout it is also useful to consider the horse's diet. Many horses cope fine on a high-fibre diet with little or no cereals. If cereals are required they should be introduced gradually.

If there is limited turnout it is essential that horses have sufficient forage when they are stabled. In the wild horses graze for up to 16 hours a day, hence domesticated horses have a natural desire to chew. If they are prevented from performing this function it can lead to anxiety and upset digestive function. To make hay or haylage rations last longer, you can provide it in a small-holed net or use products to slow down the rate of consumption such as a hay ball. In addition to this you can carefully introduce stable enrichment such as treat balls, licks, mirrors or stable toys to help keep a horse stimulated. If you are introducing food enrichment it should be included as part of the horse's balanced diet.

To help correct any type of undesirable behaviour it is necessary to consider why the horse is behaving in a particular way. As mentioned, this can be linked to the horse's natural instincts.

With regard to handling horses it is important to work with the horse to build a partnership. The horse is often behaving in a certain way because they are in pain, not coping with their environment or do not understand what is being asked of them. In order to resolve the behavioural issue we have to make changes so the horse is able to improve. All training should be conducted in a calm, clear and consistent way, following the principles of learning theory and ethology appropriately.

> **Learning theory** helps to provide principles of training and explains how positive and negative reinforcement work in establishing responses from the horse. Negative reinforcement is where something is 'taken away' when a horse displays a desired behaviour — for example, your leg is applied and when the horse moves forward the leg pressure is removed, which reinforces the behaviour. Positive reinforcement is where something is 'added', for example a treat is given when the desired behaviour is shown.
>
> **Ethology** is the scientific and objective study of animal behaviour, usually with a focus on behaviour under natural conditions.

Horses who are difficult to handle

Aggressive behaviour

It is crucial to be prepared to take precautions when dealing with difficult or aggressive horses. If you can, approach the horse from the side to make sure they see you. It is not a good idea to approach a horse directly from behind in case they don't see you and kick out in self-defence.

Fit a headcollar as soon as you can and tie up a difficult horse with a slightly shorter lead rope to reduce their opportunities to swing round or bite you as you work around them. If you are picking out a hind foot or handling a hind leg make sure you talk to the horse and run your hand over their quarters first so the horse knows where you are and you avoid surprising them. Ask someone else with sufficient knowledge to hold up a foreleg to make handling a hind leg safer if you are having difficulties.

Some fine-coated or sensitive horses display signs of aggression when being groomed as they may connect this with a previous harsh or uncomfortable experience, and may bite and/or kick as a defence. If you are gentle and use softer brushes, or even a stable rubber, rather than hard brushes, this may help the situation. In such circumstances, while you do need to take care, it is worth remembering that some horses are very sensitive/ticklish and the apparent aggression may be a reaction simply to the sensation, rather than to you in person.

Sometimes a horse may have had their tack put on roughly and had the girth tightened too quickly and may react by snapping, biting or kicking. Try and reassure them by being patient and tightening the girth slowly one hole at a time, pausing in between. This reaction can also be pain related, for example caused by gastric ulcers or tack that does not fit. Your first action should always be to investigate why the horse is reacting in this way and to eliminate pain as a potential cause.

It is sensible to leave horses alone to enjoy their bucket feed in peace, as some horses may display aggressive behaviour at feed times and may well bite or kick to 'protect' their feed.

Difficulty arising from fear, pain, or confusion

A horse has only a certain number of responses in their 'flight or fight or freeze' armoury, so, although these underlying triggers are different from aggression, responses may seem superficially similar. While you, as handler, must therefore be very careful in dealing with a horse's reaction to fear, pain or confusion, it is useful for the long term if you are able to distinguish it from real aggression and respond appropriately.

Pain can make horses difficult to handle, for example, an ill-fitting saddle causing back pain may trigger biting when being tacked up or bucking when ridden. The key is to locate the source of the pain and deal with it to eliminate it and hopefully resolve the undesirable behaviour. It is advisable to get a vet to check the horse over if there is a sudden change in behaviour to rule out any pain or illness.

With horses showing fear, confidence needs to be gained through calm, reassuring, patient handling. Gradual exposure to frightening sights and sounds in company with horses used to them is needed for scenarios like clapping, fireworks, heavy traffic, water and ditches. Bad past experiences can also generate fear, such as an accident in a lorry.

Poor training may also lead to undesirable behaviour. If training or handling is not clear and consistent, horses do not learn the responses we want. The horse is more likely to do what we want, if they anticipate a reward (for example, a reward of feed when caught). Therefore our training needs to be based upon consistent actions and rewards. When a horse is stressed or anxious they are unlikely to have the capacity to learn.

Methods of restraint

It is always best to try to resolve difficult behaviour by understanding the cause, and working in partnership with the horse to tackle the issue. However, there are some circumstances where methods of restraint can be used to provide the handler with more control and make the situation safer. In these situations you should follow the Least Intrusive and Minimally Adverse (LIMA) principles by starting with the mildest method of restraint required to maintain control of the horse in the situation. The LIMA principle focuses on ensuring the welfare of the horse by minimising unpleasant experiences caused by using strong methods of restraint where they are not required. For safety, you should always wear protective headgear, gloves and suitable footwear when handling difficult horses.

Headcollar and lead rope

For most horses, in normal everyday situations, a headcollar and lead rope will be sufficient for the handler to be able to control the horse. The headcollar should be correctly fitted with all the buckles securely fastened and the clip on the rope pointing away from their face. However, there may be times when you require a slightly stronger method of restraint, for example if you are holding a horse for veterinary treatment, dealing with a horse who is strong to lead, or loading a horse on to a lorry or trailer.

Control headcollars

Control headcollars are available in various designs but all work on a pressure and release system. If the horse pulls against the lead rope, pressure is applied on the horse's nose, when the horse stops pulling the pressure is released.

To ensure pressure is exerted in the correct place it is essential the control headcollar is correctly fitted. To ensure this method of restraint doesn't cause stress to the horse the handler must be precise with the timing of the pressure and release.

Lunge line and bridle

If a horse is strong when being held or led, a bridle can be used instead of a headcollar to provide more control to the handler. The horse can either be led by the reins, or the reins can be twisted and secured and a lunge line or lead rope can be attached to a short lead rein coupling that is clipped on to both bit rings. This will make the action on the bit rings more even. Be careful if threading the lunge line or lead rope through the bit rings and under the chin, as it acts like a curb chain and can make the horse raise their head, tightening the line even more. Leading the horse using a lunge line provides extra length with which to control them.

Chifney

If a horse is likely to rear when being led in hand or handled, a Chifney is a useful deterrent. It is a light steel ring with a U-shaped mouthpiece that is slipped into the horse's mouth and held there with a leather headpiece that goes over the horse's poll. It must be used in conjunction with a headcollar, and a lunge line or lead rope is attached to the ring under the horse's lower jaw and through the headcollar ring. If the horse tries to barge away from you, or to rear, the U-shape of the Chifney presses on the horse's tongue, thereby restraining them. Consequently the Chifney is effective in restraining a horse who is difficult to lead into or out of the field, to load, or to handle. However, before resorting to a Chifney, first check whether a bridle, instead of a headcollar, is sufficient restraint. Horses must not be tied up up directly from a Chifney as if they pull back they can easily break their jaw.

2 | Handling Difficult Behaviour

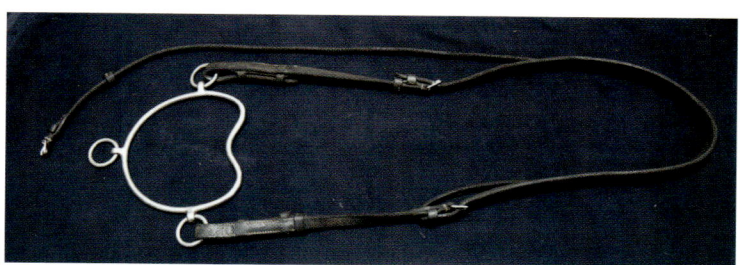

A Chifney attached to a headpiece. The U-shaped mouthpiece goes in the horse's mouth and the lead rope attaches to the ring at the bottom.

Situations when restraint may be needed

Leading a difficult horse into a field

Select the method of restraint you feel is appropriate and wear PPE. A helper to open and close gates makes it easier with impatient or difficult horses. Lead the horse through the gateway and far enough into the field to avoid being trapped between the gate and the horse if they kick out. Turn the horse to face the gate before you release them, so that they would have to swing round before galloping away, giving you time to move away. However, if at this point you offer a treat as soon as the horse is facing the gate, you can use this positive reinforcement technique to distract the horse long enough to have a better chance of letting them go safely before they pull away. If used consistently, the use of positive reinforcement training can change this undesirable behaviour as the horse learns to wait for the treat before moving off.

> *Positive reinforcement* means adding something to encourage a specific behaviour. This could be treats, clicks, scratches or praise.
>
> Positive reinforcement training means using a reward to encourage desired behaviours. The horse is rewarded as soon as they display the desired behaviour and learns (through repetition) to repeat the behaviour.

If you choose to use a Chifney to lead the horse into the field, and the horse were to pull away suddenly from you in the gateway and stand on the lead rope, there is the potential for serious injury to the horse's jaw. Likewise, if the horse were to break free when led out with a lunge line, the line could wind around their legs, causing a potentially dangerous situation. Therefore, in instances where a horse is known to pull away at the gateway to the field, you may choose to use a slip rope with a leather headcollar so the rope will fall off in the field if the horse gets away. If a horse is likely to be difficult to catch, it may in any case be easier to leave a correctly fitted leather headcollar or field-safe headcollar on the horse in the field.

Holding a horse for treatment

If you are holding a horse for treatment, you will find that some horses may well be more difficult than others, particularly if they are injured and/or in pain. Make sure that you wear protective headgear, gloves and sturdy, non-slip footwear. If you know the horse, use the methods of restraint that you know are usually effective for them. If you don't know the horse, it is wise to have several methods of restraint nearby, such as a control headcollar or a bridle, should the need arise. Ensure that the area is safe for all handlers and the horse. If in a stable, check that, if the horse rears, they will not hit their head on the rafters. Always position yourself on the same side of the horse as the vet, who will tell you if they need you to stand somewhere different. That way, if the horse swings to one side or tries to kick, you can quickly move their head towards you and thus move the quarters away from you both. Stand the horse where there is enough room for the vet to move safely around them if required. If the treatment is taking place only on one side of the horse you might find it easier to keep the horse still if you position them next to a wall so they can't step sideways. Sometimes distracting or reassuring a horse with feed will keep them quieter and more likely to stand still.

For a horse who requires treatment on a hind limb, lifting a forelimb on the same side can be an effective way of preventing them from kicking out. Stand close to the horse's shoulder,

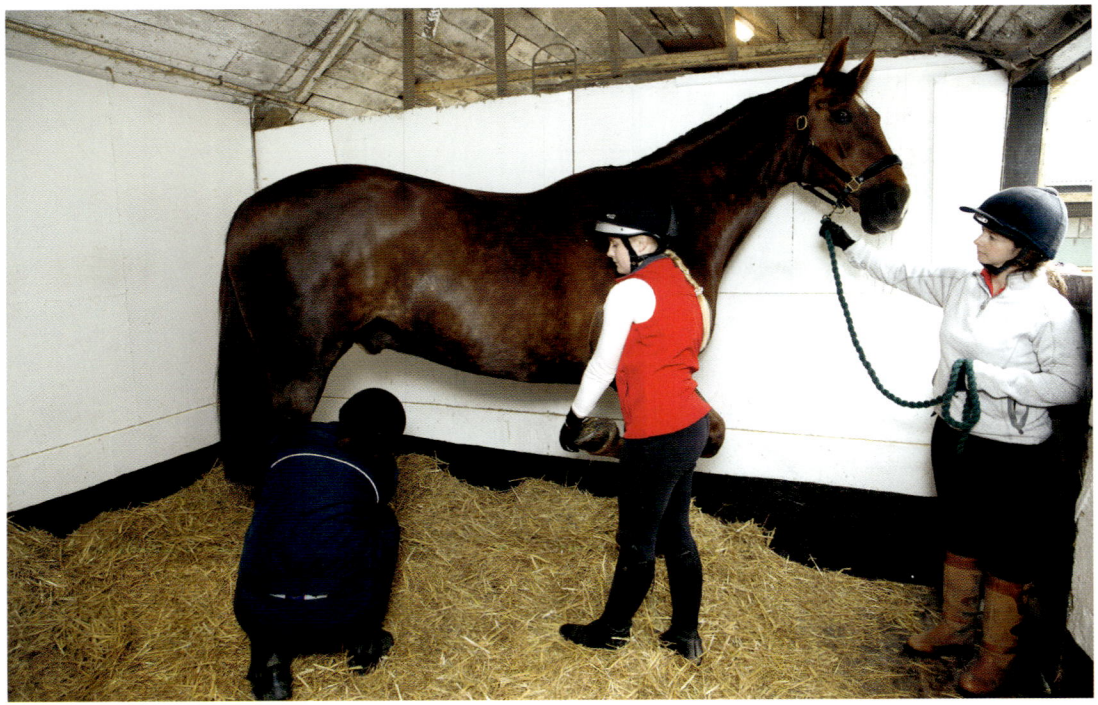

Lifting the foreleg on the same side can be an effective way of stopping the horse from kicking out while the hind limb is examined.

facing the tail and pick up the leg, making sure that you bend your knees and keep your back straight. Warn the person giving the treatment if you need to put the leg down.

Introducing a horse to clipping

Carefully introducing a horse to being clipped can make the difference between a trouble-free or stressful experience for horse and handler going forward. Time and effort should be put in when first introducing the horse to being clipped to ensure the horse has a positive experience.

If the horse has never been clipped before, a good place to start is by introducing them to the noise of the clippers. Stand a short distance away from the stable and switch the clippers on monitoring the horse's reaction. If the horse shows little or no reaction you can gradually move closer to the stable door with the clippers still running. Rewarding the horse with a treat (positive reinforcement) for standing still will help the horse to associate the clippers with something they like. If the horse reacts move further away from the stable again so the noise is quieter until they settle. You may have to repeat this over several days until the horse is relaxed and confident with the noise. If the horse shows no signs of stress you can progress to standing next to them with the clippers running.

If the horse is relaxed with this, try placing them near to a quiet experienced horse being clipped (such as in a neighbouring stable) and watch how the horse reacts.

Once the horse is comfortable with the noise of the clippers you can start to introduce the feel of them. Have an experienced handler holding the horse somewhere safe such as the stable who can reassure and reward the horse as required. Small battery operated clippers tend to be quieter and give off less vibrations, making them ideal to use. You and the handler should wear protective equipment (PPE) as described in the section above.

With the clippers turned off hold them against the horse's shoulder (rewarding the horse for standing still) and then progress to running the clippers over the horse's body. If the horse is accepting of this, the next step is to introduce the feel of the clippers when they are running.

Switch the clippers on and place your hand on the horse's shoulder. Place the clippers on the back of your hand so that the horse can feel the vibrations through your hand. Be aware that switching the clippers on near the horse can cause them to jump so practice this beforehand.

If the horse is standing still and not reacting, start to slowly run your hand over a wider area. Once the horse is comfortable with this take your hand away and place the clippers directly onto the horse's shoulder. If they move away, try to stay with them so they don't learn that moving results in the clippers being removed. Gradually move the clippers all over the horse's body (without clipping any hair) until the horse is comfortable with the feeling.

If at any point the horse appears stressed or uncomfortable with what you are doing, go back a step or even two and gradually build up the horse's confidence again. Some horses will accept the clippers quickly, but others may take several sessions.

Once the horse is confident with the noise and movement of the clippers you can try clipping a small patch of hair off their shoulder. Be aware the horse may react to the hair falling off so make sure you are in a safe position. For a first clip it is sensible to start with a small bib or trace clip and build up to taking more off over several sessions.

General precautions when clipping

When clipping the hind legs, holding on to the tail may reduce the risk of the horse kicking and enables you to feel what the horse is doing, potentially warning of kicking out sooner. Horses can be sensitive around the stifle, flank and the girth area, so make sure that you are positioned safely, close to the horse, and pay attention to their body language. When clipping around the horse's elbow and between the forelegs ask your assistant to lift a forelimb and pull it forward to tighten the looser skin around this area so you are less likely to nick the horse. You could also ask your assistant to lift a foreleg as a method of restraint while you are clipping around any sensitive areas.

Some horses will react strongly to being clipped. This may be as a result of a previous bad experience, or a severe dislike of the sound or feel of the clippers. While the best option is to continually work with the horse to help them gain confidence, there is often a necessity to clip a horse, especially if they are in medium or hard work and likely to sweat during exercise. In this situation a vet can be called to sedate the horse.

Although they may appear very drowsy and wobbly on their feet, it is unusual for a sedated horse to fall over. Extra care should be taken when working around a sedated horse as they can still react unpredictably and are very capable of kicking out with no warning. Other side effects can include sudden twitching or throwing their head up. The horse will lower their head towards the floor to help them balance, so you will need an assistant to lift the horse's head up when you are ready to clip this area. Sedated horses tend to sweat quickly, so clip the areas where the sweat glands are first.

Undesirable ridden behaviour

Some of the triggers for undesirable ridden behaviour, such as pain, may be the same as those mentioned earlier in the context of undesirable behaviour when handling. For example, jumping on hard ground may trigger limb and foot pain and uncharacteristic refusing at fences; a sore mouth is likely to lead to contact issues and perhaps rearing.

Rearing

In the wild, rearing is used as an effective fight mechanism. By going up in the air on their hind legs, the horse keeps their head safe from predators and can come down hard on predators with their forelimbs in order to inflict injury. The horse's first method of defence is to flee, but in situations where a horse is unable to do this they may resort to rearing. If a horse is asked to go past something that frightens them, for example flapping polythene, and the rider prevents the horse from fleeing from the situation, the horse may rear to avoid going near it. A ridden horse may also rear to avoid leaving the security of a group of other horses, for example, in the collecting ring or a showing line. In training, a horse may rear because they feel unable to cope with what is being asked of them and rearing acts as an escape mechanism, for example, if, in rein-back, the rider's hands become strong and uncomfortable and the horse wants to free themselves from this pressure. Similarly, with any other sudden, unexpected or jarring rein action the horse could react instinctively by leaping upon their hind legs. Pain, therefore, can also be a trigger for rearing.

The danger is that, with the weight of a rider on their back, the horse can overbalance and go over backwards, injuring both themselves and the rider. It is important that rearing does not become a learnt behaviour with the horse using it as an evasion to avoid working.

If a horse you are riding is threatening to rear, try to keep them moving forward actively as it is more difficult for the horse to rear when going forward. It is better still if you can keep the horse actively forward on a circle or figure of eight. If the horse does start to go up in the air on their hind legs, use one rein to turn their head and neck to one side to try to limit the height of the rear. However, if you can't, you need to lean forward to keep your balance; this also helps to prevent increasing backward rein pressure, which could unbalance the horse.

Rearing can happen for a variety of reasons.

Bucking or plunging

This can be triggered by high spirits, or a desire to escape pain. When a horse bucks, keep your shoulders back and body upright so that the action of the hind legs does not throw you forward out of balance. Use both reins to keep the horse's head up, as horses can buck higher with their heads down. It is also more difficult for a horse to buck if you keep them moving forward and encourage them to bend laterally, for example, on a circle. Ensure to have their saddle fit checked by a qualified saddle fitter as soon as possible to eliminate pain as a potential cause. If no concerns with saddle fit are found, contact your vet and arrange for the horse to be checked.

Shying or spinning

Try to deal with shying or spinning by keeping a horse's attention on you, contained between your leg and hand. To forestall potential shying, turn the horse's head away from the frightening object and use your leg on the opposite side from the object, to encourage them forward and past it. Some horses may like time to look at a strange object and then be better about passing it, however this must only be allowed in appropriate circumstances when it is safe to do so — it may not be appropriate to do this on a road. In an arena, try to keep the horse moving forward on a constant circle, bending them away from what is frightening them, then, if and when they start to relax and gain confidence, gradually bringing your circle nearer to the frightening object until the horse is going past it without resistance. If a horse is an habitual shyer, it is worth having their eyesight checked.

Sensible precautions with ridden horses

If a horse you ride is known to kick, consider fastening a red ribbon (carefully) around their tail when riding in company to warn other riders. (If you see a horse is wearing a green ribbon, this usually means that they are a young horse, and alerts other riders to the fact that they may be unpredictable.) If you know the horse is likely to kick when in a group or warm-up area at a competition, try to stay a safe distance away from other horses — although this can be difficult in a crowded arena! You may need to warn people who come too close.

Horses will also follow the lead of others. If one horse absconds and bucks on a hack, others are likely to follow suit. If you always gallop at the same place each time on a hack, the horse will soon learn this behaviour through repetition and always anticipate galloping at that spot.

> As mentioned earlier the best way to resolve behavioural issues is to work in partnership with the horse using calm and consistent handling methods so that they gain confidence in given situations. In situations where problems are more severe, or your handling methods are not improving a horse's behaviour, it is advisable to seek professional help from a more experienced person, or to consider contacting an equine behaviourist registered with The Animal Behaviour and Training Council (ABTC).

Summary

- Behaviour is very much influenced by the horse's lifestyle as a herd animal and by their natural instincts.

- Undesirable behaviour can often be triggered by long periods of inactivity in stables without enough forage.

- Follow the LIMA principle when considering suitable methods of restraint for a horse and be mindful of how horses learn.

- Fear, pain, learnt responses and poor training can trigger undesirable behaviour.

- Undesirable ridden behaviour is often based upon how the horse would defend themselves in their natural environment.

TRAINING TIPS

1. Offer to assist or observe vets during their visits.

2. Offer to hold horses or assist with clipping.

3. Observe experienced handlers around horses — note how they position themselves and react to what the horse is doing.

4. For more information about horse behaviour visit the BHS website.

Chapter 3

Horse Anatomy and Physiology

The components and function of the respiratory system

The components and function of the cardiovascular system

The anatomy of the lower leg and foot

Summary

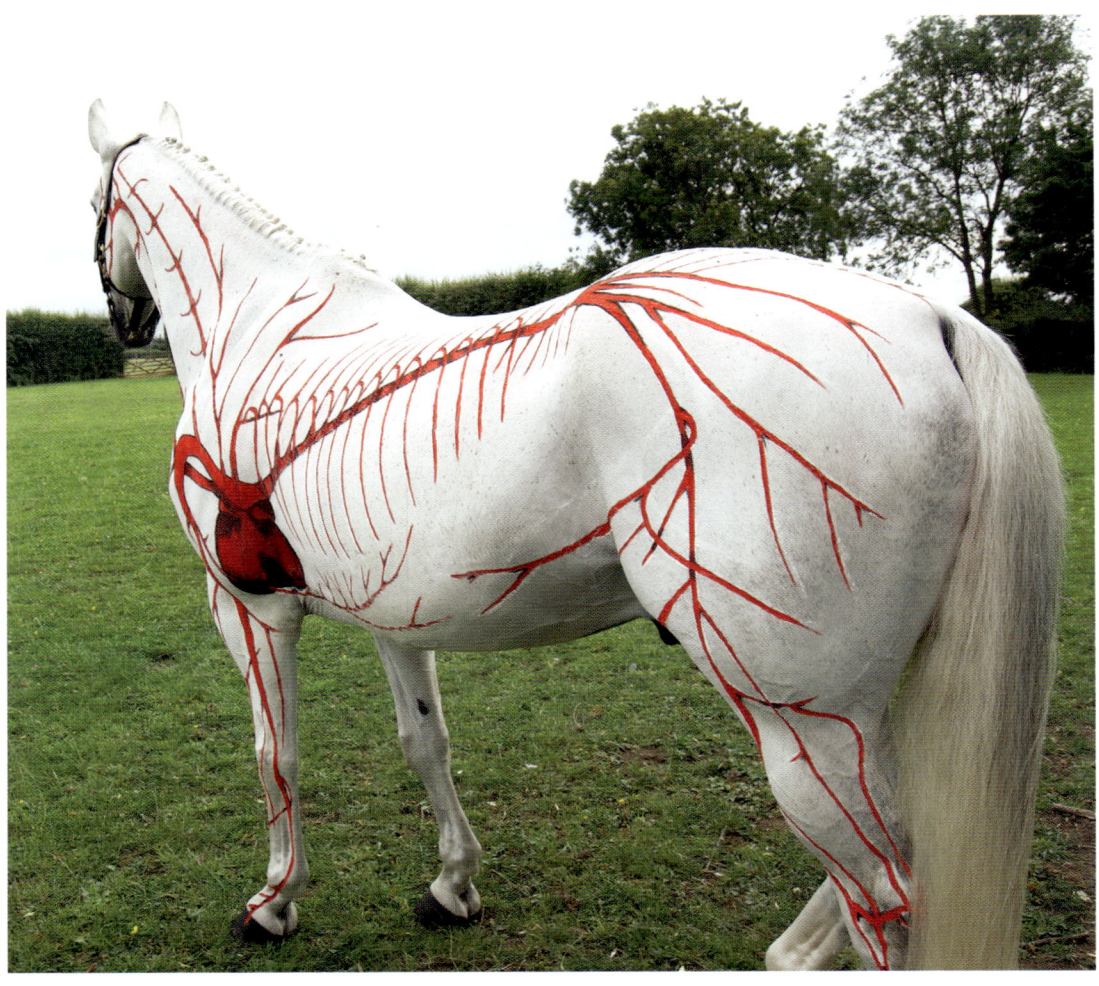

Anatomy is the branch of science that describes how animals are built. Physiology describes how they function. (Photo: Gillian Higgins).

Anatomy, which studies 'form', and physiology, which studies 'function', are closely related subjects that explain exactly how the eleven systems of the horse work in conjunction with each other. Understanding how the systems work is an essential component when working with horses. It helps us to improve performance, manage horses more effectively, train more sympathetically, reduce the risk of injury and spot when things go wrong. The systems are:

1. Inaugumentary (skin).

2. Skeletal.

3. Muscular.

4. Digestive.

5. Respiratory.

6. Cardiovascular.

7. Lymphatic.

8. Nervous.

9. Endocrine (hormones).

10. Urinary.

11. Reproductive.

In this chapter you will be learning how to explain:

- The components and function of the respiratory system.

- The components and function of the cardiovascular system.

- The anatomy of the lower leg and foot.

The components and function of the respiratory system

- The components of the upper respiratory tract are the nostrils, nasal passages, sinuses and larynx.

- The components of the lower respiratory tract are the trachea (windpipe), lungs and diaphragm.

Some facts about the respiratory system

- The respiratory system works closely with the cardiovascular system.

- Respiration is the act of inhaling and exhaling air.

- The main function of the respiratory system is gaseous exchange. This refers to the process of oxygen and carbon dioxide moving between the lungs and blood.

- Oxygen is essential for life and for the body to produce energy.

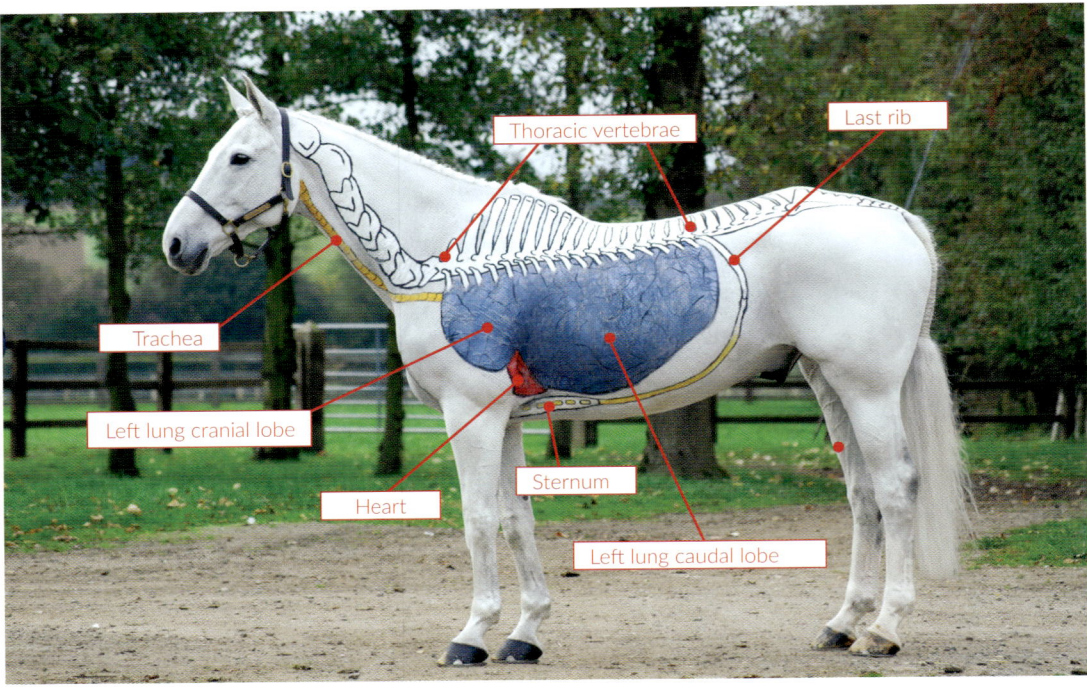

The main function of the respiratory system is to take oxygen into the lungs where it is transferred to the blood and circulated around the body by the circulatory system. Carbon dioxide is then taken from the body, delivered to the lungs and exhaled. (Photo: Gillian Higgins).

- The horse inhales, bringing oxygen into the lungs. This is then absorbed into the blood, pumped around the body by the heart, returned to the lungs and exhaled as carbon dioxide.

- The oxygenated air is drawn into the lungs through the trachea.

The upper respiratory tract

The nasal passages are connected to the trachea by the pharynx and larynx, which control airflow to the lungs. The larynx also houses the vocal cords, which allow the horse to whinny and neigh.

3 | Horse Anatomy and Physiology

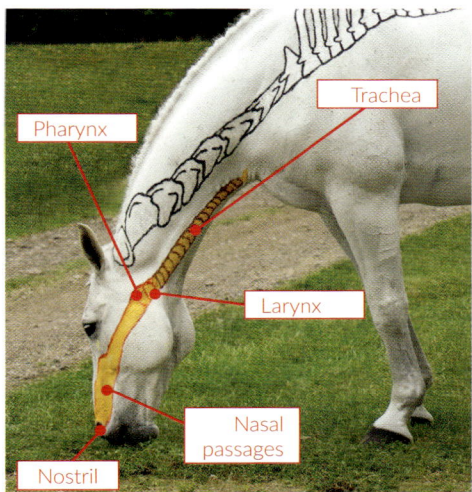

As the horse breathes in, oxygenated air is drawn into the nasal passages through the nostrils. (Horses cannot breathe through the mouth). The nasal passages are lined with a moist mucus membrane and thousands of tiny hairs called cilia. These remove dust, filter and clean the air. (Photo: David Higgins).

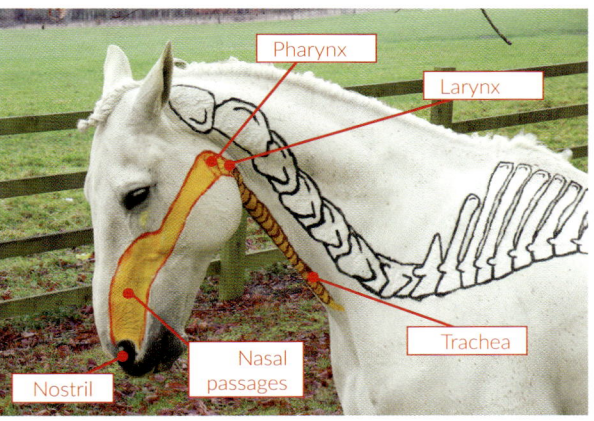

In a flexed neck outline the diameter of the pharynx is reduced. We could not run a marathon with our head on our chest! (Photo: David Higgins, taken from Horse Anatomy for Performance by Gillian Higgins).

The lower respiratory tract

The trachea

You can feel the trachea (windpipe) running along the underside of the horse's neck. It is held open by between fifty and sixty rings of cartilage and can be up to a 1m (3ft 3in) long. It is marked on the preceding photo. The trachea branches into two bronchi just above the heart. One branch leads to each lung.

The lungs

The two lungs sit comfortably within the thorax (chest cavity) encased within the ribs, sternum, spine and diaphragm. The left lung is smaller than the right to make room for the heart. The inside of the ribs and the outer surfaces of the lungs are covered with a slippery membrane called the pleura. The lungs are also lubricated with a slippery substance called the pleural fluid. This allows the lungs to expand and contract as the horse breathes.

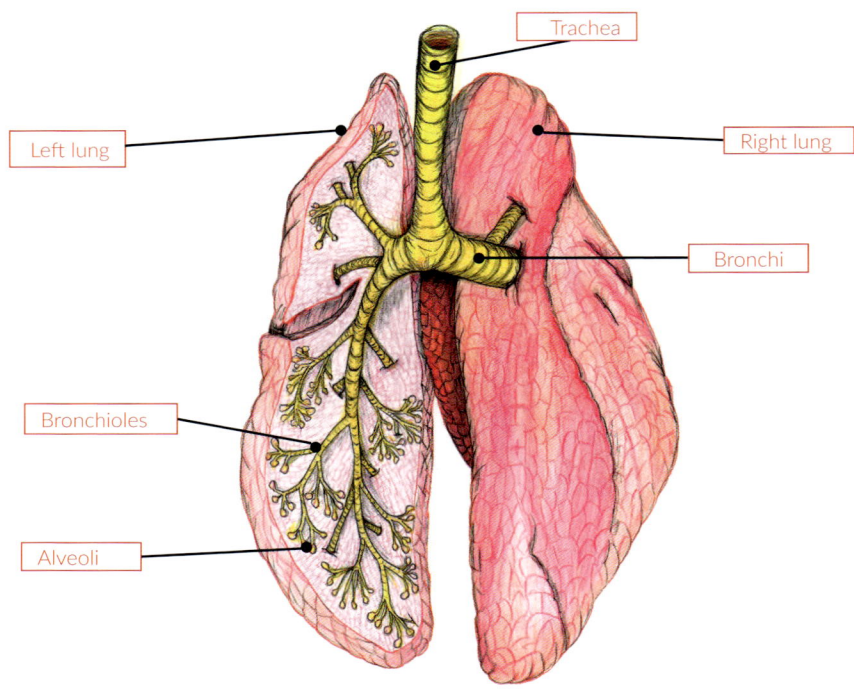

Once inside the lungs, the bronchi continue to divide and subdivide (rather like the branches of a tree). The smallest branches, of which there are thousands, are about the size of a hair and end in small air sacs called alveoli. The air sacs are covered in minute hairs. (Illustration: Gillian Higgins).

Gaseous exchange

Gaseous exchange occurs within the alveoli. This refers to oxygen and carbon dioxide moving between the alveoli and the blood.

When the horse breathes in, air floods into the lungs and makes its way to the alveoli. Here the oxygen passes through the thin walls of the alveoli and into the capillaries surrounding them. The oxygen-rich blood is transported to the heart, which then distributes it to the tissues around the body. At the tissues, oxygen from the blood is exchanged for carbon dioxide (a waste product). The carbon dioxide then moves in the opposite direction, and is transported via the heart back to the lungs to be exhaled.

The components and function of the cardiovascular system

A healthy cardiovascular system enables the horse to be energetic, strong and full of life. (Photo: David Higgins).

The main function of the circulatory system is to circulate blood containing nutrients and oxygen to the vital organs and tissues and then to transport carbon dioxide and waste products away to the lungs. The system consists of the blood, arteries, veins and heart.

Blood

Blood is the body's transport system. Bright red oxygenated blood is carried away from the heart in arteries whilst darker red deoxygenated blood is carried back to the heart in veins. The constituents of the blood are carried in a watery yellow liquid called plasma.

- Red blood cells give blood its colour and carry oxygen to the cells.

- White blood cells are part of the immune system. They help to clean the blood and fight bacteria and viruses.

- Platelets are the cells that clot the blood and stop bleeding.

- Fats, carbohydrates, proteins, chemicals and hormones are also carried in the blood.

Blood also plays a part in regulating temperature. The horse's core temperature range is 37.5–38.5°C (99.5–101.3°F).

The heart

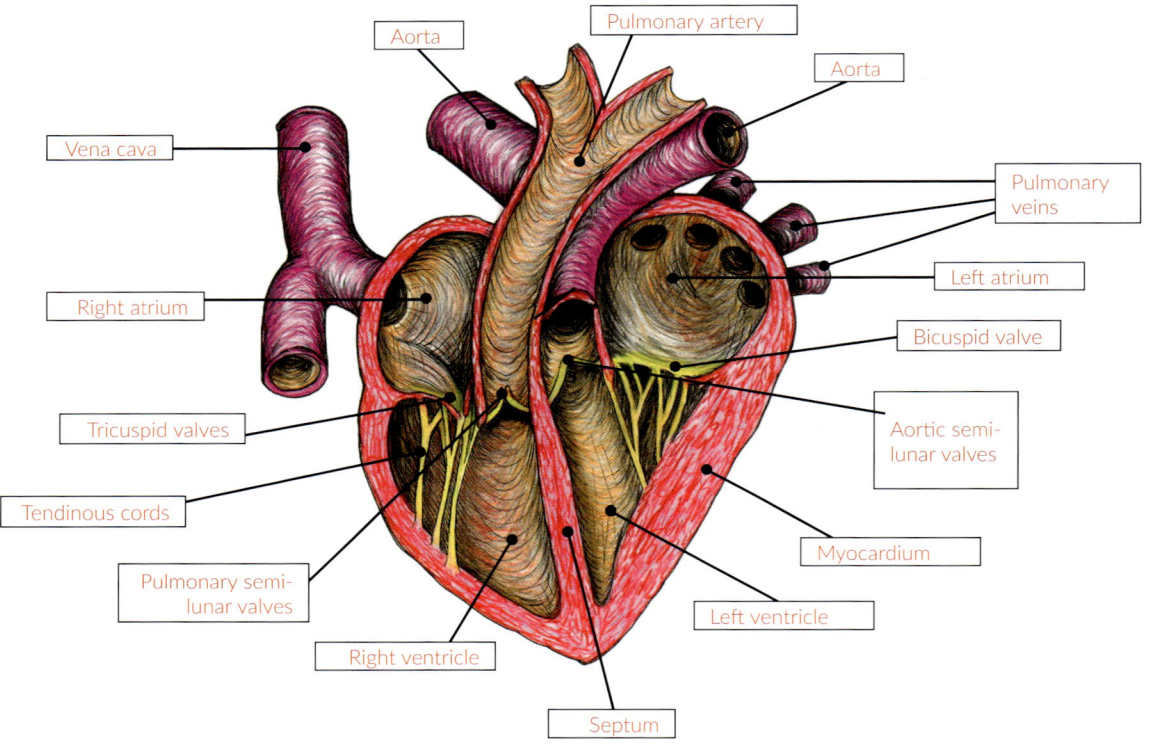

The heart works as follows. Oxygen-rich blood flows from the lungs through the pulmonary veins to the left atrium of the heart. The blood is then squeezed through a valve to the left ventricle from where it is pumped to the rest of the body via the aorta. Simultaneously, deoxygenated blood from the body enters the heart through the right atrium. It then flows into the right ventricle. It is then pumped to the lungs via the pulmonary artery where it receives fresh oxygen.

3 | Horse Anatomy and Physiology

How the heart functions. (These two images taken from Horses Inside Out Anatomy Poster Book Volume 2: The Internal Organs *by Gillian Higgins).*

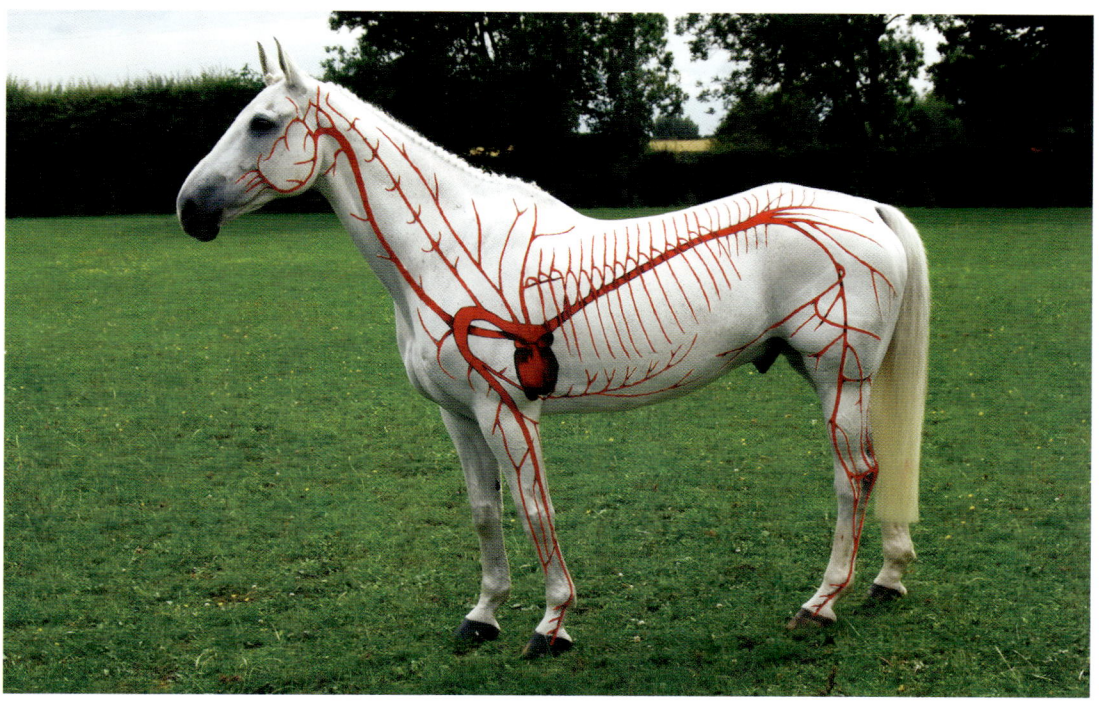

Arteries

Arteries form a branching system that carries bright red oxygenated blood away from the heart and around the body. The pulmonary artery is an exception to this rule. It carries deoxygenated blood from the heart to the lungs.

- The aorta takes blood from the left ventricle of the heart. It is the largest artery in the body.

- If an artery is cut the blood spurts out at the same rate as the pulse.

Veins

Veins form part of the branching system that transports deoxygenated blood high in carbon dioxide and waste products back to the heart. This blood is darker in colour within the veins. If a vein is cut the escaping blood will be bright red because as soon as it contacts the air it will oxygenate. However, differently from arterial blood, it will not pulse.

Pulmonary veins are large blood vessels that receive oxygenated blood from the lungs and drain into the left atrium of the heart. There are four pulmonary veins, (two from each lung) bringing oxygenated blood from the lungs to the left atrium of the heart.

Capillaries

As arteries and veins become smaller they are renamed capillaries. Oxygen and carbon dioxide are exchanged in the smallest capillaries, which are furthest from the heart.

The anatomy of the lower leg and foot

The lower leg and foot are part of the appendicular skeleton. It is a complicated arrangement of bones, joints, tendons and ligaments. The lower limb is the first part of the anatomy to absorb concussion.

Some definitions

Joints

- Are the point at which two or more bones meet.

- Are held in place by a complicated arrangement of muscles, tendons and ligaments.

- Allow movement.

3 | Horse Anatomy and Physiology

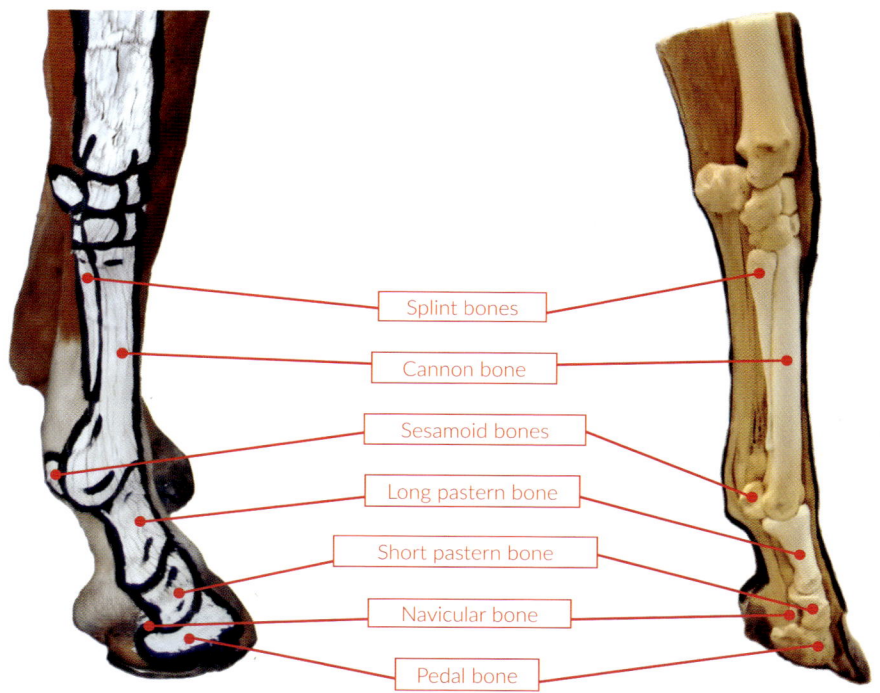

The bones of the lower legs are the same in the fore and hind limbs. They consist of the cannon and splint bones, the long and short pasterns, two sesamoid bones, the navicular bone and the pedal bone, which is sometimes called the coffin bone. The cannon bone is a strong, weight-bearing long bone. The splint bones are evolutionary remnants of what would have been the horse's equivalent of human first and ring fingers. (Photos: Gillian Higgins).

Tendons

- Are bands of strong fibrous tissue that join muscle to bone.

- Have a point of origin, which is the parent muscle, and a point of insertion into the bone. In the limb the tendons are an extension of the parent muscles located above the knee/hock.

Tendons in the lower limbs are either:

- Flexors, which flex the lower limb joints. These run down the back of the leg and are attached to parent muscles, which lie above the knee/hock and behind ulna/tibia.

- Extensors, which straighten the lower limb joints. These lie in front of the cannon bone and are attached to parent muscles, which lie above the knee/hock and in front of the radius/tibia.

Tendons of the lower limb

Because there are no muscles below the knee, all movement of the pastern and foot is controlled by the muscles in the upper limbs via the tendons. The tendons of the lower limb are long and subject to enormous forces. Healthy tendons are well defined and feel firm.

The main tendons of the lower limb, which can be seen in the diagram, are:

- The deep digital flexor tendon (DDFT).

- The superficial digital flexor tendon (SDFT).

- The common digital extensor tendon (CDET).

- The lateral digital extensor tendon (LDET).

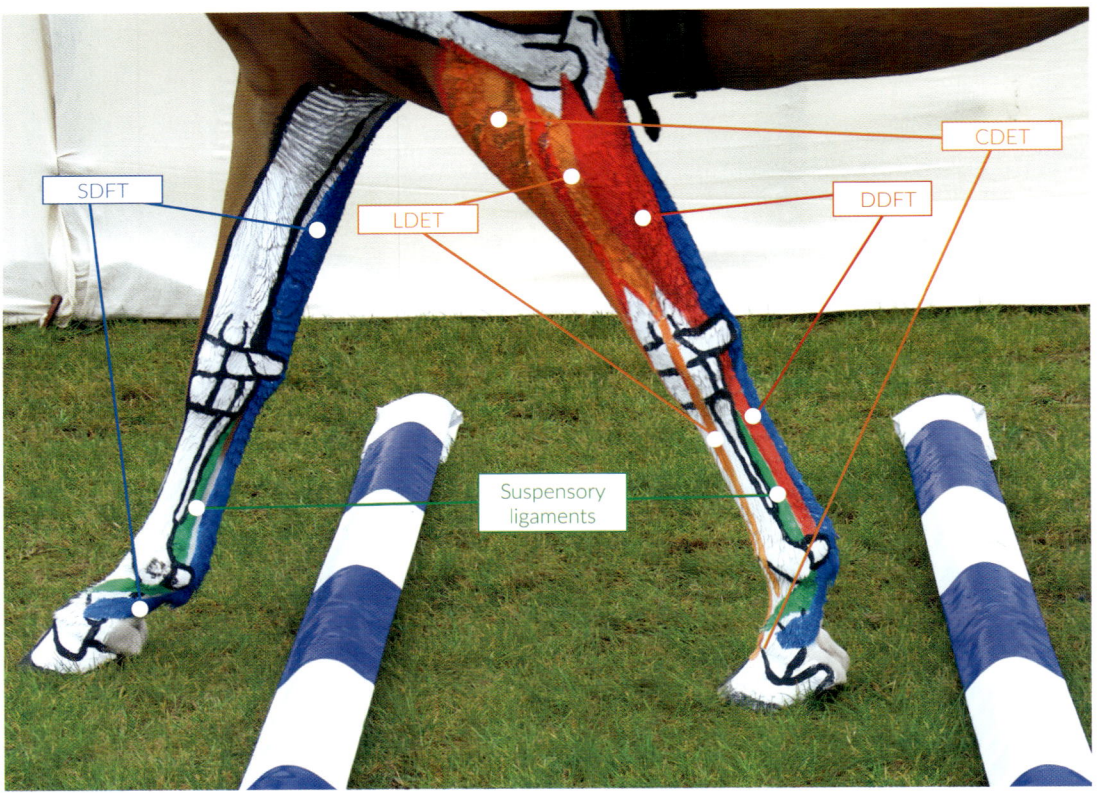

The muscles and tendons represented in red and blue are responsible for flexing the lower limb joints. The muscles and tendons represented in orange extend the lower limb joints. (Photo: Gillian Higgins).

Ligaments of the lower limb

Ligaments are bands of strong fibrous tissue that join bone to bone.

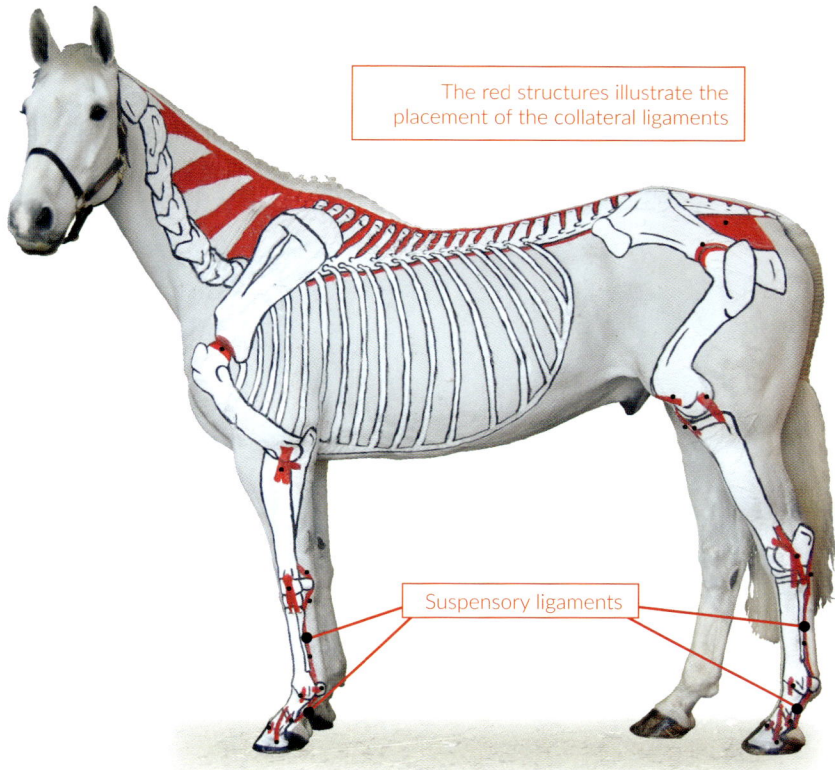

Ligaments of the lower limb.

Most ligaments within the lower limb are collateral ligaments. Their function is to unite the bones and stabilise the joint. Collateral ligaments are made up of pairs of ligaments that typically occur on the inside (medial side) and outside (lateral side) of hinge joints.

The suspensory ligament

The suspensory ligament is very different from all other ligaments in the lower limb. It lies between the digital flexor tendon and the bone. When the horse is standing, it feels very hard and is often mistaken for bone. This is an atypical ligament in its make up as it is more elastic than most. It plays a major role in support of the fetlock and, during movement, stretch and recoil of this ligament contributes to fetlock flexion.

The foot

The foot is enormously, complex, strong and resilient. A healthy hoof is crucial for soundness and, as much lameness comes from the foot, understanding its anatomy can help avoid problems.

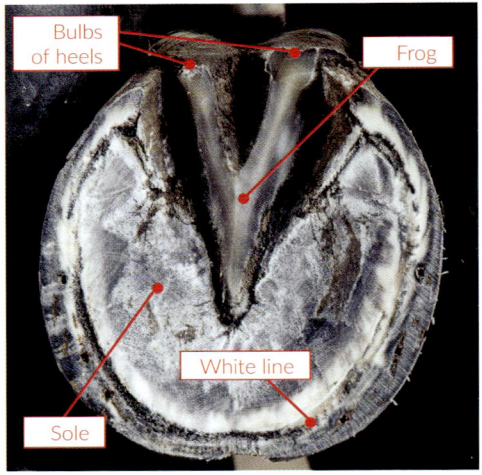 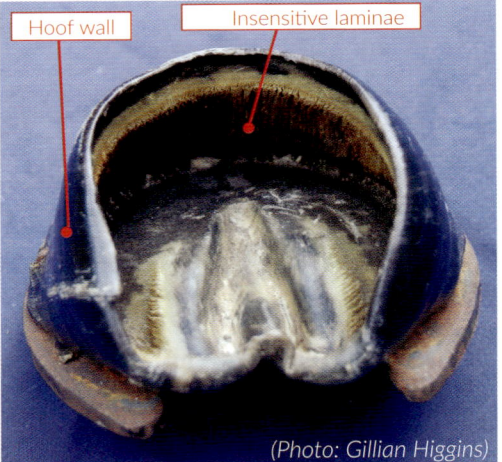

The outside of the hoof has a wall, sole and frog. These encase and protect the sensitive internal structures. The hoof wall itself has no blood supply and can be compared to our fingernails.

The main functions of the hoof are to:

- Provide a strong weight-bearing surface that is not easily worn away.

- Protect the sensitive internal structures.

- Maintain moisture.

- Provide grip.

- Absorb concussion.

- The sole should be firm and slightly concave.

- The white line joins the sole to the inner wall.

- The bulbs of the heel, together with the large digital cushion are important for absorbing concussion.

- The pedal and navicular bones lie deep within the hoof.

- The deep digital flexor tendon runs through a groove in the navicular bone then attaches into the pedal bone.

- The hoof grows downward from the coronary band.

- The sensitive and insensitive laminae hold the hoof wall to the coffin bone.

- The sensitive laminae are filled with nerves and blood vessels that help support the horse's lower leg and hoof. (Laminitis is an extremely painful inflammatory condition of the laminae.)

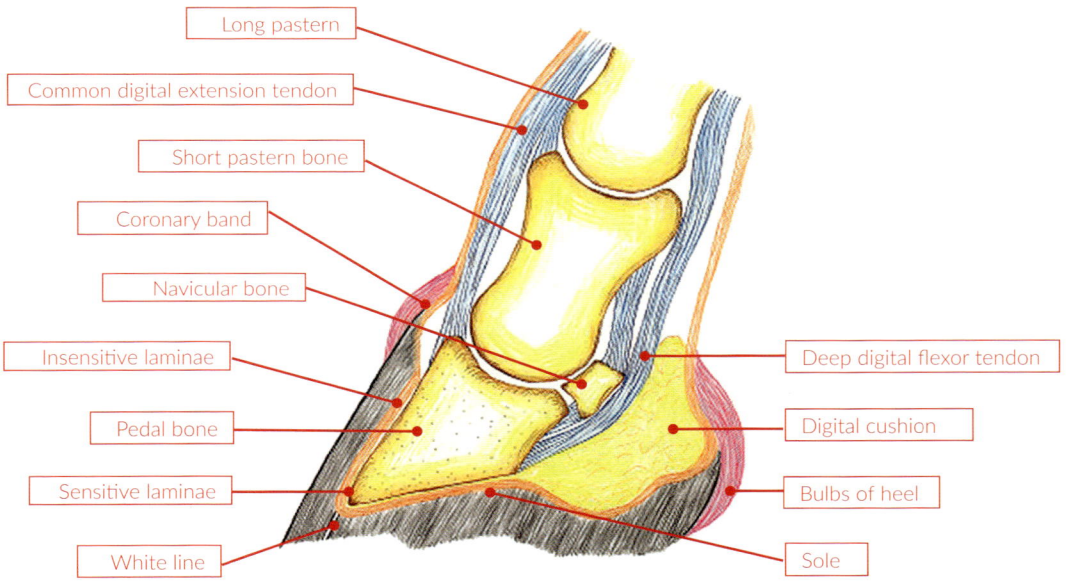

Cross-section of hoof and pastern.

Summary

- The main function of the respiratory system is to take oxygen into the lungs, where it is transferred to the blood and circulated around the body by the circulatory system. Carbon dioxide is then taken from the body, delivered to the lungs and exhaled.

- The main function of the circulatory system is to circulate blood containing nutrients and oxygen to the vital organs and tissues and then to transport carbon dioxide and waste products away to the lungs. It consists of the blood, arteries, veins and heart.

- The lower leg and foot are part of the appendicular skeleton.

- The bones of the lower legs are the same in the fore and hind limbs.

- Tendons are bands of strong fibrous tissue that join muscle to bone.

- Ligaments are bands of strong fibrous tissue that join bone to bone.

TRAINING TIPS

1. Try to feel for the position of the tendons and splint bones in the lower legs; lifting the horse's leg can make it easier to feel.

2. Practise identifying the location and function of each part of the respiratory and circulatory systems on the horse.

3. Observe and record the respiration rate of the same horse at rest, halfway through a riding session and at the end of a ridden session and compare how the rate changes.

This section has been written by Gillian Higgins, Anatomist, Sports and Remedial Therapist, Anatomical Artist, BHS Senior Coach and Author. If you have enjoyed this fascinating introduction to anatomy and physiology just visit www.horsesinsideout.com to look at the bookshop and the 'what's on?' page.

Chapter 4

Conformation, the Foot and Shoeing

Conformation defined

How to assess conformation

Conformation piece by piece

Foot balance and shoeing

Summary

Conformation defined

Put simply, this term applies to the overall outline or make and shape of a horse. As we know, horses and ponies come in all shapes and sizes and some aspects of conformation depend upon the breed and type of the horse. There are many pictures of what would be considered a good-looking or ideal horse and we need to be able to relate this to the work that we ask the horse to do. In particular it's important to be able to recognise positive and not so ideal aspects, and how they might influence the comfort of both horse and rider and the horse's potential for work when ridden.

Practice makes perfect when learning to assess conformation accurately. Although the skeleton will dictate the shape of a horse it is the length of the differing bones, angles of joints and the proportions involved that influence how this all affects the overall balance of a horse. Add to this the effort of carrying a rider then, depending upon many factors such as what we are asking the horse to do, the horse's ability to balance can be affected even more. General wear and tear upon soft tissues and joints will probably be greater on a horse with poor conformation.

Horses are remarkable in their ability to cope and adapt with the work demands we have placed upon them over the years, whether the work is ridden, driving or ploughing. Well-proportioned horses will find it easier to maintain their balance when working which, in turn, will lessen the risk of lameness and potentially have a longer, more successful working life.

The conformation of a horse is hereditary. Breed and type of horse can influence the conformation so it's useful to consider what job the horse is expected to do. Certain breeds of horse have particular ideal shapes or traits that breeders welcome and are helpful in enhancing performance and allowing the horse to work and stay sound. An example would be that a Thoroughbred will have differing ideal conformation from a draught horse with regards to length of neck and back, as they have very differing ways of travelling over the ground.

Many horses do not have perfect conformation, or may have a mixture of 'ideal aspects' and 'not so good aspects' but are still able to have purposeful working lives. Most people will know of a horse whose shape is far from ideal but has proved to be successful at competitions. When this happens it is likely that the correct level of care, attention and in some cases, adaptation to workload or how the horse is shod or trimmed, has been given to managing that individual horse.

How to assess conformation

As stated earlier, this is a skill that develops the more you do it. Having a system to follow helps as it's very easy to quickly form an opinion without allowing yourself time to really view the horse, which risks you missing something. Different people will have their own approach to assessing a horse that works for them, so asking to shadow a knowledgeable and experienced person such as a showing judge or vet could help you.

To assess a horse we need to be objective and see the horse at rest and then view how the horse moves.

Assessing static conformation

This is when we view the horse stationary and at rest, relaxed but standing square. Ideally we see the horse in an area that has flat ground and that will enable us to move around the horse safely, giving sufficient room to step back and gain an overview of their initial outline. Being able to view the horse from all sides will let you start to consider the following points.

Breed and type

- Can you tell what breed the horse is? They might be a mixture of breeds.

- Is there anything you see that is specific to a breed type?

- Start to consider the proportions, for example the size of the hindquarters in relation to the forehand — do they look as though they belong to the same horse?

- Can this help with considering the job the horse could do?

Condition

- Remember that muscle tone and condition can alter depending upon whether the horse is in work or soft condition.

- Is there any tone to the muscle and is it developed correctly? For example, is neck muscle all on the underside of the neck?

- Does the horse have any topline?

- Look for any blemishes or injuries as these might be related to how the horse moves; consider that they may be related to condition if a horse is very weak or poor.

Skeleton

- View proportions — for example, does the head look too big compared to the rest of the body, or does the back look very long compared to the rest of the horse?

- What does the middle of the horse look like? How well positioned are the ribs?

- Consider joints and angles of bones — for example, does the shoulder slope at a similar angle to the pastern? The ideal would be approximately 45 degrees with a line horizontal to the ground.

- Consider the straightness of the legs from side view, front and rear. Any crookedness may affect weight-bearing, which could encourage unsoundness.

- Does the pastern look very long or too upright and from the side does it slope at a similar angle to the shoulder and the hoof?

Feet

- Look at size and shape of the hooves, are the forefeet a pair and the hind feet a pair?

- Do the toes naturally point towards the front, or turn either in or out?

- Consider whether the horse has been shod or not, and whether this has affected the shape.

- Look for uneven wear on shoe or foot; this may indicate issues with movement.

- Is the hoof/pastern axis (see later this chapter) on both forefeet similar?

Assessing dynamic conformation

This is when we look at the horse being led in hand in both walk and trot to assess how well they move. Remember, this is normally done after assessing the static conformation whereby the natural stance of the horse, in terms of both straightness and proportions, is looked at.

Be careful that you don't let this static assessment overly influence your initial thoughts about how the horse moves. It is important to be objective when looking at the horse in action. It's also worth bearing in mind that if you found any injuries or old scars on the legs when you assessed the static conformation, these might be related to the action of the horse. An example could be a horse with signs of excessive brushing or rub marks to the inside of the fetlock area on the hind legs. They may have conformation faults that have influenced this, such as being very 'narrow behind', which means both hind legs being close together.

Where possible, try to see the horse being led in a suitable area, for example on a hard surface that is level, where there is room to turn the horse safely. Check that the horse is being led by someone competent to do so. They need to be able to lead the horse safely, especially if they need to be led up more than once for, as we know, some horses may either get excited being trotted up several times or become reluctant to move. To gain an accurate assessment it is important that the horse is active when being led and that the person leading them does not

4 | Conformation, the Foot and Shoeing

When assessing dynamic conformation the horse should be walked and trotted on a firm, level surface. This horse is being trotted up in a bridle to ensure that the handler has sufficient control.

hold on so tightly that they restrict the movement, or do the opposite and end up dragging the horse behind them!

Stand in a position from where you are able to observe the horse from the side, the rear and also from the front. Initially view the horse in walk, looking for an overview of just how easily they move. Consider that, although you are looking primarily at how the horse moves, when we look at horses we should always be looking out for subtle lameness. Remember that how the horse moves may affect their ability to stay sound. Having viewed the movement in walk, then look in trot as some faults in action show themselves more in one gait than another.

What to look for when assessing movement

- General movement — is there any abnormal movement that might raise concerns about soundness?

- When seeing a horse move, their tail should be relaxed and not clamped down or held out to the side at an odd angle.

- Sound of footfall — is it regular and even? Do you hear a shoe drag on the concrete?

- Straightness — does the horse move easily in a straight line? Do the feet follow lines similar to those of a straight train track?

- Stride length — do strides appear equal in the ground they cover? Do the hind feet meet, follow or land in front of the prints left by the forefeet?

- Limb action — are there any signs of this not being straight, such as dishing or plaiting?

- Placement of feet on the ground — is it even, or do the feet twist and does this relate to uneven wear on a particular foot, or on a pair?

- How does the horse move through the turn?

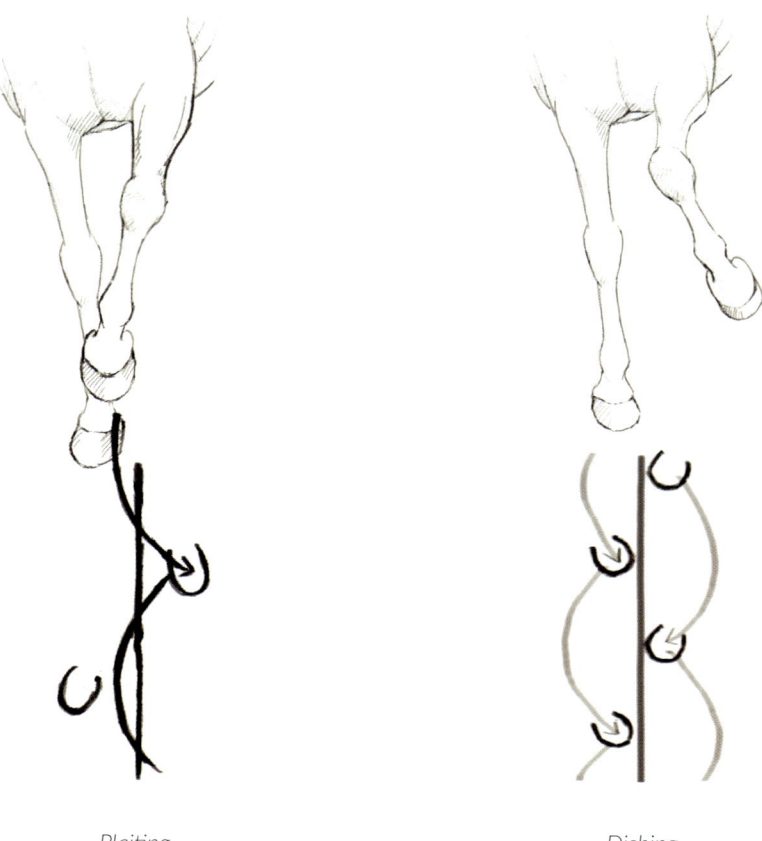

Plaiting.   *Dishing.*

Conformation piece by piece

Having assessed the horse in halt and then how they move should give you some information from which you can start to piece together an opinion upon conformation. If you struggle, try comparing it to a jigsaw. As we know, having only one piece of a jigsaw is of little use, but as you start to gather more pieces a picture starts to build.

Head

There are a number of features to take note of.

Profile. Overall the sideways profile of the head may be linked to the breed. For example, the Arab is renowned for having a concave appearance, known as having a 'dished face'.

Dished face.

Roman nose.

Forehead. This should be broad and flat, which helps allow for good side positioning of the eyes, important for allowing clear peripheral vision — remember the horse's need in the wild.

Ears. The length of the ears is mainly a cosmetic factor. However, the various positioning of the ears, along with the horse's facial expression, will tell us a fair amount about the horse's temperament at any given time.

Eyes. You've possibly heard of a horse having a 'kind eye' which suggests a kind temperament. This would be a large, clear eye, whereas it is thought that a small eye, similar to the eye of a pig, suggests an untrustworthy temperament. Consider the colour of the eye, for example, a horse lacking pigment can cause the eye to have a lot of white or blue, which is sometimes referred to as a 'wall eye'. This would be something that would cause questions about suitability for some showing classes.

Nostrils. Ideally these should be large to help with the increased intake of air that galloping work might require.

Mouth. Look at this to check whether the jaws meet correctly, and also check how deep or shallow the distance from the corner of the lips downwards is. Both of these need assessing as they may affect management of the horse. For example, an excessive 'parrot mouth', whereby the top jaw overlies the lower jaw, could mean that the molars don't meet evenly so additional tooth care will be needed to ensure the horse can eat easily, and the depth of the mouth may influence choice of bit when ridden.

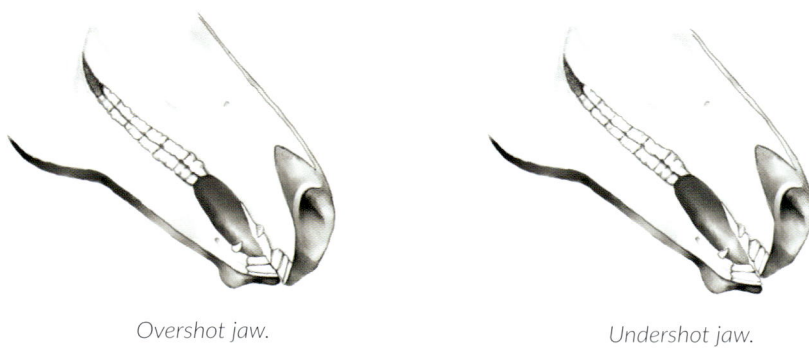

Overshot jaw.   *Undershot jaw.*

Throat. As a general guide, you would hope to be able to fit a clenched fist under the jaw at the throat. It's thought that this estimates sufficient room for the windpipe and also helps indicate the potential of ease for correct flexion at the poll when the horse is working.

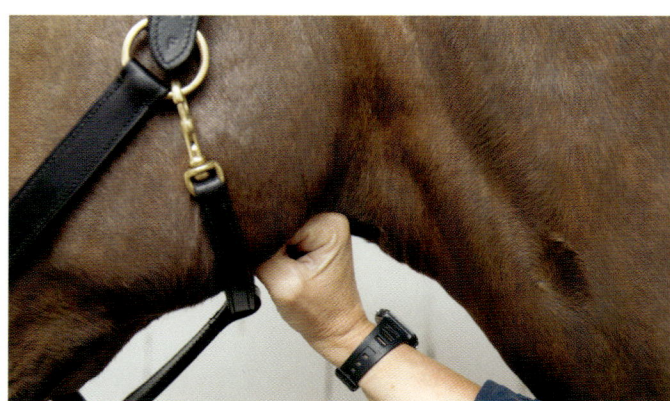

You should be able to fit a clenched fist under the horse's jaw.

Neck

Watch a horse moving freely in the gaits and you'll see how much the horse relies on the neck as a balancing tool. It moves forwards, back, up, down in or a combination of these directions, depending upon the gait, which is why we always need to ride with that elastic feel to the rein contact.

The length and positioning of the neck will influence how the horse feels to ride, but remember this is also often relative to the breed — for example, the neck of a Thoroughbred will differ from that of a native pony. An example of a poor neck might be a 'ewe' neck which, because of its positioning, can present problems with riding a horse in correct form, often as muscle develops incorrectly on the underside. When you hear terms such as this, think what a sheep looks like when it's looking up and how the neck lifts up slightly, almost looking as if it has been put on upside down!

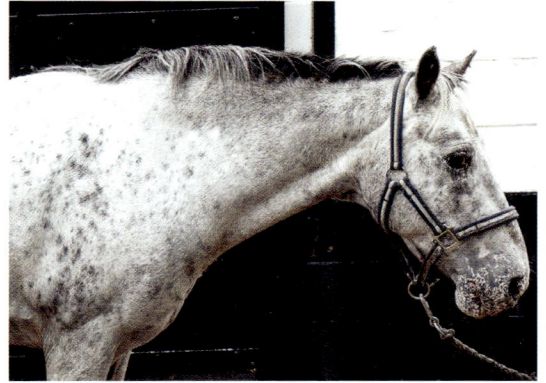

Neck set on low.

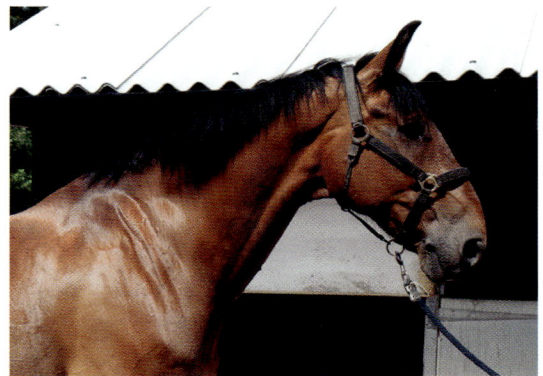

Neck set on high.

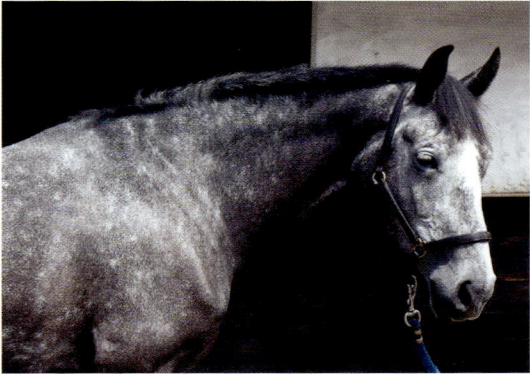

Neck set on well.

Withers

Consider assessment of this area relative to positioning of the neck and the shoulders. It's really important that you look to check with a practical approach — for example might there be problems associated with fitting of a saddle? High prominent withers can present as many problems as a pony with flat, undefined withers, but remember to relate this to the condition of the horse as at the time of assessment. An extremely overweight native pony may appear very different in this area after a controlled weight-loss diet! Equally a horse may have uneven muscle development as a result of workload, and this mustn't be confused with actual conformation.

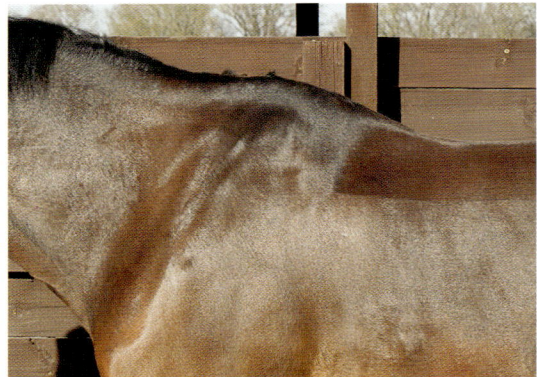

High withers.

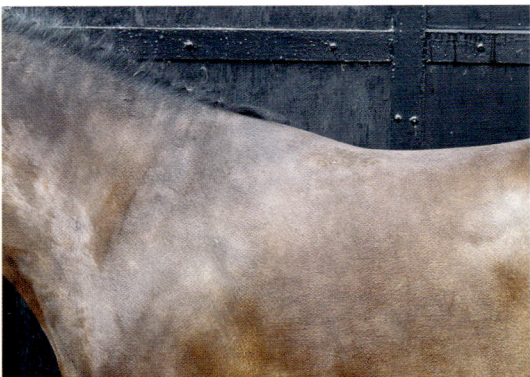

Flat withers.

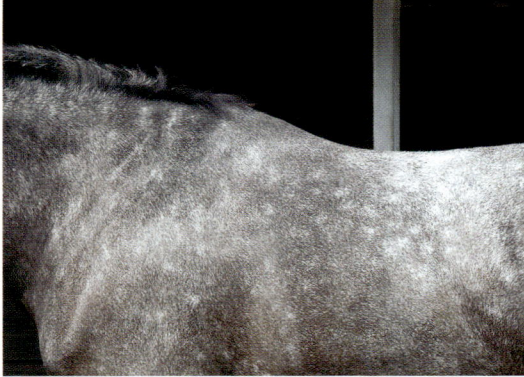

Well-shaped withers.

Shoulders

You may have heard people talk about the angle of the shoulder. To practise assessing this, see the horse standing square and imagine a chalk line drawn along the middle of the scapula. The ideal line should slope to form an angle of approximately 45 degrees to the ground and this should, in turn, relate to the slope you see when looking at the angle of the pastern and hoof, known as the hoof/pastern axis (HPA). The mechanics of how the horse moves means that a lot of weight-bearing is taken upon the forehand. For this reason, a horse with good proportions and correct, similar angles between shoulder, pastern and hooves is likely to suffer less concussion strain, wear and tear that should, in turn, help to minimise onset of lameness.

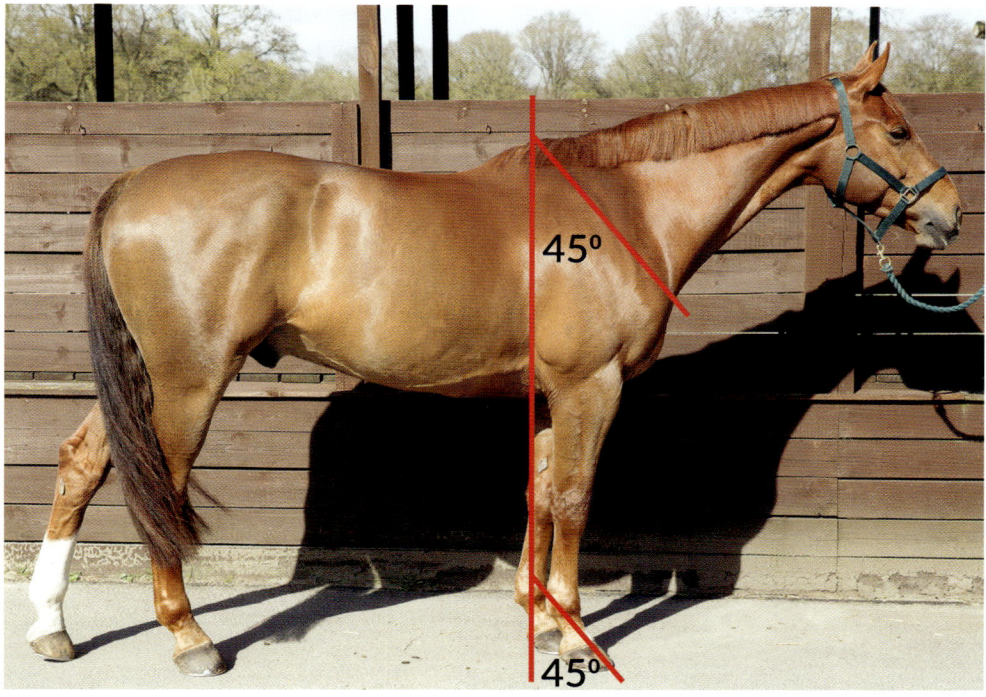

A horse with matching shoulder and hoof/pastern axis angles of approximately 45 degrees.

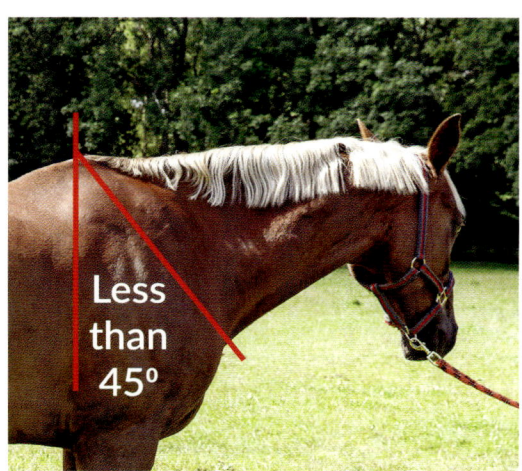

A horse with more upright angles of shoulder.

The angle and length of the scapula can influence the length of stride which, in turn, can relate to comfort and long-term soundness. Examples would be that upright shoulders are often associated with a short, choppy stride whereas shoulders with a good slope contribute to a longer stride, and are thus associated with a more comfy ride and an ability to gallop more easily.

When you look from the perspective of the job you hope a horse can do, step back and remember how the positioning of all the joints and the angles the bones are set at will influence the movement.

Chest

The chest or sternum is the starting area for the chest cavity. It needs to be wide enough to allow room for internal structures and for the horse to be able move their forelegs freely forwards to limit the risk of injury from self-inflicted wounds, such as brushing. The opposite would be an over-wide chest which can cause the horse to have almost a rolling action when they move.

Look at the chest and sternum from the side, as this might help you to see whether the horse has an appearance similar to that of a pigeon (hence the term 'pigeon-chested'); this would be considered a fault as it further increases the weight on the forehand.

Forelegs

Whether viewed from the front or side, the ideal is that they appear as an equal pair, which indicates that they should be able to carry weight evenly. Imagine dropping a 'plumb-line' down the front of each leg to help you. If the legs are not a pair because of crookedness, then there may also be increased uneven wear on the shoes or feet and a future risk of unsoundness. Ideally the knees should be large and flat, especially as the knee joint is comprised of many bones and is asked to flex with every stride.

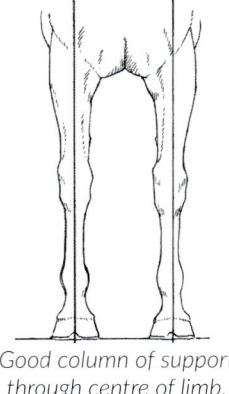

Good column of support through centre of limb.

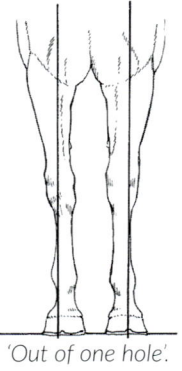

'Out of one hole'.

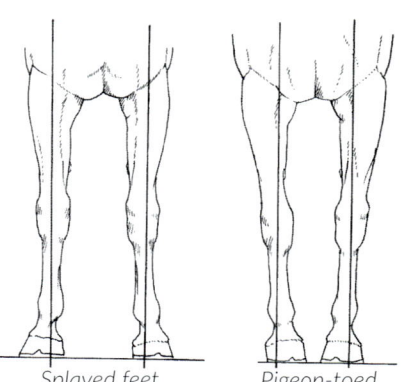

Splayed feet.   *Pigeon-toed.*

Various types of forelimb conformation.

4 | Conformation, the Foot and Shoeing

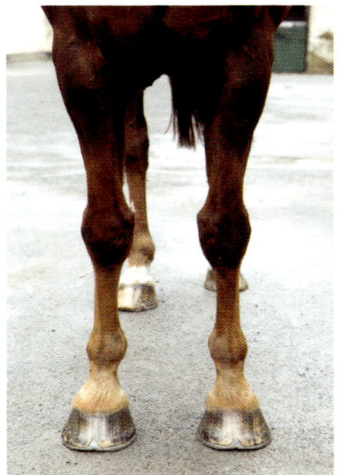

This horse has a fairly good column of support, although the off fore turns slightly to the outside from the fetlock down.

When viewing from the side, look again to see the actual stance of the horse — do they appear to lean backwards so there is a concave line along the front of the leg? This is known as being 'back at the knee' and the concern would be the potential extra strain that the horse might place on the flexor tendons. A horse who appears to have a convex line along the front of the leg is known as being 'over at the knee'. It is considered that a horse with this conformation is likely to put less strain on the tendons. There are many ways in which horse's legs differ in terms of their straightness; the main thing is to recognise such faults and how these might impact upon movement and what might possibly be done about it, such as adapting workload or speaking to the farrier about how shoeing or trimming differently might help. Remedial shoeing can't cure a fault, but might help minimise the effects of the fault.

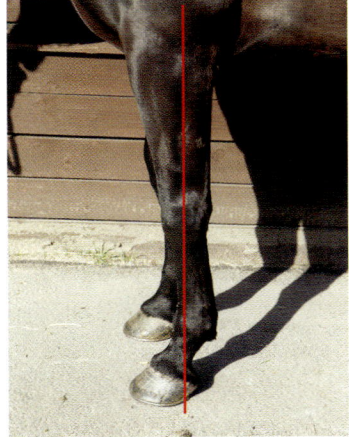

Slightly over at the knee.

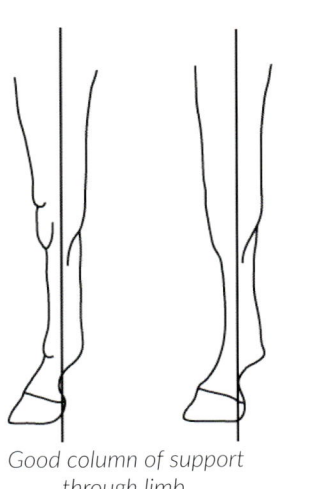

Good column of support through limb.

Over at the knee.

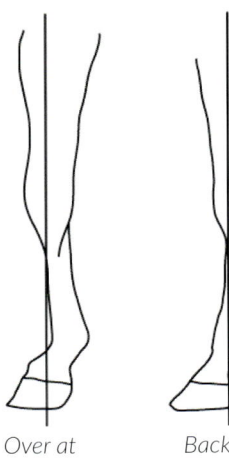

Back at the knee.

Good and bad knee conformation.

69

Feet

Correct foot balance is a term often used when assessing conformation and this can be influenced by trimming and shoeing. For this reason, when you consider the conformation of the feet think about how the foot functions and whether the shape and positioning of the foot allows for normal foot function. Remember that the foot functions as part of the shock-absorbing and anti-slip mechanism, so never undervalue the importance to this area — as the saying goes 'no foot, no horse'.

As well as looking at the shape of the feet in terms of being a pair, their proportion to the horse's size and in relation to the breed or type, don't forget to look at the quality of the feet — for example, what is the hoof wall like? If shod, is there any uneven wear on the shoe? Is the horse shod with pads and if so, is it one foot or both and why might this be?

Ideally the angle of the front of the feet should be similar to that of the pastern (the hoof/pastern axis) which, in forefeet, is similar to the shoulder. The ideal angle would be 45 degrees for the forefeet and 50–55 degrees for the hind feet.

When a horse's toes turn either in or out, this can affect the movement and, in doing so, cause uneven wear and tear, increase of risk of injury from brushing, or actual tread-type injuries. A flat foot is likely to have a weak sole that may be prone to bruising and little depth to the heel areas.

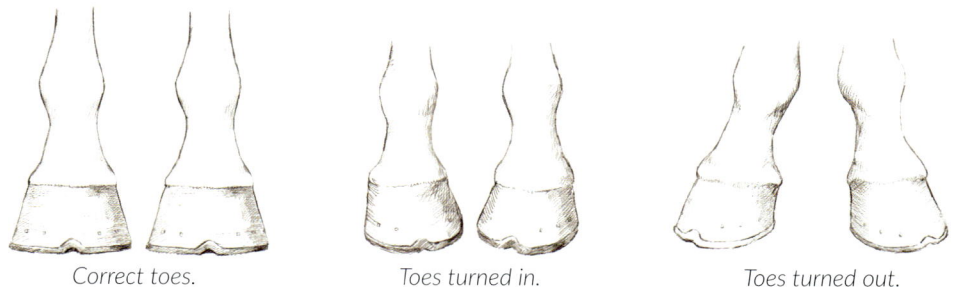

Correct toes. *Toes turned in.* *Toes turned out.*

Correct and incorrect alignment of the feet.

Middle

This is the area between the withers and the hindquarters, including the barrel and girth area. When assessing this area, consider the following aspects.

Length of back. Is this in proportion with the rest of the horse? A shorter back is considered stronger than a long back. However, both extremes can present challenges. For example, a long back could cause problems with tracking up correctly and an excessively short back might present saddle fitting problems.

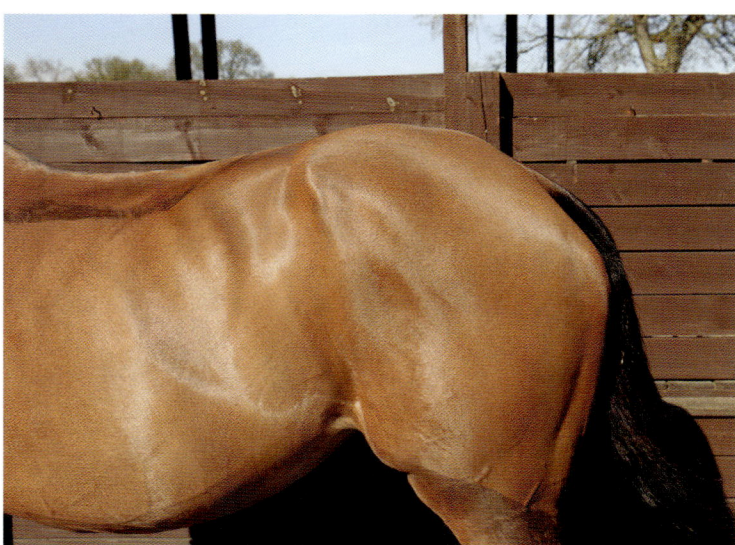

Sway back.

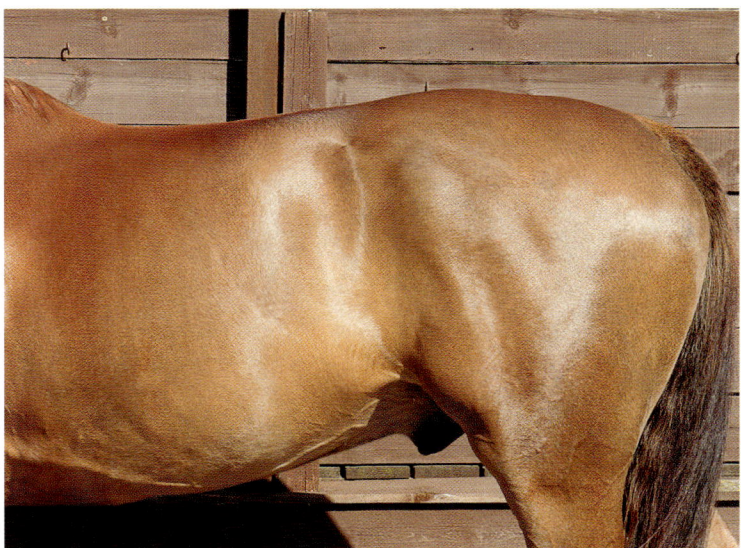

Long back with slight roaching.

Topline. Does the topline appear to run smoothly from the withers to the tail? Are there any odd contours, such as a 'roach back' which is, in the direction of the tail, an upward slope towards the loins? This could mean that the horse is less comfy to ride.

Barrel and girth areas. These areas need to look as though they belong together. Look at the ribcage to help you decide whether the horse might feel either very wide or too narrow when being ridden and then relate this to the overall picture you have gained so far. A good feature

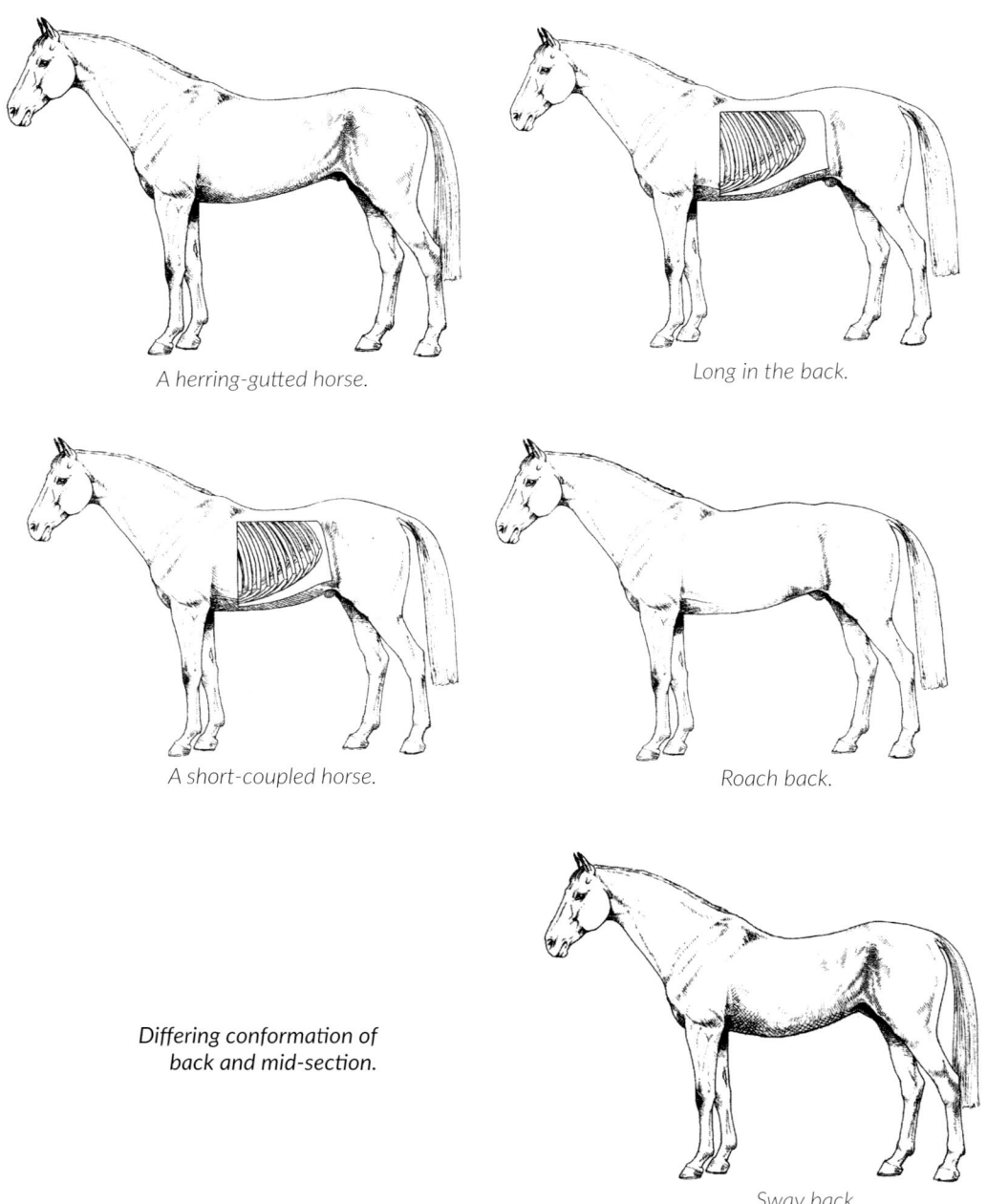

A herring-gutted horse.

Long in the back.

A short-coupled horse.

Roach back.

Sway back.

Differing conformation of back and mid-section.

here would be that the ribs appear 'well-sprung', enabling the barrel area to have sufficient room to house and protect the internal organs, but still enable you to ride the horse in comfort. Some narrow horses might make you feel as if you were sitting astride a gate!

Hindquarters

This area is considered to be where the horse gets their power or propulsion from. When assessing this area, you need to understand how to include the hind legs and, importantly, the hocks. Imagine a horse working, for example jumping when they have to bring their hindquarters under themselves in order to then propel themselves high enough to clear a fence.

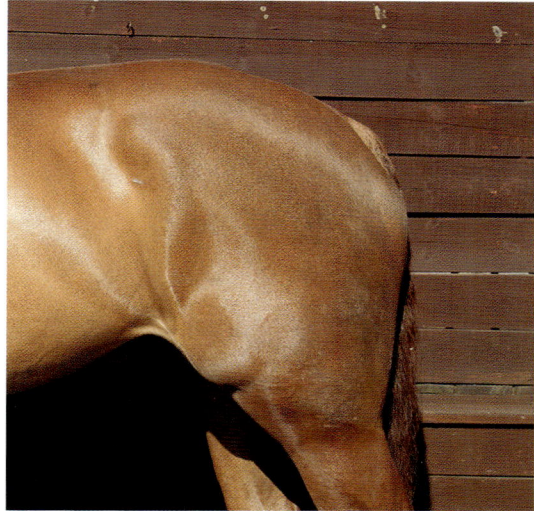

An example of a good rounded quarter.   *These quarters are less developed, shorter and weaker.*

The hindquarters should appear level at the hips, with a well-set tail, not too low as this can be associated with weak hindquarters. As with the shoulders, the hindquarters can differ upon differing breeds, for example a Thoroughbred horse's hindquarters will differ in shape from a draught horse's hindquarters.

Hind legs

There are many assessment points similar to those of the forelegs, but it is also necessary to consider the difference in the hock's action and purpose when compared to the knee. Remember that both joints need to flex, but there is additional need for both hocks to be well positioned to enable the horse to 'engage' their hindquarters. It can be helpful to imagine a straight line that runs from the point of the buttock to the point of the hock, downwards to the rear of the fetlock when you look to assess for the ideal.

One example of weak hocks would be 'sickle hocks', whereby the fetlock is in front of the imaginary line just mentioned, causing the cannon bone to slope slightly backwards. Another

Various types of hind limb conformation.

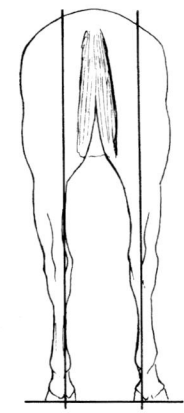 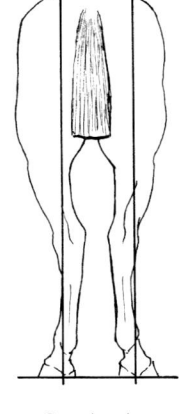 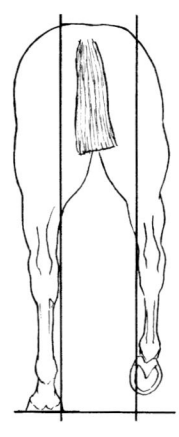 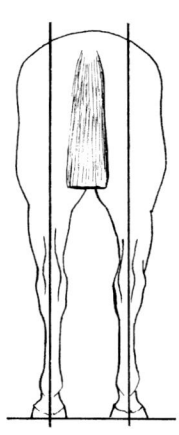

'Split up behind'.   *Cow hocks.*   *Wide behind.*   *Good hocks.*

is 'cow hocks' which means that, when viewed from behind, the points of the hocks are close together and the toes turn out. Both would be considered a weakness, as they can impact upon stride length, cause uneven wear and tear and, if very severe, affect ability to engage the hocks fully.

Various types of hock conformation.

Good hocks well supported under the body.   *Sickle-shaped hocks.*   *Hocks too high.*   *Hocks out behind.*   *Straight hocks.*

4 | Conformation, the Foot and Shoeing

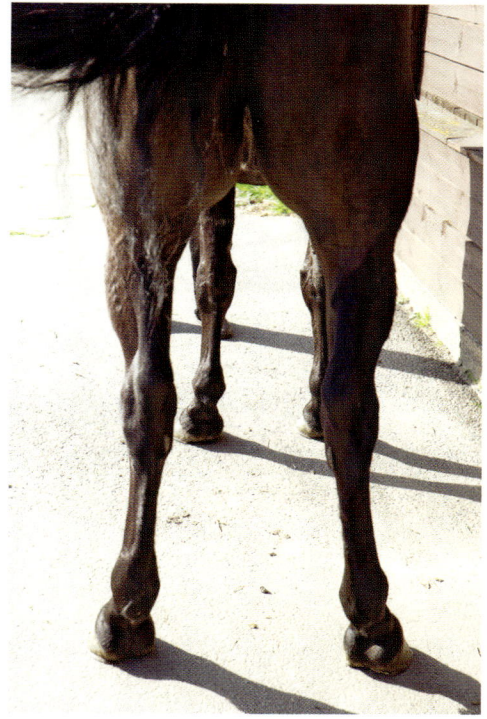

Wide behind.

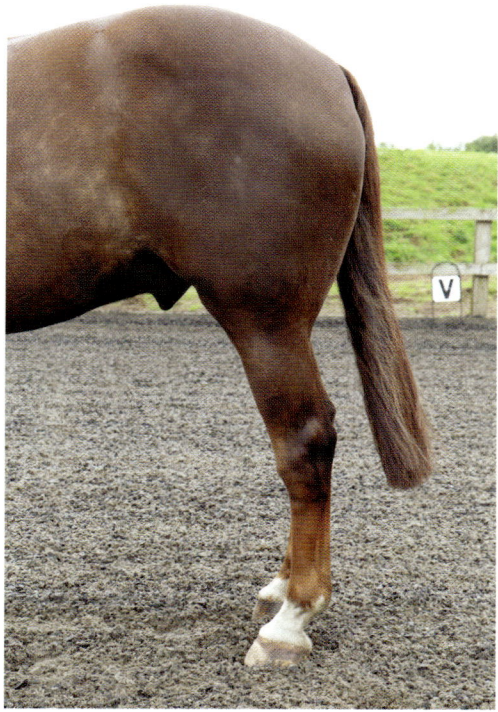

Straight hocks.

The value of experience

Overall, assessment of conformation is a skill that develops with experience. This can be gained looking at pictures of horses both standing still and in action, but it's important to really observe in practice. This allows you to learn to recognise the impact the static conformation may have on the dynamic aspect and you can then use this knowledge in helping to decide what sort of work the horse might be able to cope with.

It is worth remembering that few horses have absolute text book perfect looks and conformation, but by understanding the benefits of good conformation and the potential impact poor conformation can have, we stand more chance of enhancing horse welfare. Examples of this could be through thinking before we randomly breed from a lame horse, through adapting workloads and incorporating small changes, such as increased frequency of shoeing or trimming, or adaptation of shoe type to help with limb movement.

Foot balance and shoeing

Balance is a term often used when we talk about horses and this can range from when we comment upon a loss of 'rider balance' to describing a horse working 'in balance'. As a noun, the definition of the term balance is 'an even distribution of weight enabling someone or something to remain upright and steady'. Applying this term to the horse's foot simply means that, in the ideal horse, the feet will be suitable in proportions, size and at an angle to enhance the balance of the horse.

As research helps to inform us through increasing knowledge and understanding of the structure and many functions of the foot, we gain opportunities to recognise the impact good or poor foot balance can have, and how this may affect a horse's ability to stay sound.

What is ideal?

The ideal horse will have equal shape and size to the two forefeet, and to the two hind feet; the forefeet will appear rounder, as they weight bear more than the hinds, which are more oval in shape and tend to push as part of their action. We all know that a horseshoe should be made to fit the hoof, not the hoof to fit the shoe — if you look at an old horse shoe, you should be able to tell whether it is from a front or hind hoof by its shape. Don't be totally put off a horse if the feet are not exact pairs as many horses have feet that differ slightly, just as with humans. Provided such horses are asked to do work that they can withstand, and are regularly and correctly trimmed or shod, then any risk of future problems can be greatly reduced.

The feet should look as though they 'belong to the horse' and are correct for their breed or type. For example, if you saw a Thoroughbred with feet you would expect to see on a Clydesdale (or swop that vision round) there would clearly be a problem. Another concern would be if the feet appear what's often known as 'boxy', similar to those you might find on a donkey, the concern being that all of the structures within the hoof capsule would be very small in proportion to the size and weight of the horse. The virtual opposite of this would be 'flaring' whereby the foot widens out too much at the base, similar to a pair of flared trousers.

Poor foot conformation.

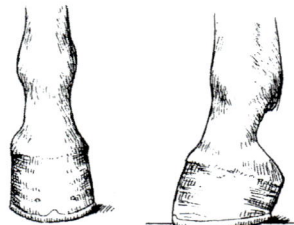

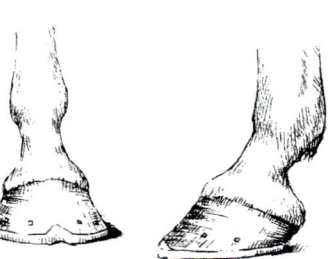

Boxy foot.

Flat foot with long toe and collapsed heel.

4 | Conformation, the Foot and Shoeing

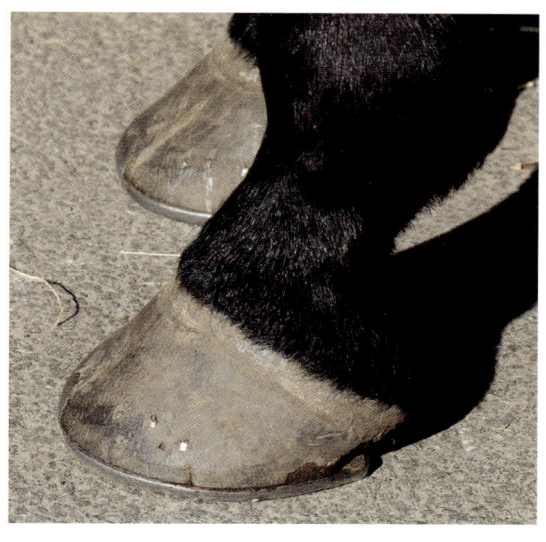
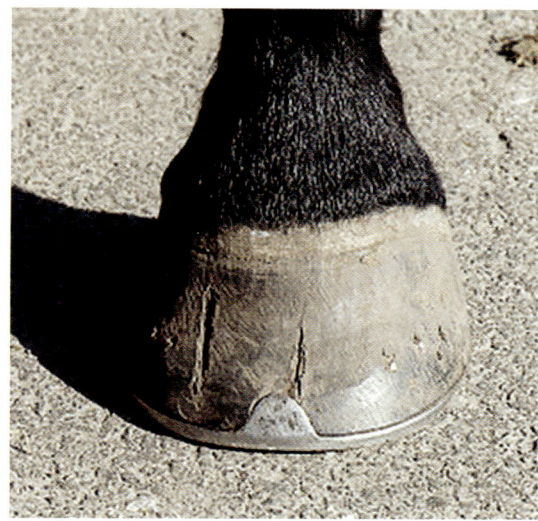

Flat feet.

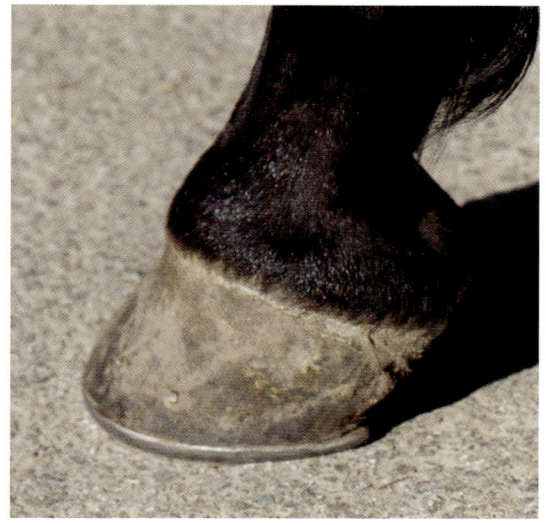

Boxy feet.

Feet have a lot to cope with. They bear weight, help absorb concussion, help provide an anti-slip mechanism and work with the circulatory system. The hooves, which help protect the inner structures, have their outer wall worn down through either workload, trimming or shoeing. A horse who has healthy feet with good foot balance will be more easily able to function well, and this will help to keep the horse sound.

Foot balance and the hoof/pastern axis (HPA)

Foot balance

The aim of assessing the foot balance is to establish whether the foot has equal proportions. This means from the front view, known as lateral and medial balance, and from the side view where you are assessing the balance between the toe and the heel.

In terms of the proportions viewed from the front, you are looking to see if there is an equal amount of foot either side of the centre of the hoof. The angle of the hoof wall at each side of the foot needs to be equal.

When you consider the toe angle it should be equal in both pairs of feet. Compare it to if you wore a pair of shoes of the same design, but the heel of one shoe had fallen off; you would not be 'landing' evenly on your feet and this would eventually make you sore. Initially the pain would probably be directly on the heel, but if you continued then the pain would travel to other parts, possibly your other leg as you started to adapt your stride. As you can imagine, having an uneven bearing surface or incorrectly balanced feet just makes everything hard work!

As the diagram below shows, the toes should not be too long, and they should point to the front when the horse is at rest. There should be an equal amount of foot either side of the imaginary line from the leg through to the ground. The reason for this is that it helps to indicate whether the weight-bearing pressure is even, for example, that the horse is taking equal weight to the left and the right side of the foot.

We also need to look at the heel area of the foot and assess whether the depth of the heel is sufficient and in proportion to the rest of the foot. As the diagram below shows, the depth of the heel is often relative to the HPA.

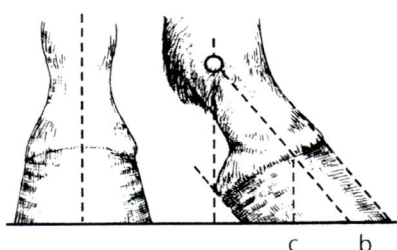

The well-balanced foot. Weight distribution should be equal in front of and behind c.

It is worth picking up all the feet, not only to see if the horse is wearing any form of foot pad or cushion, but to look at the actual bearing surface and see the heels and quality of the frog. Combined with the sole and bars, the heels work with the frog and all play an essential part in a well-functioning foot. Again, as the pictures below show, you are looking for an equal amount of foot either side of an imaginary line running down the centre of the heels to the toe area. At the same time, look for signs that the frog makes contact with the ground and that the heels are firm but slightly spongy under pressure.

While not perfect this hoof is fairly equal on both sides. The hoof is in good condition, with a well-defined frog.

The hoof/pastern axis (HPA)

As the photo and diagram below show, the ideal HPA will mean that there is a continuous slope through the hoof and the pastern. The ideal angle will differ between individual horses and also between the fore and hind legs. Having this continuous slope will help minimise wear and tear on the fetlock, pastern and coffin joints and associated tendons and ligaments.

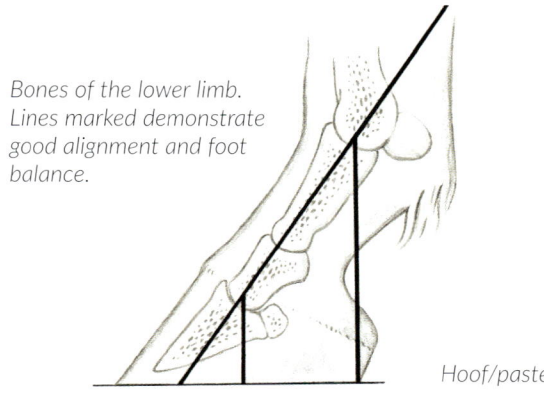

Bones of the lower limb. Lines marked demonstrate good alignment and foot balance.

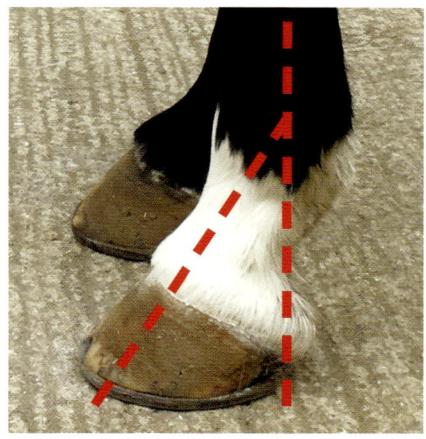

Hoof/pastern angles.

To an extent, correct trimming and shoeing can help improve the HPA for a horse, but a farrier will only be able to work with what nature supplied. If you have concerns with a horse's HPA then this should be discussed with the farrier for advice.

Good and bad hoof/pastern angles.

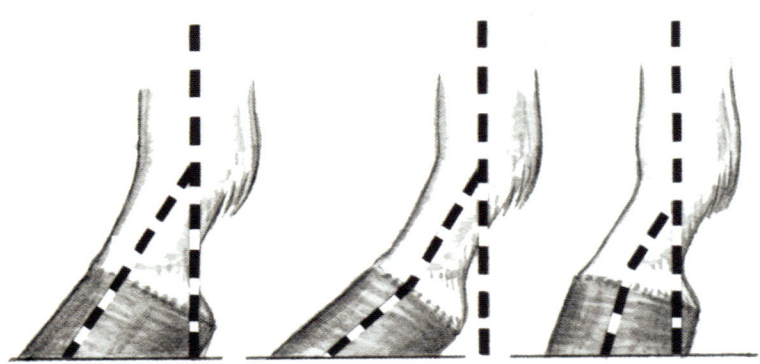

Good hoof-pastern axis

Broken back hoof-pastern axis; puts strain on the back of the leg.

Broken forward hoof-pastern axis; subjects lower limb and foot to more concussion.

Broken-back HPA can put additional strain on the back of the leg, with risk of increased soft tissue injuries.

Broken-forwards HPA can increase the concussion risk through the foot and further up the limbs.

If a horse has poor foot conformation that affects foot balance, it can impact on the long-term welfare of the horse, if the situation cannot be improved through correct shoeing or if the workload of the horse is not moderated in light of potential problems. Examples of problems include:

- Tripping or stumbling, especially if the toe of the hoof is long.

- Repetitive strain on soft tissues, such as tendons and ligaments.

- Unnecessary concussion.

- Altered stride length (from an adapted flight pattern of the limb as it moves).

- In some cases, poor performance, for example, a limited stride length.

- In some cases, low-grade pain.

How shoeing can help

To a large extent, correct trimming and shoeing will help, although bear in mind that the farrier can only work with the foot presented to them.

As you will know, preparation of the foot for shoeing has an initial stage whereby the farrier will be assessing the natural balance of the foot, and taking a view upon the amount of hoof growth that may or may not need removing to help ensure correct and even balance across the foot. The farrier will assess the bare foot on the ground and consider how this may link to the horse's movement.

If the horse is already shod, looking at the wear and tear upon the current shoe will help identify how evenly the horse is placing the foot on the ground, especially if the workload involves regular roadwork. Bear in mind how recently the horse may have been shod, as this may influence the overall amount of wear.

Excessive wear on one side suggests what is known as lateral to medial imbalance, in other words the horse is landing more heavily on that side of the foot.

Excessive wear on the toe area suggests that the horse might be dragging the limb/toe; this could mean that there are underlying problems, or it might be that the horse is just a bit lazy and has been allowed to dawdle along when being ridden.

When looking at the wear on a shoe remember to check all the feet — it might be, for example, that the toe is worn more on a right fore than on the left and maybe this is because the horse paws on concrete at the stable door a lot, for example at feed time or simply to gain attention.

Shoe types

There are many types of shoes available and you may have heard of the term 'remedial shoeing'. Remedial shoeing is shoeing that has been specifically recommended by appropriate professionals, such as through the vet and farrier working together. Use of such shoes may be short- or long-term but the key point to remember is that, in such situations, careful monitoring and evaluation of use is essential, especially as there may be a need to adapt the horse's workload too.

The foot surface, which is the part of a shoe that contacts the hoof, should be the same in most shoes. Its function is to support. Examples of altering this contact would be 'rolling the toe' of the shoe or 'seating out'; both act to remove pressure slightly from the hoof.

The actual width of the metal used in a shoe is called the web and this will depend on the size and thickness of a horse's hooves. In general the wider the web the better it is for the horse as the shoe will support and protect more of the hoof.

Recognising shoes in common use helps when assessing foot balance as it enhances an understanding of why they may be worn.

Fullered shoe

This is what we recognise as a regular shoe. As the photos show, it has the following features in its design:

A slightly sloped inner edge that helps make the shoe lighter and to continue the concave shape of the sole, so helping with grip.

A fullered edge to help with grip and to provide a bed for the nail heads.

Toe clips to help with holding the shoe in position. Normally in the centre of the front side.

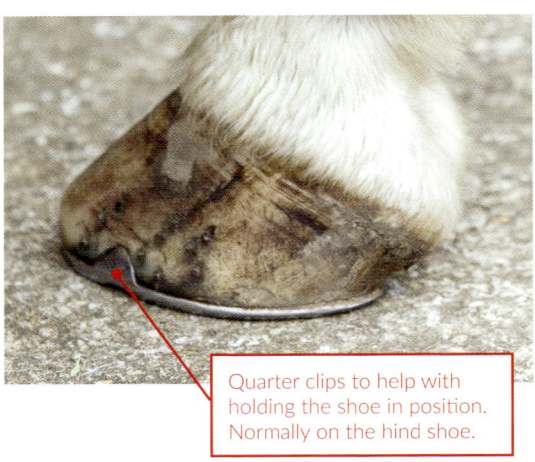

Quarter clips to help with holding the shoe in position. Normally on the hind shoe.

A fullered shoe.

There may be reasons for toe or quarter clips being offset from the normal positions, such as to minimise shoe slip or because of weaknesses in the hoof wall.

Plain stamped shoe

As the name suggests, this shoe is plain on the bearing surface to the ground with no fullering. It is wider than a fullered shoe, therefore expanding the surface on the foot. This type of shoe is more commonly used on heavier draught-type horses who are not doing fast work.

Features are:

- Flat appearance.

- No fullering in the design.

- Designed and fitted so that the actual nail holes position over the white line, which means that nails will pass through the full thickness of the wall.

A plained stamped shoe.

Natural balance shoes

These shoes are slightly square in appearance at the toe and, when fitted, are fitted slightly further back on the foot than a regular shoe. When applied they need to be fitted to both of a pair of feet. The idea is that they slightly alter what's known as the 'breakover point'. 'Breakover' is a descriptive term, often misunderstood, that is applied to the pattern of flight the foot takes as the horse's heel leaves the ground as they stride forwards, almost at the point of 'push off' into the next stage of a step.

It is thought that, with some horses, this helps improve their stride length and reduces risk of tripping as it effectively shortens the length of the toe.

Natural balance shoe.

Rolled toe

This is where the shoe has a slightly upward turn to the front edge of the toe. Such shoes do not have toe or quarter clips. The idea of this shoe is also to help reduce the breakover force.

Rolled toe shoe.

Remedial shoes

These are types of shoes intended to alleviate various conditions.

Egg-bar. This would be used on a horse who needs additional support in the heel area.

Heart-bar. Similar to the egg-bar but also applies support to the frog. Can be used in the treatment of laminitis.

Egg-bar shoe.

Heart-bar shoe.

Seated-out. This term commonly applies to a scenario when the heel area of a shoe has been flattened on the ground-bearing edge. This is done to reduce pressure directly above it on that area of the hoof. An example of use would be on a horse who is susceptible to corns, as it will still allow some protection to that area of hoof.

Racing plates

These are made of a lightweight metal (aluminium). These are very light and are used on racehorses during racing. They would not provide the support or stand up to the wear and tear of a regular shoe, for example doing roadwork. Being light, they are used as they help to reduce strain on the legs, the risk of injury and to encourage an easier flight pattern of the limb.

Racing plate.

Glue-on shoes

Differing designs of these are available. The idea is that by being glued on, rather than nailed on, there is less risk of damage to a hoof wall that may be weak. Quite often, if a hoof wall is weak then it can become damaged by nails penetrating it, which then increases the risk of the shoe coming off easily. As we know, this often risks further damage to the wall, which then makes it more difficult for a farrier to find healthy wall on which to secure a shoe. These shoes are expensive compared to a regular set of shoes.

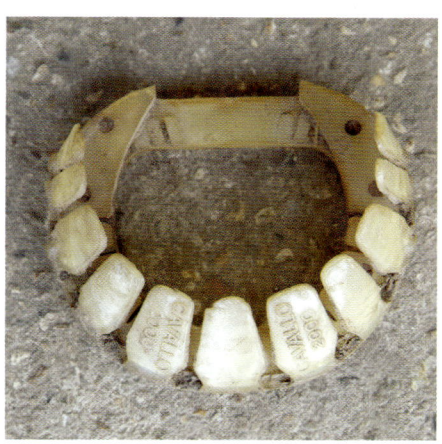

Glue on shoe.

Pads or cushions

You may have seen horses wearing pads between the hoof and the shoe. There are many types available and these would normally be used only on the advice of a farrier or vet. They are available in a variety of materials, with leather or plastic ones being the most common. Pads will vary in thickness depending upon the reason for use and more commonly will be on both forefeet, rather than just one, although it is possible that there may be a reason for there being only one. Pads tend to be used when there is need to reduce risk of injury to the frog and sole, or to very slightly help with adjustment of the foot balance.

An example of a pad.

Some opinions suggest that their use can increase the risk of shoe loss, depending upon the thickness of the pad, as it can encourage clenches to rise. However, with attention to detail, careful monitoring and good farriery advice, pads have enabled many horses to continue to have active working and competitive careers.

Summary

- Conformation refers to the overall outline or shape of the horse.

- When assessing conformation, view the horse from each side as well as the front and back.

- Foot balance refers to the proportions, size and angles of the horse's foot.

- The hoof/pastern axis refers to the slope through the hoof and the pastern.

TRAINING TIPS

1. Look at and discuss the conformation of a variety of horses with an experienced person.

2. Before you ride a horse have a look at their conformation and try to relate it to how the horse moves and what they feel like to ride.

3. Speak to the farrier or vet about remedial shoeing and its uses.

Chapter 5
Common Health Conditions

The need to understand general indicators of health

The vital signs of health

Common health conditions

Assessing lameness

Managing horses' health and biosecurity

Professional healthcare for horses (supportive/additional therapies)

Summary

The need to understand general indicators of health

To see a healthy horse enjoying themselves in safe surroundings, whether being ridden for pleasure, competition, grazing in a field or resting in a stable is very rewarding — especially if you have had involvement in any aspect of their management and care.

All animals need good health to survive and thrive and, as with humans, the topic of health covers not just the physical aspects but mental well-being as well. Horses can become distressed for a variety of reasons and, as you will know, being left in such situations often risks their condition worsening or them hurting themselves as they attempt to remove themselves from a stressful situation. Examples of such situations could be stress-induced pain caused by ulcers or trying to escape when panicking if left alone in a field, resulting in injury.

The more time you spend with horses and becoming familiar with their normal healthy behaviour patterns the more accurate and confident you will become in recognising when something 'just isn't quite right' with a horse. While all horses will be different in terms of their breed, type, age and sex, physiologically they are all fundamentally the same. Peoples' opinions upon how temperaments differ between breeds will always vary and, with some, opinions may well depend upon the last person spoken to, or horse of a particular type encountered! However, it's through continually observing a range of horses that you can start to gain valuable experience in interpreting some indicators or signs of their physical health and mental-well being. As you will know, environment affects behaviour a lot, so it's important to have knowledge of what would be considered 'normal behaviour and health indicators' to help you form a speedy and accurate assessment of a horse's health. Being accurate and quick in making correct decisions is a very important skill to acquire as it enables you to prioritise what to do first. An example would be knowing whether an injury or illness needs monitoring and reporting, or whether the vet needs to be called as a matter of urgency.

In such situations the more accurate you can be with reporting concerns, the quicker problems can be dealt with. Examples would be that quick reporting of suspected heat or swelling in a leg may help prevent lameness developing, or early identification of colic may prevent the situation worsening to a degree whereby it could become fatal.

Using your knowledge of anatomy and physiology helps to inform your management and care for horses in a way that enhances their welfare and performance. Accuracy in identifying parts of the horse, and having an understanding of how these parts function, plays a key part in being able to provide correct information when describing conditions to the person to whom you're reporting — whether it's the owner of the horse, proprietor of the yard, a vet, farrier or other health professional. This understanding is also a massive help in making observations and assessments of the health of a horse. Examples would be when monitoring the health of a new arrival in a yard, a horse who may be unwell, or when planning or adapting a fitness programme.

You will be familiar with the many routine care procedures that help to maintain health — simple ones done on a daily basis, such as keeping stables clean and dust-free, regular grooming and tack-fitting checks through to more regulated ones such as foot care or dentistry. These are all excellent opportunities for you to start to notice how a horse's normal behaviour might be when all is well in terms of health, but in slightly different circumstances. For example, when grooming you automatically check for sores, heat, swelling and note the horse's reactions — perhaps they are unusually reluctant to allow you to hold their leg while picking out a forefoot, which might mean that it is uncomfortable for them to bend their knee or fetlock.

Horses have evolved and adapted to domestication in response to our demands upon them. Most horses are now stabled, often in close proximity to each other, which can increase risk of disease spreading, especially if ventilation is not great. Consider how often people fly on a plane and then claim to have become ill as a result of the recirculation of airflow within the plane! Many horses travel to competitions, sharing transport and working in close proximity to other horses from other areas which, again, can offer an opportunity for spread of disease. These are a few of the many reasons why it's really important to be able to assess a horse's health to recognise and act upon any areas for concern as soon as possible — especially if there is risk of a disease being contagious or infectious. Domestication has many benefits for horses as long as our care for them in this environment is able to meet their needs. When a horse has been out at grass and on rest for a long period and is then brought back into a regime of being stabled it will affect the physiology of their systems, so best practice would be to make any adjustments slowly to allow the horse to adapt. In the ideal situation, the horse would be brought into the stable for short periods each day to allow an adjustment period, and their condition would be monitored. Examples of systems affected would be the:

- Digestive system; as the horse has had continual access to grass this should be mimicked through a plentiful supply of forage.

- Respiratory system; as the horse has gone from fresh air to a potentially dusty environment it would be prudent to use low dust bedding, soak hay and ensure good airflow without draughts.

- Circulatory system; as the horse has been walking freely, grazing, being stabled will restrict this so it will be necessary to ensure frequent exercise for short periods and be aware of any fluid build-up in the legs resulting from them standing still.

An incremental adjustment, using the same basic philosophy, should be in place when a horse is turned away to grass to rest for a long period.

The vital signs of health

You are probably aware of the basic health indicators that can be observed through quietly watching a horse at rest, such as regularity of droppings and regular drinking and eating patterns. These are ones that provide an overview of patterns of behaviour and any changes may be early indicators that something seems amiss. Further, more in-depth monitoring of a horse, to gain a more accurate view of whether a situation is improving or worsening, requires observation of what are known as the vital signs of health.

Evaluating 'norms'

Readings or observations are made upon the systems described below and these are used to help assess both fitness levels in a healthy horse, and state of health in horses suspected of being unwell. Since individual horses may differ slightly in their precise 'norms', it's important to be able to know what is 'normal' for an individual horse at rest.

Temperature

Measurement tells you the state of the body's internal temperature — a healthy range (at rest) would be 37.5–38.5°C (99.5–101.3°F).

A rise in temperature could:

- Occur naturally during exercise (exertion), especially in hot weather.
- Indicate fever.

Pulse

Indicates the rate of the heartbeat, which shows how well the circulatory system is working — a healthy range (at rest) would be 28–44 beats per minute.

A rise in rate is likely to:

- Occur naturally during exercise (exertion).
- Occur naturally when excited.
- Occur naturally if in pain.

Respiration

Indicates how many breaths are taken in a rest period, which indicates how easily the horse is able to take in air for use as oxygen — a healthy range (at rest) would be 8–16 breaths per minute (bpm).

A rise in rate is likely to:

- Occur naturally during exercise (exertion).
- Occur naturally when frightened.
- Occur naturally when in pain.
- Occur when affected by disease.
- Occur alongside a rise in temperature.
- Occur when anaemic.

How to measure vital signs

If you have never done this before then ideally get someone who is competent to help show you how, and use a patient, resting horse who hasn't just been ridden — that way you should find it easier to get accurate readings, sometimes referred to as 'base rates'. Have someone hold the horse or, if you are on your own, make sure that the horse is secured and remember to warn the horse before you start taking the temperature. It is best to take the respiration rate first, followed by the pulse and then take the temperature last. With nervous horses, or a horse who is not used to having their temperature taken, pulse and breathing rate may increase if temperature is taken first.

Measuring respiration

Equipment. A stopwatch or timer on your phone, or watch with a second hand.

Preparation. This is normally done visually and is best done when the horse is quiet, in a non-dusty environment and at rest — unless it is being taken as part of monitoring the 'recovery rate' after a horse has been exercising.

Method. Stand to the side of the horse, facing towards the hindquarters. Look at the flanks to observe them moving in and out as the horse breathes. An inhalation and exhalation count as one breath. Watching the nostrils flare each time a breath is taken is another method.

Count the breaths taken over 30 seconds and then multiply the amount by two to get the number of breaths per minute.

Measuring heartbeat (pulse)

Equipment. A stopwatch or timer on your phone; a stethoscope (but it can be done without).

Preparation. If you have access to a stethoscope, then make sure it works and that you have it on the correct way. You should hear clearly when you gently tap the head end of the instrument. If you accidentally wear one 'back to front' the earplugs will be in the wrong direction. It might also be an idea to try listening to your own heartbeat or finding your own pulse first.

If you don't have a stethoscope then you can use your fingertips and find the horse's pulse by applying pressure on certain arteries that run close to the skin surface — avoid using your thumbs as they have a fairly strong pulse themselves and you don't want to read your own pulse by mistake!

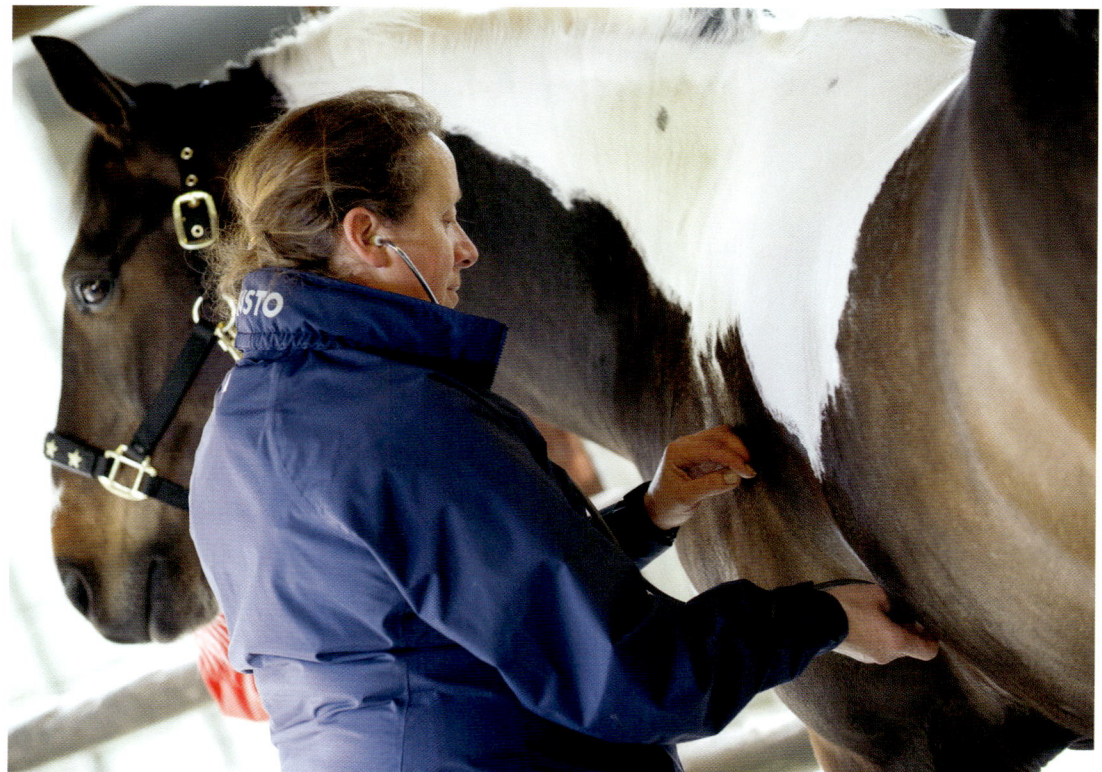

Use the stethoscope on the left-hand side of the horse, on the girth area behind the elbow.

To measure heartbeat by stethoscope. Standing on the left-hand side facing the girth area, gently place and hold the stethoscope on to the girth area approximately a fist's width behind the point of the elbow. If you don't automatically hear the heart beat then try sliding the stethoscope forwards or lower down, or standing the horse with the left leg slightly forwards, as both these actions can help.

To calculate the rate: a beat can be heard as a 'lub-dub' sound. Count each 'lub-dub' as a beat for 30 seconds then multiply by two to get the average beats per minute.

To measure the pulse. The pulse is the blood flowing in response to the heart beating. To measure by hand at the mandibular artery: standing at the left side of the horse, steady the horse's head with your spare hand then curl your fingers and place the tips of your fingers in the groove on the underside of the jaw and press them towards the jawbone. You should then feel a thin, cord-like structure as you press against the jawbone, and should feel the pulse beating. As with reading the heartbeat, read for 30 seconds then multiply by two to give the average pulse (heartbeat reading).

Measuring temperature

Equipment. Stopwatch or watch with second hand, thermometer, cotton wool or wipes and petroleum jelly.

Preparation. First, make sure that you know how to read the thermometer and check that it is clean. Digital thermometers are most commonly used. Switch it on and check that the battery is working. Then, place a small amount of petroleum jelly on the end of the thermometer (this is to help make insertion into the rectum smoother).

Method. Which side you stand on will depend upon where the horse is in the stable and whether you are left- or right-handed. The main consideration is to be gentle, but make sure that you don't drop or let go of the thermometer. If you let go of the thermometer it can be sucked into the horse's anus, which would then require you to call the vet to locate and extract the thermometer. Stand to the side of the horse and, with your spare hand, give the horse a scratch to relax them and gently move the tail away from you and hold it to the side. Then, keeping the thermometer horizontal, place it gently into the anus. Applying a slight rotation to it as you do so will help it enter. The thermometer should be pressed gently against the wall of the rectum to ensure the temperature reading is from the horse and not from a ball of dung. A digital thermometer is often quick to register a reading and should omit a 'beep' at the appropriate point. Make sure that you rotate the thermometer gently as you remove it. Briefly wipe the thermometer before reading the result, then clean thoroughly and put it safely away.

If using a glass mercury thermometer take care, as the mercury contained within the thermometer is poisonous, so it could cause a significant hazard if the thermometer were to be dropped and broken. Before you use it, shake the thermometer in a downward motion to

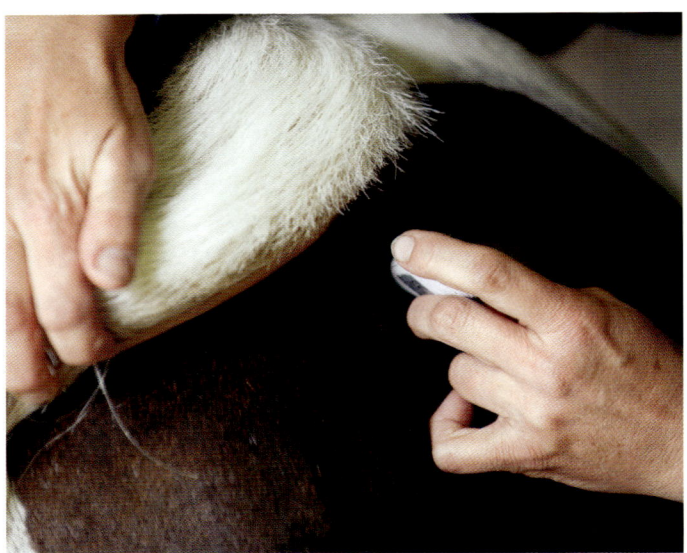

Stand to the side and keep hold of the thermometer whilst taking the horse's temperature, when the thermometer beeps it is ready to be taken out and a reading can be taken.

ensure that the mercury (grey liquid inside the glass) is towards the base end as this will help ensure an accurate result. You will need to leave the thermometer in the anus for 2–3 minutes; when you remove the thermometer, wipe it before reading. To find the reading, slowly turn the thermometer until you can see the line of the mercury against the scale.

Maintaining health records

As stated earlier, every horse is an individual and you must use your knowledge of each horse's normal health indicators to check that all is well and that each is within what could be considered a normal healthy range. It's accepted that some of these ranges may differ, subject to how fit a horse is, but when a reading differs from a horse's normal range it could indicate that there may be something wrong — in which case increased monitoring of health needs to be put in place over a period to see whether a condition improves or worsens. An increase in temperature can often be the first indicator of illness before any physical symptoms are shown. Isolating a horse with a high temperature while you monitor them, can reduce the risk of spreading disease and prevent further outbreaks.

Health records need to be up to date as they can prove invaluable in providing speedy access to information. Examples could be needing information in an emergency situation (for example, for the vet), to discuss information with an owner or, if a horse is to be sold and is moving to a new yard, to inform others. Implementing the use of a Care & Emergency Plan (a template can be found on the BHS website) for each horse on your yard can save time in an emergency.

Routine health records

In addition to recording of TPR, routine health records also relate to procedures or health routines that are regularly undertaken to maintain a horse's general health.

Examples of such would be:

- Vaccinations.

- Dentistry.

- Testing-led deworming programme.

- Shoeing or trimming.

- Veterinary medications, especially prescription only medications (POMs).

- Dietary adjustments.

- Additional therapies, such as physiotherapy treatments.

Passports

All horses, ponies, donkeys, mules and zebras must have a passport and microchip. This is applicable across the United Kingdom as stated in the following regulations:

- The Equine Identification (England) Regulations 2018

- The Equine Animal Identification (Scotland) Regulations 2019

- The Equine Identification (Wales) Regulations 2019

- The Equine Identification Regulations (Northern Ireland) 2019

The legislation states that owners or keepers with the primary responsibility for the care of the horse, have a legal duty to ensure that the horse is correctly identified. If there is any likelihood that, when euthanised, a horse is intended for human consumption then some medications authorised by vets and known as prescription only medications (POMs), may need to be recorded upon a horse's passport by the vet administering the treatment. If the passport has been signed stating that the horse is not intended for human consumption, then medications don't need to be recorded in the passport.

Common health conditions

Many health conditions affect horses. Being able to make a quick and accurate assessment of a condition in the early stages will be really useful. While, in most cases, further help may be needed, it's wise to consider the following points as part of your initial assessment:

- Is the horse in pain or suffering?
- Is the horse in immediate danger?
- Will I need help and who needs to be told?
- Is veterinary advice urgently needed?
- Is the condition likely to be contagious or infectious?
- What adjustments might be needed to the normal daily care and management of the horse?

Approaches to managing certain conditions continue to alter as research discovers more about health and informs professionals, such as vets, upon the most appropriate treatment for differing situations. Listed below are some common conditions, with brief notes relating to current thinking on diagnosis and treatment. In addition to participating in the nursing process while a horse is actually unwell, and following all veterinary advice, you should be mindful of ensuring that nutritional levels are adapted as appropriate, and that a period of convalescence and a gradual return to normal work levels will be necessary for any horse who has endured a period of significant ill health.

1. Equine flu

A very infectious and contagious viral illness causing disease of the respiratory system that affects both the upper/lower respiratory tract.

Symptoms

Initial cough, dullness, loss of performance, appetite and general disinterest. Raised temperature, sometimes nasal discharge.

Actions

Seek veterinary advice for accurate diagnosis and appropriate treatments. Implement strict isolation and care procedures, cease work and adjust diet. Follow vet's advice throughout. Monitor and record progress. Importantly, close monitoring and observation of other horses in proximity. Restrict all movements to minimise risk of further spread. A vaccinated horse should show less severe symptoms if they become infected as an infected horse will shed less of the virus. Vaccination can also help limit the spread of the disease. Vaccination is discussed later in this chapter.

2. Strangles

A highly contagious disease of the upper respiratory tract caused by a bacteria called streptococcus equi. It can be easily spread directly through horse to horse contact and indirectly, for example through contaminated equipment.

Symptoms

Initial depression, fever (temperature rises) and nasal discharge. Loss of appetite. Horse uncomfortable, with posture lowered and nose stretched forward. Painful jaw area with difficulty swallowing. As condition develops swellings appear under the jaw. Bacteria form abscesses, which can burst outwards in this area. In some cases, a condition known as bastard strangles can develop whereby bacteria spread through the lymphatic system and can form swellings elsewhere.

Actions

Seek veterinary advice for accurate diagnosis and appropriate treatments and advice upon later return to work. Implement strict isolation and care procedures, cease work and adjust diet. Follow vet's advice throughout. Monitor and record progress. Importantly, maintain close

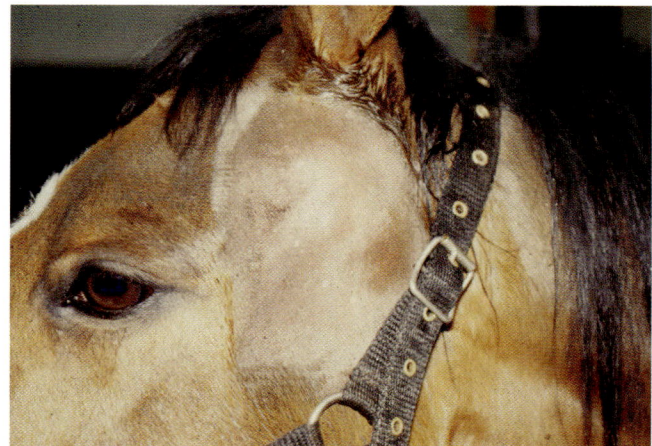
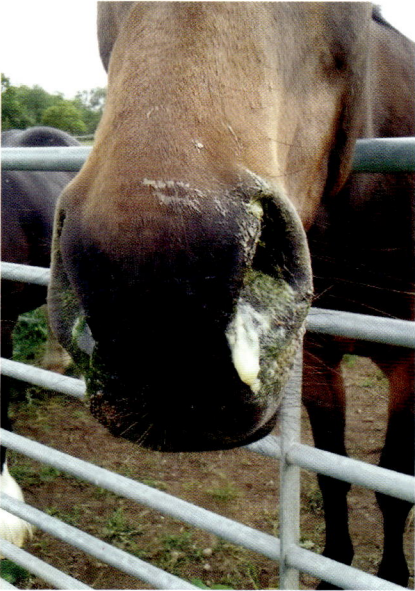

Thick nasal discharge is a symptom of strangles. Later, abscesses may form around the jaw and upper neck.

monitoring and observation of other horses in the proximity. Restrict all movements of horses to minimise risk of further spread.

Strangles Carriers

Occasionally infection can remain in a horse who has had strangles. The horse has fully recovered and will not be showing any signs but is still infected and able to spread the bacteria to other horses. These horses are known as 'carriers'. You cannot tell if a horse is a carrier just by looking at them. Your vet is able to carry out a test called a guttural pouch endoscopy to confirm, where they will check for dry balls of pus known as chondroids. The chondroids are removed from the guttural pouch and antibiotics may be prescribed to kill any remaining bacteria. Horses are re-examined after two weeks to check if they are free from infection.

3. Ringworm

A highly contagious fungal condition affecting the skin, that can be transferred through direct and indirect contact. Classed as a zoonotic disease, which means it can be transferred between species, so humans are at risk of infection.

Symptoms

Raised scab-like patches of hair varying in size appear, which fall off leaving a bald area to expose the skin. Lesions in the skin can cause itchiness. If severe in spread the horse may be dull in outlook.

Actions

Seek veterinary advice for accurate diagnosis skin/scab sample and appropriate treatments. It is really important to not 'self-medicate' prior to the vet taking a sample for analysis, as this could make results inaccurate. Implement strict isolation and monitoring procedures. Work does not need to cease on health grounds, but this can delay recovery because of continual re-application of tack increasing risk of further spread. Reduce grooming as this will also increase area of spread on the skin. Follow vet's advice throughout. Continue to monitor and record progress. Importantly, carry out close monitoring and observation of other horses in proximity. Ideally restrict movements to minimise risk of further spread.

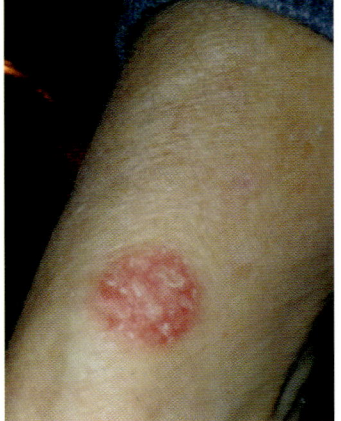

Ringworm can spread from animal to human. Here, a person has contracted ringworm.

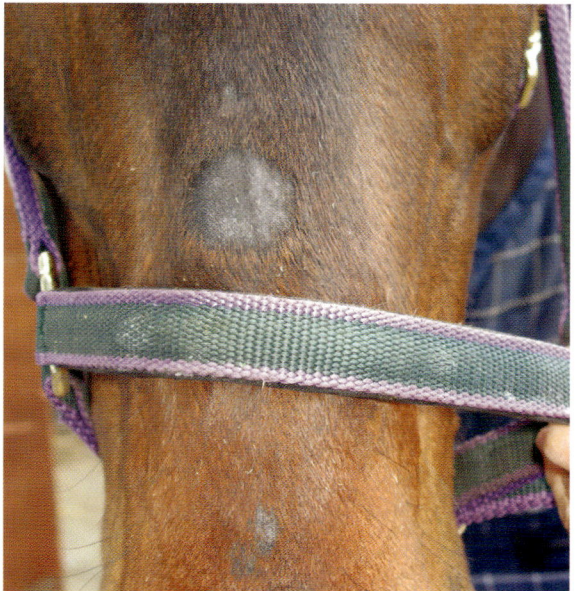

Examples of ringworm on horses.

Anything that has come into contact with the infected horse such as tack, saddle cloths, grooming kit items, headcollar and rugs should be disinfected. As ringworm can live in wood, stable walls or fencing should be disinfected, or a wood treatment applied that will kill the fungus. Anyone treating a horse with ringworm must observe bio-security measures such as wearing disposable gloves, disinfecting footwear and changing clothes between treating the infected horse and non-infected horses.

4. Tetanus

A disease caused by the bacteria Clostridium tetani, which is found in the soil. It can enter the bloodstream via a wound, which offers the ideal environment for survival as it does not require oxygen, enabling the bacteria to multiply anaerobically at a rapid rate. This produces a neurotoxin that targets the horse's nervous system.

Symptoms

The incubation period is 7–21 days.

- Stiffness in head and limbs.
- Progressively worse muscle spasms in the limbs.
- Reluctance to move.

- Flaring of the nostrils.

- Prolapse of the third eyelid.

- Hypersensitivity reaction to light, sudden movement or noise.

Actions

Seek urgent veterinary advice if Tetanus is suspected as it is often fatal. Tetanus is preventable by following a vaccination programme.

5. Equine atypical myopathy

Also know as seasonal pasture myopathy (SPM), this is a very serious debilitating condition that destroys the muscles. It can be fatal as it often affects the muscles of the heart and diaphragm. The cause is predominantly linked to horses eating sycamore seeds and seedlings.

Symptoms

Affected horses will often be found out at pasture unwilling to move. During the initial stages symptoms can progress very quickly and can lead to the horse having difficulty breathing and standing. Other signs include general lethargy, muscular stiffness with tremors or spasms and dark-coloured urine. Some horses exhibit signs similar to colic. Most cases of atypical myopathy occur during the autumn when seeds dropped on the pasture are eaten, or during the spring when the sycamore seedlings are growing.

Actions

Seek immediate veterinary advice for accurate diagnosis and appropriate treatments. Implement care procedures. Follow vet's advice throughout, and monitor and record progress. Remove other horses from the grazing area and increase monitoring of them.

6. Exertional rhabdomyolysis syndrome (ERS)

Previously referred to as Azoturia and such names as 'Monday morning disease' or 'tying up'.

It is a very painful condition whereby the muscles of the hindquarters stiffen and, if untreated, it will worsen quickly. It normally occurs and is noticed when the horse is being exercised — often after a rest day, hence the old name 'Monday morning disease'. It may be noticed at the beginning of exercise or at the close if, for example, a horse works excessively hard and then is not cooled down correctly.

Symptoms

Reluctance to move forwards, possible stumbling of the hindquarters. Muscles across the hindquarters become hard and tense. Consequent pain can produce signs of sweating with an increased respiratory rate. Obvious signs of discomfort or lameness. The horse may glance towards their hindlimbs, so it is important that this action is not confused with colic symptoms.

Actions

Immediately cease working the horse and cover the hindquarters to keep them warm. At the time of occurrence limit horse's movement as much as possible. (If on a hack, arrange transport for return to yard.) Veterinary attention will be required as soon as possible and advice will be needed for accurate diagnosis, appropriate treatments and further clear advice upon later return to work. Follow all such advice and monitor and record progress. Return to work will need to be gradual because of possible muscle damage and it's likely that the horse will need careful attention to diet in the future and some form of exercise on their day off.

7. Equine metabolic syndrome (EMS)

This is a reduction in the normal response to insulin, or insulin resistance. Can occur in young to middle-aged horses who are genetically predisposed to the condition. Other factors that may contribute are obesity or horses on a high-calorie diet and little exercise.

Symptoms

The development of abnormal fat deposits (sometimes described as pockets/bulges/pads) usually seen around the crest, behind the shoulder, the hind quarters (especially at the tail head) and above the eyes, is one of the most common signs of EMS. However, some horses and ponies may still be suffering with insulin dysfunction even if they're at a healthy weight.

Actions

Seek veterinary attention and treatment. Follow vet's advice on diet control, grazing and exercise.

8. Pituitary pars intermedia dysfunction (PPID) or Cushings

A hormonal disease caused by changes in the pituitary gland, most commonly found in older horses.

Symptoms

Excessive hair growth, often abnormally long in length, and coat hair not naturally falling out

A pony with a distinctive thick, curly coat associated with Cushings, the coat will not naturally fall out through moulting so is constant throughout all seasons.

through moulting throughout the seasons of the year. Increased drinking and urinating. Often increased sweating even when stationary, sometimes leaving the coat hair damp. Lethargic in temperament and often prone to other health problems. Horses or ponies with PPID can be more prone to laminitis

Actions

Seek veterinary advice for accurate diagnosis and appropriate management such as medication to help manage the symptoms. Adaptations to workload will depend upon each situation, but there will be a need for increased monitoring on a daily basis, especially owing to the increase in thirst associated with this condition.

9. Laminitis

A painful metabolic disorder that reduces blood flow to the foot, causing inflammation of the sensitive laminae in the hoof. Many causes contribute to this condition, such as EMS or PPID, in addition to an irregular diet or excessive weight.

Symptoms

Most commonly seen in the forefeet, it can start with the horse showing very subtle signs see infographic opposite.

The subtle signs of laminitis
If you're concerned about your horse contact your vet

 Reluctance to turn

 Change in behaviour / temperament

 A shortened stride / a stiffened gait

 Reluctant to pick up their feet

 Shifting weight from foot to foot

 Abnormal heat at the hoof wall or coronet

 Being careful on hard or stony ground / preferring to walk on soft ground

 A strong pounding digital pulse

www.bhs.org.uk
For further advice contact **welfare@bhs.org.uk** or call **02476 840517**

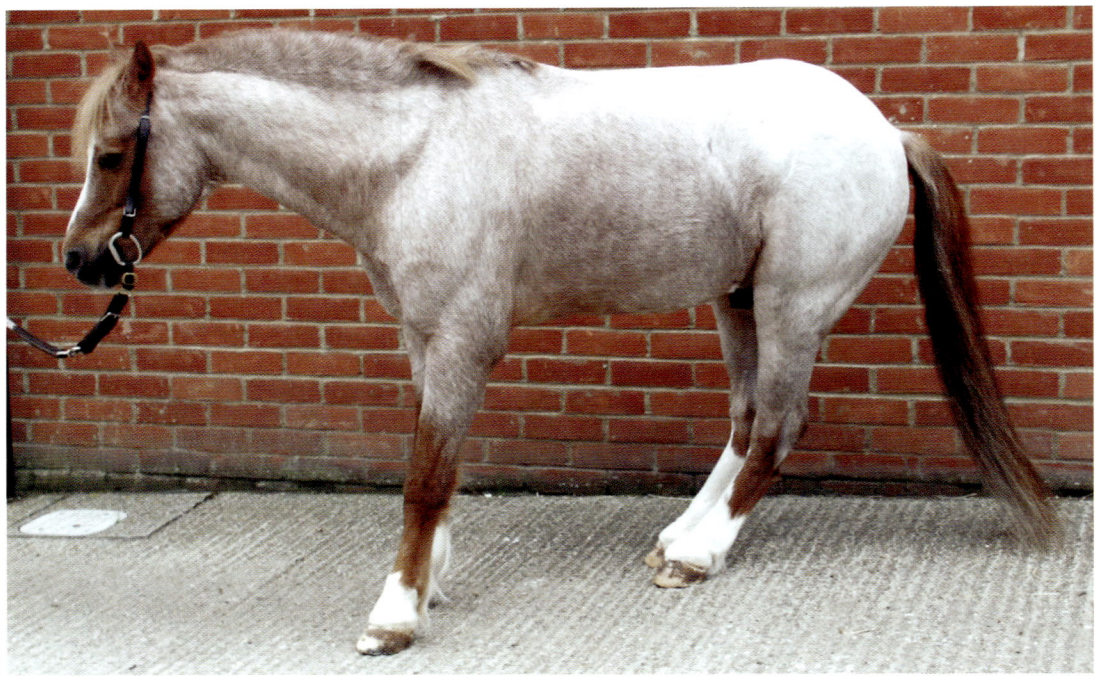

A pony showing a laminitic stance.

When moving, the stride can become short and pottery, with a reluctance to move forwards. There may be an increase in the pulse and respiration rate in response to the pain if it is very severe. At rest the horse may adopt a backwards stance, in an effort to remove the weight from the front feet through leaning backwards and straightening the front legs.

Actions

Seek immediate veterinary advice for an accurate diagnosis and appropriate treatment and management of the horse. Horses will often require pain relief.

If the horse is being kept at grass, bring them off the grass to restrict their access. A deep shavings bed will provide support for the hoof as well as cushioning the horse's weight when standing. Follow the vet's and farrier's advice with regard to diet, hoof care and exercise and monitor and record progress.

10. Equine asthma (EA)

EA, previously referred to as recurrent airway obstruction (RAO), is a term used to describe horses with chronic respiratory signs ranging in severity from mild to severe. It is a chronic respiratory condition commonly caused by sensitivity to dust or mould spores. It is less common in grass-kept horses who live in a relatively dust-free environment with natural ventilation although some horses can be affected by pollen.

Symptoms

Initial cough, frequently at start of exercise and sometimes in the stable. Rarely causes a rise in temperature or appetite loss, but a rise in respiratory rate and often loss of performance when under exertion.

Actions

Seek veterinary advice for accurate diagnosis and appropriate treatments. Remove cause, for example, if stabled improve ventilation, reduce dust, steam hay or provide an alternative such as haylage. You may also need to consider the dust levels in arenas during prolonged dry weather. Moderate work and adjust the diet accordingly. Follow the vet's advice throughout. Monitor and record progress.

11. Equine herpes virus (EHV)

EHV is a highly contagious airborne disease. There are nine strains of EHV but the most common are EHV-1 and EHV-4.

EHV-1 can cause respiratory disease (especially in young horses) and neurological disease in horses of any age, sex and breed, and pregnant mares to abort.

EHV-4 can also cause respiratory disease and occasionally abortion.

Symptoms

Not all horses will show the same signs, some may show mild signs or if they are silently carrying the virus potentially no signs at all.

- Respiratory symptoms – clinical signs of EHV-1 and EHV-4 respiratory disease are very similar to equine flu and can include:

    » High temperature, above 38.5°C.
    » Nasal discharge.
    » A dry cough.
    » Loss of appetite.
    » Reduced performance.
    » Lethargy/depression.

Once infected, horses can show signs of disease within 24 hours, but symptoms usually begin within 4-6 days. For some horses, this may be longer.

- Neurological symptoms:

    » Affected horse can appear weak.
    » Inability to pass urine or droppings.
    » Poor limb coordination (the hind limbs are usually more affected).
    » In severe cases the horse may be unable to stand.

These signs occur as the virus damages the spinal cord.

- Abortion

    » Pregnant mares can suddenly and unexpectedly miscarry their unborn foal.

Actions

Isolate the horse and call the vet immediately. All horses that have had direct or indirect contact with the infected horse should be closely monitored and their temperatures taken twice a day. Isolation procedures should be followed.

12. Sweet itch

This condition is an allergic reaction to midge bites, causing itching which, in turn, causes the horse to react with excessive rubbing. Horses often rub their mane and the top of their tail bald and also rub bald patches on the skin, which become sore.

Symptoms

Midges usually bite along the top of the horse including the head, mane, withers, rump and tail. Signs of the horse rubbing in these areas will be seen; the skin is likely to become bald, crusty and sore and, over time, the skin will thicken and becomes wrinkled. There may also be dandruff and, in some cases, weeping sores may develop.

This horse has rubbed their tail as a result of sweet itch.

5 | Common Health Conditions

Actions

Seek veterinary advice for management of affected horses. Horses affected can be kept stabled during dusk and dawn when the midges are at their worst during the summer months (April to October). Specially designed rugs are available that will cover the whole horse; these protect the horse from the midges and also prevent them from becoming sore through excess rubbing. When turned out and ridden, applying fly repellent can prevent the horse from being bitten. When horses are affected, soothing lotions can be applied to relieve itching and reduce inflammation.

13. Colic

This term applies to symptoms of any sort of abdominal pain in the horse, all of which must be taken very seriously. Many factors can cause colic, ranging from sudden change in diet to impacted food within the intestines, or a build-up of gas produced in the intestines. Some cases of colic may result from displacement of the intestine, which restricts blood supply to that area, causing sections of the intestine to die.

Symptoms

The five REACT signs are the most common and important indicators of colic. The signs include:

- Restless or agitated:

    » repeated attempts to lie down,
    » frequent rolling,
    » box-walking,
    » unexplained sweating.

- Eating less or droppings reduced:

    » eating less than normal or not eating at all,
    » passing fewer droppings than normal or not passing any at all,
    » changes to the consistency of droppings.

- Abdominal pain:

    » pawing at the ground,
    » kicking at the belly,
    » watching or looking at flanks.

- Clinical changes:

    » increased heart rate,
    » rapid respiration rate,
    » changes in the colour of the gums,
    » reduced gut sounds or no gut sounds at all.

- Tired or lethargic:

    » lying down more than normal,
    » lowered head position,
    » dullness and depression.

Actions

Colic cases can quickly deteriorate so early recognition and prompt veterinary attention is vital to increase the chance of recovery for the horse. Seek immediate veterinary advice for accurate diagnosis and appropriate treatments. Remove all feed. Place horse in a safe area in case they should wish to roll. Follow vet's advice throughout. Monitor and record progress.

14. Worm burden

Even horses who appear healthy might be hiding a heavy worm burden as some signs are difficult to see and there are many different types of worms that affect horses, all with slightly differing life-cycles. For this reason it's very important to make sure that there is a testing-led deworming programme to reduce the risk of infestation through preventative measures, such as removal of droppings at least twice a week and good pasture management and to reduce the risk of resistance to the dewormer.

Symptoms

Loss of condition and weight, and general lethargy, with poor appetite and diarrhoea. In some severe cases an extended appearance to the belly with ribs showing. There may be frequent bouts of colic.

Actions

Seek veterinary advice, especially if the horse has other health problems. Utilise Faecal Worm Egg Counts (FWEC) and saliva or blood tests to help ascertain worm egg levels and reduce the risk of dewormer resistance. Resistance to dewormer occurs when a proportion of the worms inside the horse are no longer killed by the dewormer.

It is essential that dewormer drugs are only used after testing and as part of structured programme of worm monitoring and control that is developed in partnership with your vet.

FWEC should be carried out between spring and autumn. Following the results of the FWEC, or if advised by your vet, when you give your horse a dewormer it is recommended checking that the treatment has worked and that the dewormer did its job, killed the adult worms, and has significantly reduced egg numbers in your horse's faeces. Because of its importance in detecting dewormer resistance, many labs offer this reduction test free of charge. Talk to your vet about performing Faecal Worm Egg Count Reduction Testing (FWECRT) at least once per year to check that the different dewormer drugs are still working on your property.

Tapeworm antibody tests measure the antibodies to the tapeworm present in the horse's saliva or blood. The frequency of testing should be determined with guidance from your vet and based on the horse and the herd's risk. Based on the results of these tests your vet will advise you if the horse does not require deworming, or if they require dewormer what type.

15. Lymphoedema

Also known as 'filled legs', this is a gravity-dependent collection of lymphatic fluid causing swelling of the lower legs, often arising from lack of movement.

Symptoms

More commonly found in the hind legs, although some times in the forelegs: swelling occurs from the coronet upwards, particularly at the rear of the fetlock. Normally happens when a horse stands in with reduced exercise; the horse should not register pain with this condition.

Actions

Report to stable manager. The filling should reduce with exercise, so try to reduce the amount of time the horse spends in the stable. In some cases, applying stable bandages when the horse is stabled overnight can help to reduce the swelling, but this does not stop the fluid collecting. If a horse develops filled legs and has not previously suffered from this, seek veterinary advice.

16. Lymphangitis

Lymphangitis is an inflammation of the lymph nodes and lymphatic vessels. It can occur when bacteria enter the lymphatic system via a cut or skin lesion, causing the lymphatic vessels to swell and narrow.

Symptoms

It more typically affects a hind limb, which will swell and become painful. In some cases the swelling may reach to stifle, with the leg reaching twice its normal size or more. Initially, when an area of the swelling is pressed with a finger, a dent will appear in the skin surface. This is known as a 'pitting oedema'. If the lymphangitis is untreated, the swelling will worsen and become firm. Lameness and rise in temperature might be present, depending upon the onset and, in severe cases, serum might ooze from the skin pores.

Actions

Seek veterinary advice for accurate diagnosis and appropriate treatments. Implement care procedures. If sound, lead in hand to help increase circulation. Vet will advise upon reintroduction of gentle exercise.

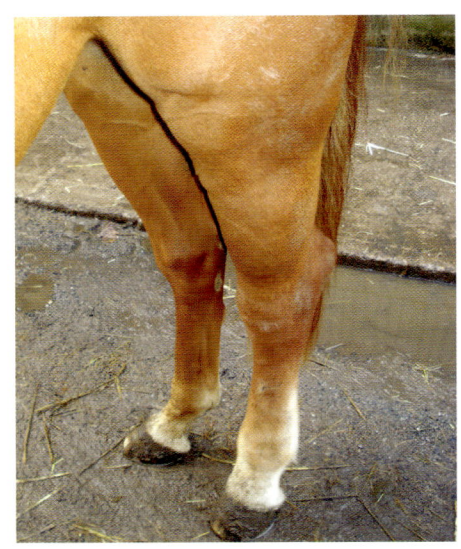

Lymphangitis in a hind leg.

17. Windgalls

Can be divided into two forms. Articular windgalls are associated with the fetlock joint, and tendinous windgalls with the flexor tendon sheath. Can be common in middle-aged and older horses.

Symptoms

Known as synovial enlargements, these are fluid-type swellings that appear behind the fetlock joint as a result of over-secretion of the joint fluid, often caused by workload or by upright conformation. Fluid in the fetlock joint is kept in place by the joint capsule and it is a swelling of the joint capsule that makes articular windgalls appear. Tendinous windgalls are slightly higher up above the fetlock joint and appear as a thickening. They can occur on all legs, but more commonly the hinds

Action

If the horse shows discomfort, or the windgalls are newly developed, seek veterinary advice on

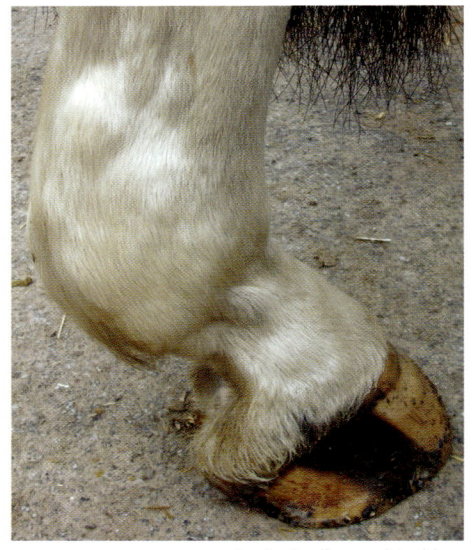

A windgall on a hind leg.

management. These do not usually cause unsoundness but are a sign that the joints may be undergoing some wear and tear. It is important to monitor the horse and ensure they are shod frequently and, if necessary, the workload is moderated.

18. Splints

These are caused by direct trauma, such as a kick to the splint bone, or from workload when the horse is still immature. Can frequently occur in young horses who work on hard ground.

Symptoms

Usually found on the inside of a foreleg between the splint and cannon bone, or on the splint bone itself, but can be found on any leg on the inside or outside. If recently formed, there will be heat and swelling on the leg, and it may be painful if pressure is applied. When splints are forming, they can sometimes cause shortening of stride, an unwillingness to work and lameness. If a splint has already formed there will be a cold, hard bony lump that is not painful to the touch.

Actions

If the horse is sore, reduce workload and seek veterinary advice. Implement care procedures and monitor. If symptoms persist or worsen, seek further veterinary advice.

19. Tendon injury

If a horse suddenly becomes lame when being ridden, especially if jumping, doing fast work or where the going is deep or boggy, it could be an indication that the horse has a tendon injury. This can happen particularly if the horse is tired or unfit.

Symptoms

Lameness, with heat and swelling usually down the back of the leg from the knee to the fetlock. Horses may also suffer less severe tendon injuries, and may not be lame, but have slight swelling and heat. However, if they continue to work, the condition can worsen.

Action

Seek veterinary advice for accurate diagnosis and appropriate treatments. Immediately cool the area by cold hosing or applying an ice pack or boot. Repeat regularly and follow a care plan in line with veterinary advice. The vet may decide to scan the leg for more specific diagnosis. The horse is likely to require box rest initially, then gradual introduction of walking in hand.

When assessing lameness see the horse firstly in walk, then in trot. It is good practice for the handler to wear their hat and gloves, a bridle can be used on the horse for extra control if required.

Assessing lameness

Being able to notice when a horse is lame is important. When vets assess a horse as being lame, they are measuring how lame the horse is. They often describe the level of lameness as a proportion of how lame the horse appears, for example one-tenth would indicate a horse being less lame than one described as six-tenths lame. This measurement is used as a guide for ascertaining the level of discomfort and in the diagnosis of reasons for lameness, in addition to re-assessing progress with the horse at a later stage.

Recognising an obvious pronounced lameness is easier than one that is very slight or intermittent and it's only through having knowledge of how a horse should move, practising looking and being observant that you can develop confidence in assessing lameness.

Having prior knowledge of a horse may help, but you have to be careful that this doesn't influence your decision when making an assessment. In addition, if the horse has a fault in their action when they move this may be a result of poor conformation and not an unsoundness.

How to make an assessment

At halt

In an ideal situation this would be done in a secure area on level, hard ground with the convenience of having someone to stand the horse up prior to leading them in hand for you to view. Make sure all of the horse's feet have been picked out prior to any assessment.

Initial assessment in halt will involve quietly observing the horse at rest to check how comfortable the horse is. Allow for the fact that, when relaxed, most horses will rest a hind leg, but look to check that the horse is happy to bear an even amount of weight on each leg. An example of when to be concerned would be if a horse was reluctant to stand with the complete base of their foot contacting the ground, such as when being asked to move over, they don't put either the heel or toe on the ground.

Based on what you see at halt, if you suspect a problem on a particular leg then, as long as it doesn't cause the horse further discomfort, pick up the suspect leg and check the foot in case there is something in it, or the shoe has slipped badly.

In movement

Get someone to lead the horse, first of all in walk as, if the lameness is severe, it may not be necessary (or safe) to see the horse in trot. Make sure they are competent to lead the horse safely (wearing hat and gloves, using a bridle if required) and in doing so, are able to control the horse and keep themselves positioned at the side of the shoulder. This will let you see the horse fully and prevent them from dragging the horse behind them or getting left behind if the horse is overly fresh!

It's important to view the horse from the side, the front and from behind. First, see how the horse moves in a straight line.

Assess by:

- Looking for any abnormal limb movement.
- Checking whether stride lengths are equal.
- Listening for equal footfall/beat.

If the lameness is very subtle, then look as the horse is:

- Led in walk through a turn in direction.

- Lunged on a circle.

Signs of suspected forelimb lameness.

The head will raise as the lame limb touches the ground (to help you remember, think how you would 'hunch' upwards to alleviate the pressure if you had a stone between your sock and your shoe) or try seeing how the head will nod downwards as the sound limb contacts the ground.

Signs of suspected hind limb lameness

This is often more difficult to assess. Generally there will be asymmetry (unequal movement) as you view the horse from behind. This means a hip will either lift excessively high, or drop lower when the horse moves. To ascertain which hind leg may be the lame one takes practice, and considering other factors such as the stride length and ability to bear weight.

What to do if a horse seems lame

First, cease work immediately. While recognising that older horses may sometimes initially appear stiff when being ridden first thing in the morning, lameness is lameness, so it is important to know when and whom to ask for further opinion and advice.

The following factors need to be taken into account to establish what to do next:

- Who should be notified? (Could be a senior member of staff, horse owner/yard owner — or a combination of all.)

- Age and history of the horse.

- Onset of lameness, was it sudden or gradual?

- Has the horse been lame before recently?

- Rest the horse as required.

Establishing any previous history can help, for example, is it a recurring lameness? If it is, remember that accurate diagnosis by a vet will enable the prescription of pain relief if required, alongside ensuring that correct and appropriate treatment takes place.

Managing horses' health and biosecurity

When it comes to health, we would all agree that the saying 'prevention is better than cure' is very true — especially when it concerns horses. Humans are able to tell each other if they start to feel unwell, whereas horses are totally dependent upon our ability to pick up those early warning signs and act upon them to stop a condition worsening and/or spreading disease.

Keeping horses healthy is made much easier if preventative measures are put in place, such as a yard having an isolation procedure for any new arrivals, following a vaccination programme against certain diseases and adhering to routine procedures such as a testing-led deworming programme for all horses. It's helpful to have some understanding of the differing terms that get used when discussing health.

Definition of terms

Disease. An abnormal condition or disorder of a structure, or how something functions.

Contagious. Means that the disease can be transferred (passed from one horse to another) and in some cases to humans (when they are known as a zoonoses).

Direct contact transfer. Means that the disease can transfer through physical contact, for example horses being in contact with each other.

Indirect contact transfer. Transfers through horses coming into contact with the same thing, such as sharing grazing areas or equipment.

Airborne contact. Means that the disease can transfer through the air (such as equine flu), by horses sneezing, coughing and the disease travelling through atomised bodily fluids, such as nasal discharges.

Infection. Results when a disease-producing organism invades the body's tissues.

Infectious disease. An illness resulting from an infection, not always contagious.

Notifiable. Term applied to specific diseases, where it is a legal requirement in Scotland, England and Wales to notify the Animal & Plant Health Agency (APHA) at Defra or the Department of Agriculture, Environment and Rural Affairs (DAERA) in Northern Ireland when such disease has been confirmed. An example would be equine viral arteritis (EVA). Whenever such diseases are suspected immediate isolation and veterinary advice is essential. A list of notifiable diseases can be found on the Defra and DAERA websites.

Vaccination

The main purpose of vaccinating horses is to prevent the spread of disease. As with humans, as research continues to develop and inform, the range of available vaccines widens. Best practice would recommend relevant vaccination for all horses but the specific requirements may vary depending upon situations. An example would be that a horse kept solely for pleasure would have a differing requirement placed upon them as compared to brood mares and horses who race or compete at affiliated competitions. Competition horses who travel frequently to various venues would be considered a higher risk because of close proximity to other horses, especially if sharing transport.

A horse must be in good health prior to being vaccinated and, as each vaccine differs in composition, the vet will best advise upon any workload restrictions or moderation for the period after the vaccine has been administered.

Currently equine influenza (flu) and tetanus are the diseases against which horses are most commonly vaccinated in the UK. Vaccines are also available for Strangles and EHV.

Currently, an example vaccination schedule for flu and tetanus would be:

- First vaccine.

- Second vaccine 21–92 days after the first vaccine.

- Third vaccine 150–215 days after the second vaccine.

- An annual 'booster' injection is required for flu (not more than 365 days from the third vaccination). Tetanus requires a 'booster' every two years – the vet will advise you which vaccination a horse requires.

The vaccination date and details must be recorded in the horse's passport and signed by the vet. If the vaccination is not done within the allowed time-frame the vaccination programme will have to be re-started to ensure full coverage.

Vaccination rules can vary for competition horses depending on the governing body so make sure you are familiar with the rules.

Strangles and EHV vaccines

Vaccination is available for both the respiratory disease and miscarriage caused by EHV-1 and/or EHV-4. There is no vaccine registered to prevent EHV-1 neurological disease.

Vaccination is recommended for horses:

- Under the age of five as they may be particularly susceptible to the respiratory disease caused by EHV-1.

- Breeding studs or in areas with pregnant mares.

- Horses in facilities with frequent equine movement, including livery yards.

- Horses in venues where equestrian sports and disciplines take place.

Managing biosecurity

Alongside horses kept in a yard having their relevant vaccinations as a means of preventing the spread of disease, common sense precautions such as keeping everywhere tidy and reducing dust and dirt levels will help to keep the environment healthy. Good ventilation, routine cleanliness of equipment and regular use of disinfectant, cleaning feed bowls and limiting the sharing of equipment — especially water buckets/bridles (because of saliva) will all help in reducing the spread of contagious disease.

Each time a horse is off site and in close proximity to others there is risk of contagion. Participating in activities such as sponsored rides and competitions will always involve an element of risk. You would not allow a horse in your charge to stand too close to strange horses for fear of them being kicked but think how often, for example at a children's rally, you might see ponies being allowed to say 'hello' to each other by their young riders, with no idea of the risk of disease being spread. Not allowing your horse to drink from a random trough at an event, or to graze shared areas, will also help reduce the risk of mistakenly bringing home an unwelcome disease.

Isolation

This is when a horse is temporarily kept separately from other horses. It is commonly done to help prevent a disease spreading when a horse first arrives at a yard, or when it is suspected that a horse is unwell and there is uncertainty as to what is wrong. There may also be occasions when a horse needs isolation for other non-contagious situations. An example would be if they were unwell and needed to be in a quieter area of a busy stable yard.

As discussed earlier, being herd animals, some horses get upset when kept isolated — however, best practice would recommend that any new horse arriving at a stable yard should be isolated initially. Use enrichment to provide mental stimulation and keep the horse occupied. This can include visual enrichment such as placing other horses in their sightline, or feed enrichment like hay balls, which encourages foraging and extends time spent eating. This short-term situation for the horse is better than a whole yard going down with disease. The time for which to isolate a new horse is subjective, as each situation differs: an approximate guide would be 21 days, but where any doubt exists about the horse's health, it is best to seek veterinary advice.

It could be that there's been an outbreak of a disease in the local area, in which case, as a minimum the period for isolation would need to be the same as the incubation period for that disease. It is recommended that all new arrivals to a yard should have a faecal egg worm count (as a minimum) to check the horse's worm burden before being turned out to pasture. There are also tests available to help detect strangles carriers.

To isolate successfully would entail doing all that could be done to avoid transmitting a disease from horse to horse. Horses can often be 'carriers', which means they can transmit some diseases without exhibiting symptoms themselves. Often, when a horse is first isolated, some signs may not be apparent so it's really important to be vigilant about hygiene. Wearing separate clothes/overalls when dealing with the isolated horse and using an appropriate disinfectant-based footbath — even wearing disposable gloves and washing hands both before and after coming into contact — are all key factors in successful management, as are:

- Following veterinary advice.

- Informing those who need to know of the situation.

- Isolating the horse downwind from the stable yard to help minimise the travel of any airborne organisms (or at least sectioning off an area of the yard).

- Restricted access, with the fewest possible people caring for the horse — ideally one person.

- Keeping all equipment separately.

- Disposing of any bedding/waste materials correctly.

In terms of the isolated horse's welfare, it is important to ensuring that they are comfortable, with normal needs being met, such as appropriate type/depth of bedding, access to water and hay and good ventilation. In fact, standard care procedures should be practised, augmented by following veterinary advice specific to the individual case.

This may include such issues as:

- Monitoring the horse's intake of water, hay and feed.

- Adjustment to feed and exercise (as required).

- Noting droppings (number of and the texture).

- Recording temperature, pulse and respiration (TPR) (if appropriate).

- Checking for warmth.

> *Preventative management of a horse's health can be done through a combination of keeping the horse in a healthy environment, preventative planning, being able to interpret the vital health signs that might indicate something is wrong and responding accordingly to each situation. Always know to whom you should report any concerns, or from whom to seek advice and, importantly, remember to follow veterinary advice.*

Professional healthcare for horses – allied professionals

You have probably heard riders saying their horse feels sound but hasn't schooled as well as they normally do, or 'doesn't feel quite right' and then state how much better they feel after a 'treatment'. It may be that there was a very subtle lameness that the rider was unable to identify, or a soreness that was being masked by the horse's basic willingness to work.

Current UK legislation (Veterinary Surgeons Act 1966) states that vets are the only people legally allowed to make a diagnosis of an injury/disease and to give advice or prescribe on the course of treatment to be given. Therefore, any treatments must have veterinary permission before being started. Responsible professional practitioners will welcome working alongside veterinary advice as this enables a diagnosis to be confirmed prior to starting a programme of treatment. Traditionally, the vet was the main person who would have actually treated horses, but now we have equine dental technicians, physiotherapists, chiropractors, osteopaths to name a few.

It's important that, when considering using such help, homework is done to establish credibility in terms of their qualifications and experience, what the treatment may involve and how might it benefit the horse. The common aim with all allied professionals is to work for improvement that will help support rehabilitation, for example when there has been an injury, or to maximise potential for performance. Specific exercises combined with rest or moderated exercise may be suggested as part of the after-treatment — hence the need to fully understand what the additional therapy is hoping to achieve.

There are many associations to which allied professionals can affiliate and potentially join as members. Each association will have different rules for membership based upon an individual's qualifications, so it is wise to check what the differing levels of membership are.

The following text gives summaries of some of the main allied professional roles.

Dentistry

It is advisable that a horse's teeth are checked a minimum of once a year by either a vet, an equine dental technician registered with the British Association of Equine Dental Technicians (BAEDT) or a category 2 member of the World Wide Association of Equine Dentists (WWAED). Members of these associations have passed approved exams to attain their qualifications and have agreed to abide by performance guidelines and a code of conduct and are all fully insured.

Musculoskeletal therapies

Physiotherapy

Physiotherapy works upon function (how the body works) and movement (how the body moves) and uses a physical approach to restore, maintain and promote well-being. It uses science to inform working practice and delivery. A chartered physiotherapist who works with horses will have initially trained and qualified as a human physiotherapist.

Chiropractors

Veterinary chiropractic therapy is a 'hands on' therapy whereby manipulation is used. Its primary focus is on the spine and its effect on the nervous system to relieve pain, improve joint function and reduce muscle spasm. It does not replace traditional veterinary medicine but can help with treatment and care.

Osteopathy

This involves using a range of physical manipulation to stretch and massage muscle tissue and bones.

Acupuncture

This consists of inserting fine stainless steel sterile needles into specific parts of the body and is commonly used for the relief of musculoskeletal pain and can influence the function of internal organs. Being an invasive procedure that requires a thorough knowledge of veterinary anatomy and physiology, legally, it can only be undertaken by a qualified veterinary surgeon who has undergone special training in the technique.

Quality of Life

Quality of life is important for any horse of any age and is defined by their overall physical and mental well-being.

This can sometimes be difficult to assess, especially if you see that horse every day. The BHS has a quality of life indicator with a check list to help you monitor the condition of a horse to help identify/indicate areas of concern.

Physical well-being

The physical well-being of your horse has many factors that will affect how you view their physical health. For example, are they recovering from an injury? Are they an older horse? Do they have a short-term or chronic condition?

The following list will help you identify if the horse is comfortable or needs veterinary assistance:

- Is the horse maintaining a healthy weight?
- Can the horse still perform normal movement with ease, for example rolling, getting down or standing up?
- Is the horse as active as normal?
- Have you noticed a change in their movement?
- Are they stiff or reluctant to walk?
- Do they lay down for long periods, or not at all?
- Can the horse stand comfortably on all four feet?
- Has the horse lost weight or muscle condition taking into consideration their age and workload?
- Is the horse happy to accept the bit?
- Does the horse feel different when ridden?
- Has the horse's eating and drinking habits changed?

If any of these questions have raised concerns, you should speak to a senior member of staff or the vet who will be able to assess the horse and put in place a plan of action to help improve their condition.

Mental well-being

To determine if horses are 'happy', you first need to understand what is important to them.

For a free-ranging feral horse, a positive emotional state would come from the interaction with their herd. This can look different for the domesticated horse, but the need for social interaction remains the same. So how do you know if a horse you look after is happy?

The table below highlights positive and negative pointers that can help you monitor any change in their emotional well-being. However, it is important to note that no two horses have the same influences in life, such as intensity of work or physical health.

Positive	Negative
Greets you in the same way each day	Is withdrawn, dull or depressed, for example, stands in the corner of the stable head down
Spends most of their day grazing or eating roughage	Not interested in food
Interaction with other horses, for example, they can see other horses from their stable, share a field or can see other horses from their field	Stereotypical behaviour such as crib biting, box walking or weaving
Mutual grooming with other horses and regular grooming from owner	Stays away from other horses in the field or is grumpy when groomed
Express themselves in the usual way	Has become generally grumpy or aggressive
Happy and attentive when ridden, driven or exercised	Grumpy when being tacked up or objects to being ridden, driven or exercised (this could also be physical)
Have a relaxed expression on their face both in the stable and when moving or ridden, driven or exercised	Tension around their muzzle and eyes

Quality of life indicator

It is important, when using this list, to understand that if you recognise any of the conditions on the list you must seek advice, as a slight change in behaviour can indicate that veterinary attention is needed, that may potentially result in improved quality of life for the horse.

The horse:		
1.	Does not interact with people in the same way as before (for example does not come to greet their handler in the stable in the morning).	[YES/NO]
2.	Does not interact with other horses in the same way as before (for example keeps their distance from the rest of the herd).	[YES/NO]

3.	Is withdrawn, dull or depressed (for example stands in the corner of the stable with head down).	[YES/NO]
4.	Has changed their behaviour significantly (for example has become aggressive).	[YES/NO]
5.	Does not seem to enjoy life (for example a change in character, such as showing signs of stress).	[YES/NO]
6.	Is not eating their normal amount of hay or forage (for example a significant amount of hay is being left).	[YES/NO]
7.	Is not as active as normal (for example stiff movement, reluctance to walk or reduced performance).	[YES/NO]
8.	Has a dull, staring coat.	[YES/NO]
9.	Is losing weight.	[YES/NO]
10.	Is having diarrhoea often (for example for 3 or more days).	[YES/NO]
11.	Is not drinking enough water.	[YES/NO]
12.	Is experiencing discomfort or is not able to urinate (for example attempts to urinate but nothing happens).	[YES/NO]
13.	Needs help to move or get up (for example struggles to rise from lying down).	[YES/NO]
14.	Is experiencing pain.	[YES/NO]
15.	Is not weight-bearing on one or more limb(s) (for example cannot comfortably stand on all four limbs or is resting a foreleg).	[YES/NO]
16.	Is sweating without exercise (and it's not an excessively hot day).	[YES/NO]
17.	Is blowing (panting) without exercise.	[YES/NO]
18.	Is trembling or shaking.	[YES/NO]

If you are in any doubt as to a horse's quality of life then you should speak to a senior staff member and a vet should be consulted. Keeping a diary and taking photos of the horse to record their health and behaviour is useful. Sometimes, when we see horses every day, we may find it difficult to make comparisons or notice the small declines in health.

Euthanasia

There are many reasons why a horse may have to be euthanised, including illness, an accident, change in owner's circumstances or because old age or a pre-existing condition has led to their quality of life deteriorating.

It is important for anyone who works in the industry and horse owners to be aware that due to serious injury or illness, euthanasia may have to be opted for unexpectedly in horses of any age. Dealing with an emergency is difficult enough without having to make some very hard decisions quickly and under pressure. By being prepared and understanding the processes and options available, you are making appropriate plans and this will help to make a difficult decision a little easier.

Euthanasia methods

Euthanasia by lethal injection

The lethal injection can only be administered by a veterinary surgeon. In some cases, the horse may be sedated beforehand. The injection consists of an overdose of anaesthetic drugs which causes the horse to gradually collapse, experiencing a rapid loss of consciousness followed by cardiovascular arrest. Occasionally the horse may take 2–3 gasps of breath following collapse and loss of consciousness. This is a common and involuntary nervous system response to the euthanasia drugs. It may take a short time (60–90 seconds) for the heart to stop, and there may be some involuntary muscle twitching or leg movement which can prove distressing to the owner. However, the horse will not be conscious during this time and is completely unaware of what is going on. The vet will monitor the horse's pulse until it has stopped.

Once the injection is administered, the horse will tend to fall quite slowly, but this can be unpredictable meaning that the safety of the vet and handler must be considered. However, a skilled handler can influence the direction in which the horse falls. Many vets will allow the owner to hold the horse, if they wish to, while the injection is given, but will then take hold of the horse and ask the owner to stand back, giving plenty of space.

Euthanasia by free bullet

This must be carried out by a vet, knackerman, hunt kennel or slaughterman, who has a licence to use a firearm. In some cases, the horse may be sedated and this can only be administered by the vet if given by injection. The muzzle of the gun is placed against the horse's forehead and the bullet discharged. This will euthanise the horse instantly with the animal falling to the ground. The horse's limbs may make sudden twitches; these are normal reflexes after death and the heart will still beat for a short while even though there is a loss of consciousness. The noise of the gunshot will be of no detriment to the horse who would've been completely unaware as the process will be instant. Once the horse is on the ground, blood may be discharged from the wound and the amount can vary between individuals.

An equine abattoir may also be an option to euthanise a horse as owners will be paid for the carcass. However, abattoirs are not an option for every horse as many will have been signed out of the food chain (this information will be included in the horse's passport) either at the wishes of their owner or because they have received certain medication during their lifetime. As the horse would also have to travel, it is essential that they are fit to do so.

Friends at the End

'Friends at the End' is a BHS initiative designed to make sure that no horse owner has to face the loss of their equine companion alone.

The BHS Friends at the End scheme can provide support for horse owners facing this difficult decision. Every member of the team has received training from bereavement counsellors, so they have a genuine understanding of the loss and grief that come when a horse dies. They aren't there to take the place of a counsellor or vet, but they can offer an extra source of support both via the phone and on the day, they are also happy to help with making arrangements.

The BHS Horse Care & Welfare team is always willing to talk to owners about euthanasia and provide any information, advice and support that may be needed at a difficult time.

Summary

- A horse's vital signs of TPR (temperature, pulse and respiration) are a useful indication of health — if a horse is showing any signs that they may be unwell, when you take TPR you should be able to see whether they have deviated from their normal values — for example, a rise in temperature could indicate that something is wrong.

- For the reasons described above it is good practice to keep a record of each horse's normal TPR. Other records to keep include vaccinations, dentistry, testing-led worming programme, shoeing, trimming and previous medical conditions or injuries.

- There are many health conditions that can affect horses; if a horse is unwell you should always seek advice from a vet. However, it is useful to be familiar with common conditions, especially those that may be contagious or infectious so that swift action can be taken to prevent the spread of disease.

- When assessing lameness, pick out the horse's feet, check for any abnormal signs at halt, then see the horse in walk and trot. With foreleg lameness the horse will raise their head as the lame leg hits the floor. With hind leg lameness there will be unequal movement in the hips; the horse may either drop the lame hip or raise it higher.

- The purpose of biosecurity measures is to prevent the spread of disease. The measures include isolating new horses arriving on a yard and isolating any horses who show signs of a contagious or infectious disease. In addition to this, biosecurity also includes taking precautions when taking horses away from their yard to competitions. Precautions include preventing horses from drinking from communal water troughs (and supplying your own source) and preventing them from coming into direct contact with other unknown horses, for example, not letting your horse say 'hello' to another at a competition.

- There are a number of healthcare professionals who can provide supportive therapies for horses; these include; physiotherapists, chiropractors and osteopaths. Current legislation states that only vets can diagnose problems and that any consequent treatment should have veterinary permission.

TRAINING TIPS

1. Try to assist or observe vets or allied professionals when they visit the yard.

2. Watch horses being trotted up for the vet, or for your supervisor or manager so you can start to recognise which leg they may be lame on.

3. Practise taking TPR on a variety of horses.

4. For more information on common health conditions visit the BHS website.

Chapter 6
Feeding

Nutrients

Nutritional intake and different types of work

Forage

Important considerations when feeding

Supplements

Considerations when creating diets

Summary

Nutrients

All mammals require six essential nutrients in order to survive:

1. Water.

2. Carbohydrates (structural and non-structural).

3. Protein.

4. Fat.

5. Vitamins.

6. Minerals.

These are unable to be produced or synthesised by the animals themselves and so must be obtained from the diet.

The specific quantity required varies dependent on the animal's digestive physiology and how efficiently it can digest and utilise each nutrient. Horses require the largest part of their diet to come from structural carbohydrate, with smaller amounts of protein and fat.

Water

Every cell in the body needs water to perform fully. Like us, not drinking enough can mean that horses with insufficient water intake don't work or perform well; in more extreme situations dehydration can result in serious illness and disease. An average 16hh horse will drink between 30 and 70 litres (53 and 123 pints) of water a day (approximately two to five standard plastic buckets full).

Carbohydrates

Carbohydrates are the primary source of energy for the horse and are the largest constituent of many feeds. Grass, hay, haylage, sugar beet and cereals are composed largely of carbohydrates, but they do vary in the type of carbohydrate. There are three different groups of carbohydrate, although the basic building block of each is the same thing — glucose. What differs is how the glucose is held together and therefore how easily the horse can access it.

Simple sugars (non-structural carbohydrate) are found in plant cell walls, so are a component of grass. These are quick and easy for the horse to digest by enzymes in the small intestine so provide 'fast-release' energy.

Storage carbohydrate (non-structural) describes starch found in cereals, and fructans found in grass under certain growth conditions. The horse has a limited capacity for starch absorption in the small intestine.

Structural carbohydrate or fibre (cellulose) is the main structural component of plants; it is tough and not able to be broken down by the horse's system on its own, but is fermented by the bacteria in the horse's large intestine to release volatile fatty acids that can be absorbed and used for energy. This route provides up to 70 per cent of the horse's energy by way of a 'slow-release' energy system, trickling it in steadily over time.

If fed in too high a quantity, both simple sugars and starches can exceed the ability of the small intestine to break them down and use them; what happens in these cases is that they pass through to the large intestine where the bacteria ferment them. This causes huge problems as it results in stronger acid being produced, upsetting the normal balance of the large intestine, and can contribute to colic or laminitis. This is why any cereal must be fed in small quantities across multiple feeds to allow it to trickle through and be digested fully in the small intestine.

The amount of carbohydrate in grass will vary depending on the types of grasses and time of year.

Protein

Protein is used for growth and repair of all body tissues (including muscle) and is an essential component of hormones, enzymes and antibodies. Contrary to what many people believe, it is not normally used as an energy source and high levels of protein will not cause weight gain or excitability. It may be used as an energy source in extreme situations (for example, when an animal is starving and has no dietary carbohydrate) but physiologically this is a very inefficient way to obtain energy.

Protein is made up of building blocks called amino acids, some of which the horse can synthesise sufficiently by themselves (and which are consequentially called 'non-essential') and some that need to be supplied by the diet ('essential'). When we talk about the quality of protein we are referring to the essential amino acid content as well as how easily it can be digested. Some of the essential amino acids that you may see listed on a feedbag label are lysine, methionine and threonine.

Some groups of horses have a higher than normal requirement for protein; these include growing, pregnant and lactating individuals and those doing medium to hard work. If feeding these horses it is particularly important to make sure that the diet supplies enough good-quality protein. An important point to make is that although protein is used as part of muscle growth and repair, feeding elevated levels will not increase muscle development. Once the horse's protein requirement has been met any extra protein cannot be used; it is only through appropriate schooling that muscles will develop further.

Good-quality grass and conserved forage will normally meet the protein demands of horses for maintenance or light work. However, at times where grass quality is reduced, it may need to be supplemented. Likewise, horses with an elevated protein requirement (as mentioned above) will need to be given additional protein. Examples of feeds that are good sources of protein are alfalfa, soya bean meal, linseed and peas. When reading a feedbag label, looking only at the crude protein (CP) percentage will not tell you about the quality of that protein. A well-formulated bagged feed should have sufficient quality protein to match the type of horse it is marketed for – however, without having grass/hay analysed for protein content, it is not possible to feed completely optimum levels of protein based just on content of bagged feed. Purpose-formulated protein supplements may be a useful way to supply good-quality protein when pasture or the diet is deficient. A nutritionist will be able to give tailored advice for each specific horse and situation.

Fat

Fat is an essential component of the horse's diet; it is required to allow absorption and utilisation of fat-soluble vitamins (see below). Fat is broken down in the small intestine to fatty acids and glycerol, which are then absorbed for use. Essential fatty acids; linoleic acid and α-linolenic acid are required as components of some biochemical pathways. Deficiency of essential fatty acids in horses has not been reported, so it can be assumed that, under normal circumstances, grass and hay would meet demand. The common reason for feeding additional fat is to increase the energy density of the diet and provide calories

Feeding oil is a method of providing fats to horses.

in an alternative way to feeding cereals. Because of the slower release of energy from fat than from carbohydrate, fewer adverse behavioural responses are seen. As fat is very energy-dense it means that lots of calories can be fed in a small volume, helpful for weight gain or where a horse's appetite is reduced.

There are many sources of dietary fat; some are more palatable than others and some people disagree with using fish oil to feed herbivore horses. Some fats and oils have higher proportions of omega oils, particularly omega-3, which may have additional health benefits; examples are linseed or fish oil. When feeding large quantities of fat or oil it is important to balance the amount of vitamin E in the diet as this acts as an antioxidant when free radicals are produced during the metabolism of fat.

Vitamins and minerals

Vitamins

Vitamins are organic compounds that, although not required in large quantities, have essential functions in all body processes. Deficiencies can result in ill health and are linked to specific conditions. The converse can be equally dangerous as excess of some vitamins can cause toxic effects. There are two main groups of vitamins:

> Fat-soluble — vitamins A, D, E and K.

> Water-soluble — vitamin C and the B complex (B vitamins also carry individual names, for example, B1 is known as thiamine).

There are some vitamins that can be produced by the horse themselves; others that can't be (such as vitamins A and E) are often found in sufficient quantities in fresh good-quality grass. The microbial population in the large intestine also produces Vitamin K and the B complex vitamins. Provided that a horse has access to plenty of good-quality fresh forage, and has no gastrointestinal problems, these should not require supplementation.

Vitamin D is synthesised in horses' skin when they are exposed to sunlight (the process needs around six hours per day) so during the winter or when horses are stabled for long periods they may require some supplementation through the diet.

Minerals

Minerals are inorganic compounds that are essential to normal body function. As with vitamins, deficiencies can lead to ill health, while excesses can become toxic. They are all required in small amounts, but are further classed as either macro- or micro-minerals, the latter (also called trace elements) being needed in even smaller amounts than the former.

The minerals of key importance are:

Macro-minerals	Micro-minerals/trace elements
Calcium	Iron
Phosphorus	Copper
Sodium	Zinc
Chloride	Manganese
Magnesium	Iodine
Potassium	Cobalt
Sulphur	Selenium

Quantities

For both vitamins and minerals the amount a horse requires depends on many factors, the main ones being their age and what work they are doing (including breeding status). The next consideration is how much their basic diet provides; in the case of good-quality fresh pasture a significant contribution is made from that source; however, local soil conditions and plant varieties can mean deficiencies, which can be identified by lab analysis. (Trace minerals such as copper and selenium usually require supplementation, especially when the horse is in work). During winter, or when horses do not have free access to pasture, the level of vitamins and minerals in conserved forages decline the longer they are stored. Another consideration is that vitamins and minerals influence each other and, by feeding the wrong proportion of one compared to another, you can prevent them from being utilised fully.

An easy way to 'balance' the horse's diet is to use a feed balancer or specific broad-spectrum vitamin and mineral supplement. While excess of some vitamins and minerals may cause toxicity it is unlikely that these products will oversupply any to the extent of causing a problem. Balancers are also useful for those horses that are overweight and are on a controlled diet as it helps to ensure the horse is receiving the correct balance. It is always best, however, to balance them on the basis of exact requirements rather than guessing. A good nutritionist will help to formulate a suitable plan and advise as to which product(s) are suitable.

Nutritional intake and different types of work

Once you have worked out how much fibre a horse needs for maintenance (two per cent of the horse's body weight), you then need to factor in additional energy requirements for work. The first consideration must be to assess body weight and condition (fat score) and only to increase dietary energy if it is really needed. In the majority of cases, when you are given a new horse to care for, a diet will already be in place. The best rule of thumb is to monitor things for a couple of weeks and assess how the horse is responding to the existing regime: are they

Classification of Work	Number of hours worked per week	Work breakdown for an hour session (maximum time and percentage)	Example of activities	Riding school work per session (based on 1-3 hours daily 4-6 days a week*)	Maximum % of daily ration to come from concentrate feed*	Typical energy content of bagged feeds (MJ/kg DE)**
Light-low	1-3 hours	Up to 15 mins trot Up to 5 mins canter	Hacking Occasional schooling		Up to 10%	
Light-medium	3-7 hours	Up to 25 mins trot Up to 10 mins canter Occasional jump	Hacking Occasional schooling Low-level dressage Low-level Riding Club/Pony Club Occasional showing	Beginner horses – mainly walk and low speed trot, occasional canter	Up to 15%	8-10 MJ/kg DE
Light-high	5-7 hours	Up to 30 mins trot Up to 12 mins canter Up to 3 mins poles/jumping	Faster hacking Regular schooling Low- to mid-level dressage Riding Club/Pony Club Low-level showjumping Schooling for polo Short sessions on the gallops Regular showing Endurance rides up to 40km (25 miles)	Intermediate horses – up to 30 mins trot, up to 10 mins canter, up to 10 mins poles/jump	Up to 20%	
Medium	5-7 hours	Up to 30 mins trot Up to 15 mins canter Up to 10 mins poles, jumping, fast work	High-level dressage (Advanced +), Riding Club/Pony Club Medium level showjumping (Newcomers +) Low-medium level eventing (up to intermediate) Low-medium goal polo Early racing training Endurance rides up to 80km (50 miles)	Advanced horses – equivalent of high-level recreation but more hours per week	Up to 25%	10-11.5 MJ/kg DE
Hard	5-9 hours	As medium plus up to 1 hour extra over the week of speed work; increase in galloping and jumping duration	High-level eventing High-goal polo Racing Endurance rides over 80km		Up to 40%	11.5 MJ/kg DE and over

* The remaining percentage should come from forage (grass, hay, haylage) and where possible – particularly for light work – concentrate feed should come from higher-energy fibre sources.

** Feeds marketed as suitable for these different work levels tend to supply energy within these ranges, so if you look at the digestible energy (DE) content it gives a guide. DE is stated on feedbags in the UK as mega joules (MJ) per kilogram (kg) of feed.

losing or gaining weight? Could some of the ingredients be adjusted to improve the horse's health?

In a situation where you have no knowledge of the horse's previous diet and need to create a diet from scratch, the safest option would be to provide fibre at maintenance levels initially and then add further energy as indicated by weight change. It is, however, still very useful to have an idea as to how much energy a horse may need to be fed to cope with different work intensities. It is really important to be able to classify accurately the amount of work the horse is doing and, in relation to feeding, it is safer to underestimate it to avoid overfeeding and weight gain, or metabolic disruption. The table over the page provides an overview of different work levels as well as giving a guide to how much of the horse's diet may need to be supplied through ingredients that provide more energy than grass or forage alone. The percentage of concentrate linked to different work levels is simply a guide as to the maximum a horse is likely to need at each level, and should not be seen as an automatic amount or target. If the horse is maintaining their body weight and is healthy then feeding less than these guideline amounts is completely fine.

Some examples of suitable diets for a range of horses

EXAMPLE 1

16.2hh 10-year-old sports horse doing Riding Club activities, Novice dressage or 90cm showjumping a couple of times a month. One-day event 90cm once a month. No known metabolic problems: lives out in the summer; in winter is stabled overnight with 8–10 hours turnout.

Estimated body weight:	600kg (1,320lb)
Maintenance requirements at two per cent of body weight:	12kg (26.4lb)
Work level:	light-high
Maximum concentrate inclusion in diet based on work level:	20 per cent

Summer suggestions

As the horse lives out it can be assumed that they are getting their fibre requirement from grass (however, the grass quality must be monitored to not over- or under-supply their needs). It is possible they may need to be given a small amount of additional bagged food to supply vitamins and minerals as well as to support the extra energy needs of their work. Assuming the grass they get is of average quality then a good place to start would be with up to 20 per cent (2.4kg/5.3lb) concentrate made up of fibre feeds such as alfalfa or sugar beet or a low-starch complete feed and a low-calorie balancer. It would be best to split this bucket feed between at least two separate meals per day.

Winter suggestions

As the grass quality declines in the winter, and because this horse has only a few hours access to it, it is unlikely that their fibre needs will be met. This horse would need around 12kg of hay or haylage, some of which could be given in the field. The remainder of their summer diet could be kept the same through the winter, provided they maintain their weight.

EXAMPLE 2

15hh 12-year-old riding school cob, working 2–3 hrs a day, 6 days a week. Does mainly beginner lessons, with up to 6 hours a week of intermediate lessons. Puts weight on easily. Lives out all year round; in winter has ad lib average quality haylage in the field.

Estimated body weight:	500kg (1,100lb)
Maintenance requirements at two per cent of body weight:	10kg (22lb)
Work level:	light-medium
Maximum concentrate inclusion in diet based on work level:	15 per cent

Summer suggestions

It is likely that, during the summer, this horse will receive all the calories they need from grass; in fact if the grass quality is high they may still be oversupplied and need to have some restriction to grazing. It is, however, important that they receives a balanced diet, which could be given as either a low-calorie balancer or a broad-spectrum vitamin and mineral supplement in a small quantity of low-energy chopped fibre (chaff). If the grass quality declines (for example, in hot weather) and the horse starts to lose weight, they may need a small amount of additional fibre from items such as hay or haylage, chaff, fibre cubes or sugar beet.

Winter suggestions

It may be easier to manage this horse's weight in the winter, because of the lack of nutrition from the grass, and the colder weather making more demands of their energy. If the haylage they receive is of average quality it is likely that you will need to feed some additional bucket feed – up to 1.5kg (3.3lb) of good-quality fibre or a low-starch complete feed for horses in light work. They should continue to be given a balancer or vitamin and mineral supplement.

EXAMPLE 3

16.2hh 15-year-old Thoroughbred doing dressage at Elementary level, competing most weekends. Also hunts a couple of times a month in the winter. Tends to be hard to keep weight on. Has previously had gastric ulcers. Stabled overnight all year round with 8–10 hours turnout per day.

Estimated body weight:	600kg (1,320lb)
Maintenance requirements at two per cent of body weight:	12kg (26.4lb)
Work level:	light-high
Maximum concentrate inclusion in diet based on work level:	20 per cent

Summer suggestions

This horse will probably be easier to manage during the summer as their work level is slightly less and good-quality grazing will help. As they are only out at grass for part of the day they will need additional good-quality hay or haylage when they are stabled. As they have a history of gastric ulcers it is advisable to minimise the amount of time that their stomach is empty; combined with the fact that they struggle to maintain weight it may be wise to provide them with ad lib hay/haylage and try to maximise the amount of time the horse is turned out for. Can be fed up to 20 per cent (2.4kg/5.3lb) concentrate, although it may be that, during the summer, they do not need the maximum amount because of the grass in the diet. Use fibre feeds to help protect against further gastric ulcers: alfalfa and sugar beet are good additions, as are complete feeds that are fibre-based and cereal-free. As always, make sure that the diet is balanced.

Winter suggestions

In the winter the loss of the grass component of the diet will probably need to be substituted with other ingredients. As they are being fed ad lib hay/haylage the only way to do this is by increasing the bucket feed. Increase it to the maximum of 2.4kg (5.3lb) using the same feeds as during the summer. If they are still not holding their weight then take time to find higher-energy fibres and possibly add some fat/oil too.

EXAMPLE 4

16hh 8-year-old sports horse doing intermediate eventing; competes most weekends through the season. No known metabolic problems. Stabled overnight all year round with 8–10 hours turnout per day. This example will only talk about diet during the eventing season.

Estimated body weight:	550kg (1,210lb)
Maintenance requirements at two per cent of body weight:	11kg (24.2lb)
Work level:	medium
Maximum concentrate inclusion in diet based on work level:	range=25–40 per cent; will base this example on a figure of 35 per cent

Dietary suggestions

This horse's energy requirements are reasonably high so they will almost certainly need additional bucket feed. As they have access to grazing each day it is likely that, during the summer, some energy will be supplied from grass (how much depends on grass quality). By providing good-quality hay or haylage the remaining energy can be supplied by feeding up to 3.85kg (8.5lb) bucket feed. A high-energy complete fibre feed could be used, or one containing some cereals and starch. It would be sensible to start with the fibre sources at say 25 per cent (2.75kg/6lb) and only add more cereal if the horse is not maintaining their weight. The addition of some oil may be beneficial as an extra energy-dense feed. This horse's protein requirements will be slightly higher than average because of the requirement for muscle development and repair, so make sure the feeds chosen have a good-quality protein profile. A vitamin and mineral balancer is essential to ensure optimal performance.

Forage

Variability of grass

Grass is very tricky to gauge in terms of energy content as one field can change through the year according to temperature, rainfall and grazing pressure. If the mix of grasses in a field is known you should have an idea of the average energy it will provide under normal conditions. There are certain reasons related to times of the year when this will change:

1. Winter — when the temperature drops below 5°C (41°F) grass stops growing actively so there will be less grass to eat, containing less energy.

2. Young vs. old grass — as grass grows and gets older it gets harder and has more structural parts that the horse finds hard to digest; this means that spring grass is more energy-dense than late summer grass.

3. Hot, dry weather — in these conditions grass growth slows.

4. Spring and autumn — when there are bright sunny days combined with the temperature being low grass stores lots of sugar; this means that when eaten it is incredibly energy-dense and can cause problems for horses at an excessive unhealthy weight or those known to suffer from conditions such as laminitis or colic.

It is essential that access to grazing is managed appropriately and supplementary feeding is considered in response to variation in grass quality. The best way to manage this is to think ahead and be ready to alter management accordingly. This is particularly important when managing overweight and laminitic animals; by being aware of when flushes in grass sugar levels occur the risk of an episode can be reduced, which is much better than dealing with the consequences.

Forage alternatives

There may be times when a horse is unable to eat long fibre such as hay or haylage, making it very difficult to meet their nutritional needs. This is common in older horses whose teeth are no longer capable of cutting and grinding it up. The difficulty faced is balancing the need to supply sufficient energy that can be ingested and utilised efficiently while still supporting the health of the horse's gastrointestinal tract. The bulk of the diet should still be made up of fibre so it will be necessary to look to alternative forms of fibre. For horses with dental problems it is necessary to provide food that does not need extensive chewing; short fibre or mashes will be ingested easily and can be readily broken down once in the digestive tract. Feed such as sugar beet is already the right consistency and can safely be fed in relatively large amounts daily (for example, for a 500kg horse 2.5–5kg/5.5–11lb dry weight). Pelleted feed such as alfalfa, low-starch horse and pony cubes, high-fibre cubes and grass nuts are easy to make into a mash by soaking with some warm water; it might be necessary to experiment with how much water and the length of soak to get the best results. Using this as a base diet in place of hay or haylage you can then adapt the remainder of it in the same way as for any other horse. Just remember to make sure it is balanced and all the required vitamins and minerals have been accounted for. You may find the horse eats their forage replacement part of the diet a little faster than they would the equivalent hay or haylage, so lots of small buckets through the day can help to space it out and avoid the gut being empty for long.

Alfalfa pellets.

High-fibre cubes.

Preparing forage for horses with health problems

There are two main situations when you may need to prepare hay or haylage before feeding it.

Horses who suffer from respiratory problems

This may be a diagnosed condition such as Equine Asthma or simply that the horse in question is sensitive to dust. The aim is to improve the hygienic quality of the hay (reduce dust, mould spores and bacteria), while preserving the nutrient value within it. Two main methods can achieve this; soaking or steaming.

Soaking is cheap and can be done anywhere, using any bucket/tub/trough that will allow the hay to be fully submerged (this is important). The hay needs to be kept submerged for no more than 30 minutes; this will be long enough to prevent the dust from becoming airborne, thus minimising irritation to the respiratory tract. If your horse is on a controlled diet soaking the hay for 6-12 hours in cold water or 1 hour in warm water will reduce the calorie content by leaching out the nutrients. It is also important that hay is fed soon after soaking as, if it dries, then you lose the beneficial effect. Another point to consider is that after water has been used for soaking it is full of nutrients and some bacteria. This can be an environmental pollutant and disposal in large quantities down a drain is not desirable. Furthermore, water used once for

Hay must be fully submerged when soaking.

soaking must not be re-used for soaking more hay as you will simply increase the bacterial load of the new hay.

Steaming is best done using a commercially available machine that ensures high enough temperatures are reached, and steam is delivered efficiently to all parts of the hay. Although they initially require financial investment, these machines are easy to use. The real benefit of steaming compared to soaking is superior improvement in hygienic quality combined with minimal nutrient loss. As with soaked hay, steamed hay should be fed soon afterwards to gain maximum benefit.

A hay steamer.

Horses who suffer from metabolic problems (for example, laminitis) and require low-sugar diets

The challenge with this type of horse is to be able to feed sufficient volume of fibre to maintain gut health. Soaking hay is a reasonably effective way of reducing the sugar content of fibre. Obviously, the lower the sugar content of the hay before soaking the better chance you have of reducing overall sugar intake. The sugar that needs to be removed is the simple sugar (as described earlier), in particular water-soluble sugar (WSC), which is a type that is quickly digested and causes peaks in blood-sugar levels. There have been a number of studies carried out to work out the best conditions for soaking, but results vary and it is not always possible to predict losses. The times vary with ambient temperature and water temperature; usually, greater WSC reduction should happen in warm weather using tepid water (times range from around 6–12 hours in cold water and one hour in warm water). Soaking for 12–16 hours is safest for these types of horses. However, in warm weather you shouldn't soak for more than 6 hours as the bacterial load can increase.

Feeding routine/management

To maximise nutrient utilisation while minimising metabolic disorder it is of paramount importance to consider how and when to physically provide feed. We all know the importance of keeping a good routine to minimise stress (a trigger for colic) but this is simply the starting point of things that must be considered. The points discussed in the following section are applicable to all horses, but are particularly important in managing feeding routines for horses with metabolic problems.

Important considerations when feeding

Fibre availability

As horses have evolved to graze for up to 16 hours to maintain gut health it is important to mimic this as closely as possible. Access to grass should always be strived for, except in cases of veterinary concern. Failing that, conserved fibre should be available to the horse for as much of the day as possible to allow a steady trickle through the gut. Exceptions are overweight horses or those who put on weight easily; however, by sourcing low-energy fibre, more bulk can be fed. When horses are stabled, every effort should be made to split their fibre evenly throughout the day and night to avoid long periods between top-ups (meaning that a larger amount should be provided overnight).

Feed size and frequency

When giving bucket feed you must consider the total quantity required over a 24-hour period then try to break it down into regularly spaced small 'meals'. As a rough guide you should feed no more than what would fit inside a rugby ball at one time (this being the approximate stomach size for a 16hh horse). This is particularly worth considering when you need to put weight on a horse; by supplying high-energy nutrients in small quantities you will give the digestive system the best chance to fully digest and absorb them. Likewise when feeding cereals/starchy feeds, in order to avoid them overwhelming the ability of the small intestine to break them down (causing hindgut dysfunction), keep the quantity per feed as small as possible.

Feeding before exercise and travelling

Often people are anxious about feeding in relation to events such as exercise or travelling. It is important to discuss feeding fibre and concentrates (such as cereals) separately. Remember the basic concept that horses are trickle feeders. Without fibre passing steadily through the digestive tract, health problems such as EGUS (equine gastric ulcer syndrome), hindgut acidosis and colic are more likely. Considering that stress is a huge factor in the cause of these disorders, the combination of a stressful situation with no fibre transit can push the balance towards disorder even further. Fibre in the hindgut also acts as a fluid reservoir and can help to keep the horse hydrated.

There is no need to withdraw grass, hay or haylage prior to exercise, when dealing with the majority of horses. In fact, to prevent EGUS the best advice is to ensure that the stomach has a fibre layer on top of the acid to avoid splashing during work; this can be done by feeding a couple of handfuls of chopped fibre immediately before exercise.

When travelling horses there is no need to withhold fibre. By providing hay or haylage throughout the journey horses may be more relaxed, and it will have a protective function for their gastrointestinal tract. It is, however, important to consider hygienic quality as it is hard for the horse to avoid inhaling any dust and mould in a confined space. Similarly it is essential to ensure safe positioning of haynets or bags. If taking extra haynets, they should not be transported tied to the outside of the vehicle where they are exposed to exhaust fumes and other debris.

When thinking about bucket feed composed of ingredients other than just fibre (especially cereals) things are a little different. As they are processed in the gut differently from fibre you must leave enough time for them to pass through the stomach and begin to be broken down in the small intestine. If this is not done the risk of EGUS, hindgut acidosis and colic increases greatly. A good rule of thumb is to leave 1–1½ hours after giving this type of feed before exercise or travelling. With horses who become excited or stressed when travelling (possibly on a competition morning) it is important they are able to have this time to eat and digest the feed before any stressors begin. For example, many start to become alert and visibly on edge when they are plaited or see a lorry being moved around.

Supplements

When to give supplements

There may be certain circumstances in which a horse requires additional support to their diet in the form of specific vitamins, minerals or other functional ingredients. These may include:

- Being unable to obtain all essential nutrients from their normal diet.

- Poor hoof quality.

- Stiffness or reduced mobility.

- Specific deficiency as diagnosed by a vet.

- Specific condition for which a vet recommends support through dietary supplementation, for example, gastric ulcers.

There are a myriad of products available to buy and if you believe the marketing there is something to improve every ailment a horse can have. In reality, many are not formulated based on evidence of what works and how much is actually needed. Sometimes urban legend circulates about particular ingredients having incredible properties, which is what drives the market need for companies to sell it, rather than evidence that it has been proven to work. The best advice is to use only supplementation following discussion with a vet or nutritionist; these people will be aware of which conditions can benefit from help in this way, and they should know which active ingredients have some evidence behind them.

There is a wide variety of supplements available.

Which supplements have evidence behind them?

General vitamin and mineral products

There is a wealth of research around what horses need in terms of specific vitamins and minerals (although not conclusively for all). This means that a good company will be able to formulate one that should be beneficial. You must, however, remember to match them with the horse's needs. Supplements should be used on the basis of an identified deficiency and the dose worked out based on the strength of the product and the amount needed to balance the rest of the diet.

Supplements for hooves

There is published evidence about the use of supplemental biotin for improving hoof growth. Between 10 and 30mg per day for a horse has shown some improvement; for horses with very poor horn quality more may be needed. Biotin is often combined with ingredients such as methylsulfonylmethane (MSM/bioavailable sulphur), methionine (essential amino acid) and zinc (involved in keratin production) that are used by the body as building blocks for hoof horn.

Supplements for joints/mobility

The efficacy of joint supplements is much debated and initial evidence comes from human research. The ingredients most commonly used are glucosamine (stimulates collagen and may help reduce joint inflammation and cartilage breakdown) and chondroitin sulphate (may protect the joints through anti-inflammatory action and improved quality of synovial fluid). Some encouraging research exists in horses both using joint tissue in the lab and biomechanical analysis of joint movement. However, there is not conclusive evidence that chondroitin sulphate is effectively absorbed and utilised in the horse. Omega-3 fatty acids (found in some fat and oils) may provide anti-inflammatory support to joints but currently there is limited evidence of this in the horse.

Probiotics

A *probiotic* is defined as a live micro-organism (bacteria, yeast), the supply of which results in a health benefit to the animal. Legally, suppliers are not allowed to use the term probiotic unless they have solid research proving that the strains are alive, get to the right place in the gut still alive, and do have a positive impact. The yeast Saccharomyces cerevisiae is the most common one used in supplements. Ingredients such as Saccharomyces cerevisiae have been shown to improve fibre digestion in the large intestine. When choosing a product, look for one that states the bacteria/yeasts included, how much of them are in it, and talks about keeping them alive through the digestive tract.

How to choose supplements

First, supplements should only be used when there is an identified need. This may be by a vet or a nutritionist identifying a deficiency. By feeding them without good reason and careful consideration of the existing diet you may unbalance the diet or spend unnecessary money on an ingredient that does not really do much. Another consideration must be whether they contain any ingredients banned under competition rules. As with human athletes, it is very easy to make a mistake with a minor ingredient.

Once you have confirmed the genuine need for supplementation, take time to research your options and, if possible, choose a product that has some real published evidence behind it. Make sure you find out which are the active ingredients needed to support the horse and compare the inclusion rate across possible supplements. Often these ingredients are expensive and if you find a cheap version it is likely that the quantity or quality of the active component may be lower too. On the flip side, more is not always better; what is needed is the optimum amount, in a form that the horse can use efficiently.

To spend money efficiently you need to work out the cost per unit of active ingredient and choose the best on balance. This is made difficult as companies display inclusion in different ways, some as a percentage of the whole tub, others as a concentration (for example, 1g of active ingredient per 50g of supplement). You need always to work out the amount in weight of the active ingredient that the horse will receive per daily dose, then you can work out how long a tub will last, how much that costs per day and which brand has the correct amount of active ingredient. Some cheaper examples may have to be fed at a much higher rate to deliver enough of the active ingredient, meaning they are not cheaper in the long run.

Considerations when creating diets

The most important thing to remember is to treat each horse as an individual. Next, if after a few weeks the diet is not working then make a change (ensuring that it is done slowly to allow the gut and bacteria to adjust). Remember that, like us, horses' needs may change over time and so a diet that worked last year may not work long-term; make sure you take the time to regularly re-evaluate each horse's needs. The attraction of new products and media pressure can make you feel that you must make changes; if the diet is working don't change it unless there is real evidence that something else will enhance it.

Choosing components for the diet

Once you have developed an outline plan of what you wish to feed it can be a daunting task to select feeds and brands from the large number on the market. There may still be a large number that, at first glance, answer the same need. Your choice should be based on several things.

Cost

The full price per bag is a starting point, taking into account the size of bag — most feed is sold in 20kg (44lb) bags but some are smaller. The next thought should be to compare ingredient levels between products. In the UK, how much energy the feed supplies is normally expressed as mega joules (MJ) of digestible energy (DE) per kilogram of feed (a value in the form of, for example, 15 MJ/KG DE), so a feed that has a slightly lower DE value will need to be fed in a larger quantity per day to match the energy supplied by another at a higher DE value. If you work out the cost per day for each feed you may then start to see a price difference between bags.

EXAMPLE

Feed 1 supplies 10MJ/KG DE — Cost is £18.99 for a 20KG bag.

Feed 2 supplies 15MJ/KG DE — Cost is £19.99 for a 20KG bag.

1. You will need to feed 1.5KG of Feed 1 to provide the same energy as 1KG of Feed 2.

2. The cost per KG of Feed 1= 95p; for Feed 2=99p (price per bag divided by 20).

3. To feed the horse the same energy from each feed (let's say 15MJ DE per day) this would mean feeding:

    Feed 1 — 1.5KG costing £1.42.

    Feed 2 — 1KG costing 99p.

So while Feed 1 seems cheaper at the start, when you consider what is actually supplied, Feed 2 works out to be more cost-effective. A cost calculation exercise is worth doing in relation to any ingredient that is important for the horse's nutritional needs. Particularly when purchasing feed for a yard, small differences in cost per bag can add up significantly.

Guarantee of quality (including reference to prohibited substances)

Good feed manufacturers will provide quality assurance as to the hygienic quality of their feed; make sure you look out for this information when choosing a brand. There is a scheme run by the British Equestrian Trade Association (BETA), called NOPS (naturally occurring prohibited substances)

The BETA NOPS logo.

which aims to give recognition for companies who reduce the risk of feeds being contaminated with prohibited substances that are not allowed under competition rules. Feed manufacturers can apply to be audited and, if they comply, they may use the scheme logo on feedbags. If you are feeding horses who compete under the rules of various disciplines this is an important consideration.

Clean Sport for Horses

If you are competing or looking after competition horses, it is essential that you understand the rules and guidance around anti-doping.

The Clean Sport initiative is dedicated to producing a detailed approach to keeping sport clean from prohibited substances.

The FEI's Clean Sport for Horses encompasses the Equine Anti-Doping and Controlled Medication Rules (EADCMR) that apply to all equine and human athletes from grass roots to the highest level.

It involves regulating and testing for the use of prohibited substances that have the potential to affect equine or human performance, health or welfare and the integrity of equestrian sport.

Under these rules the athlete is considered the 'person responsible' for the horse they compete on. They must ensure that the horse has not been given any Prohibited Substances. If your horse tests positive you could receive a fine, lose any winnings or be disqualified from competition.

You can find further information on the Clean Sport regulations and the Prohibited Substance list on the FEI Clean Sport website.

What can you do?

- Always use a registered feed business operator (FBO).

- Look for the BETA NOPS logo on the label of feed bags and supplement containers. It will ensure that the company has met the required levels of hygiene and traceability.

- Always double check the ingredients labels of feeds and supplements.

- Check that any containers are properly sealed in a tamper evident way.

- Store feed and supplements in a secure container away from possible contamination from rodents and spillages.

- Use separate stirrers when mixing multiple feeds.

- Keep storage containers, feed buckets and utensils clean.

Condition scoring

Body condition scoring (BCS, also known as fat scoring) is a recognised method of evaluating the body fat on a horse. Vets, nutritionists, welfare professionals and researchers use it to make both single time point evaluations and to monitor horses over time. The most commonly used scale is from 0–5 where 0 is emaciated and 5 is obese. It is a method advocated within the government produced codes of practice for keeping horses (one for each UK nation) and may be referred to as a way of highlighting when welfare has been compromised and a horse is either too thin or too fat. No horse should ever score 1 or less, or be a score of 4 or greater. The aim is that all healthy horses remain at around a score of 2.5–3. There may be medical requirements for a horse to be slightly less than this, such as recurrent laminitics, but this should be in consultation with a vet. The fat score will assess the condition of the horse externally, but excess fat can also be stored around all the internal organs that we can't see. What you see is literally the tip of the iceberg, as horses start to store fat around all the internal organs that we can't actually see.

Some challenges with using this method are that it can be difficult to be accurate because it is subjective; each person who carries out an assessment of a horse may have a slightly different viewpoint. For this reason, when any comparisons are being made over time, it is best for the same person to repeat the measurements. If BCS is being used as part of managing a horse's weight, taking actual measurements such as belly girth, heart girth and rump can add some objectivity, as well as weighing the horse on a weigh bridge, if available.

Because of the way that horses carry fat in different parts of the body, and because some have different 'problem' areas than others, the BCS system is split across multiple body areas; the neck, the back/ribs and the hindquarters. For each of these areas you should view the horse from all angles and use your hands to feel the muscle tone (or lack thereof) and fat pads. A score should be given for each part; half scores (for example, 3.5) may be used. It is impossible to BCS accurately from a photograph and, if a horse has a long coat, much can be hidden from the eye. In the same way that it is more dangerous for humans to carry fat round their middle than on the hips, in horses some deposits are more dangerous than others, for example, a very fat crest.

The neck. Look and feel for fat forming along the crest; as it gets fatter it becomes solid and can flop over slightly to one side. Make sure you can tell the difference between muscle and fat. If you are looking at a stallion, remember they will have a more defined crest, which is normal.

The back/ribs. Pay attention to fat pads developing behind the shoulder; you should be able to see the shoulder-blade. You should be able to feel, but not see, the ribs fairly easily with light

Complete Equestrian Volume 3

0 EMACIATED

- No fatty tissue can be felt
- Skin tight over bones
- Shape of individual bones visible
- Marked ewe-neck
- Very prominent backbone and pelvis
- Very sunken rump
- Deep cavity under tail
- Large gap between thighs

1 THIN

- Barely any fatty tissue
- Skin more supple
- Shape of bones visible
- Narrow ewe-neck
- Ribs easily visible
- Prominent backbone, croup and tail head
- Sunken rump; cavity under tail
- Gap between thighs

2 LEAN

- A thin layer of fat under the skin
- Narrow neck; muscles sharply defined
- Backbone covered with a very thin layer of fat but still protruding
- Withers, shoulders and neck accentuated
- Ribs just visible
- Hip bones easily visible but rounded
- Rump usually sloping flat from backbone to point of hips, may be rounded if very fit
- May be small gap between thighs

3 MODERATE

- A thin layer of fat under the skin
- Top line developing and becoming more rounded
- Withers rounded over tips of bones
- Shoulders and neck blend smoothly into body
- Back is flat or forms only a slight ridge
- Ribs not visible but easily felt
- Thin layer of fat building around tailhead
- Rump beginning to appear rounded
- Hip bones just visible.

4 FAT

- Muscles hard to determine beneath fat layer
- Spongy fat developing on crest
- Fat deposits along withers, behind shoulders, and along neck
- Ribs covered by spongy fat
- Rump well rounded
- Spongy fat around tailhead
- Gutter along back
- From behind rump looks apple shaped

5 OBESE

- Horse takes on a blocky, bloated look
- Muscles not visible as covered by layer of fat
- Pronounced crest with hard fat
- Pads of fat along withers, and behind shoulders
- Extremely obvious gutter along back and rump
- Flank filled in flush
- Lumps of fat around tail head
- Very bulging apple shaped rump
- Inner thighs pressing together.

Condition/fat scoring chart produced by Dengie.

pressure. Look and feel along the top of the spine and withers; there should not be a channel or gutter and you should be able to feel the bones under the surface.

The hindquarters. The points of the pelvis should be easily felt and just visible under the surface. When looking from behind there should be a nice curve across the top; neither a gutter in the middle nor sunken flesh on either side. Feel for fat build-up at the top of the tail.

People sometimes find it hard to differentiate between a very fit horse and a thin horse; a condition score of 2 may be assigned to a very fit racehorse as such horses will carry very little extra body fat but are heavily muscled and in peak condition for their exercise needs. The equivalent thin horse at a score of 2 will potentially have little muscle and lack the vitality of a fit racehorse.

Summary

- There are six essential nutrients: water, carbohydrate, protein, fat, vitamins and minerals.

- Structural carbohydrate (fibre) should be the main energy source; protein is used for growth and repair.

- A diet must be balanced with vitamins and minerals.

- Forage quality varies dependent on time of year, mix of grasses, local soil conditions and grazing pressure.

- Some horses may need special consideration when feeding long fibre — soaking, steaming or partial/complete replacement with alternatives.

- By managing how and when feed is given it is possible to maximise the efficiency of the diet while minimising digestive health problems.

- Supplements should only be used when there is a real need, then chosen based on evidence.

- Take time to evaluate cost-efficiency of feeds and supplements by identifying active ingredients, the amount of them required, then calculating the cost per weight of the final product.

- BCS is a great way to monitor the effectiveness of a diet and how a horse's body changes over time.

TRAINING TIPS

1. Read as many feed bags as possible — compare the name and marketing language against what is actually in the feed.

2. Always read the ingredient labels not just the marketing information; check what is included and what the nutritional breakdown is.

3. Pick a supplement in your feed room and investigate it. Why is it being used? What is the active ingredient? What evidence supports that active ingredient? Compare it to other similar products on the market in terms of cost and additional ingredients.

4. Try to practise BCS on as many horses as possible. When starting out, if possible, compare notes with a vet or someone who is very experienced in using the method.

5. For more information about how to practise BCS visit the BHS website.

Chapter 7

Fitness Training

Initial considerations for a horse who has been out of work

Factors to consider when designing a fitness programme

Fitness programme

Caring for a horse after strenuous exercise

Summary

Fitness Training

It is important that horses are properly prepared for the type of work they will be expected to do. If a horse is not fit enough there is a much greater risk of injury. Usually you will be improving a horse's fitness rather than starting from scratch, as most horses in work will have a level of fitness that has been developed from the work they are currently doing. However, you should know the process of getting a horse who has been out of work fit, and should understand the values of each stage of a fitness programme. Each horse is an individual and will require a fitness programme tailored to their needs, and the amount and type of work a horse will require can be dependent on a number of factors including body condition, breed or type and the horse's age and experience. Throughout any fitness programme — and afterwards when maintaining fitness — the horse should be monitored to ensure they are coping with the work and that their fitness is improving.

As well as making sure a horse is properly prepared for competition or any type of strenuous work, consideration also needs to be paid to how to care for the horse after strenuous exercise. Caring for the horse properly can minimise the risk of them becoming lame, stiff or sore, and the risk of illness such as colic.

Initial considerations for a horse who has been out of work

If a horse has been out of work there are a few things you should consider before starting to bring them into work. These include:

Checking that they are sound. Before starting work the horse should be trotted up to check that they are sound. If you are in any doubt about the horse's soundness always ask for a second opinion from someone more experienced.

Tack. If the horse has been out of work they may have put on weight or have lost muscle tone. As a result their tack may not fit as well as it did previously. Tack should be checked, ideally by a saddle fitter, to ensure that it is still comfortable for the horse to work in.

Stabled environment. If a horse has been turned out for the period during which they have been out of work and you are now intending to stable them for longer periods, they will need to be acclimatised to this environment. Although we all do our best to make sure that horses in our care are kept in environments where dust is at a minimum, it is inevitable that, when stabled, they will be exposed to more dust than when they are turned out. If the horse was previously eating just grass, their diet will also change to include more hay or haylage, so this will also need to be introduced gradually. Therefore it is a good idea initially to bring the horse in for a few hours each day and leave them stabled before turning them back out again. This can be done while you start to introduce work.

Factors to consider when designing a fitness programme

Type of horse. Horses who can comfortably canter at the required speed and duration for the competition they are entering will require less fitness preparation than others. Thoroughbred horses are naturally athletic and usually fall under this category. However, Warmbloods and heavier types of horses are likely to exert themselves more when cantering at the speed required for competition, so they would require more conditioning to prepare them for their competition.

Age/Experience. A horse who has been fit before will gain fitness slightly faster than a horse who has not been fit before.

Previous Injury. If a horse has been off work because of injury, they may need a specialist programme for recovery to be able to return to full fitness. In this situation advice should be sought from a vet. Particular care should be taken when exercising horses on deep surfaces if they have had a muscle, tendon or ligament injury, and on hard surfaces if they have had a bone or joint injury.

Body condition. Horses who are underweight or overweight will need a fitness programme designed alongside a diet plan. If a horse is underweight, they should be given sufficient time to gain weight before being brought into work. If a horse who is slightly underweight starts work, the work should be light until they gain the required amount of weight. Extra time should be allowed within a programme when improving the fitness of an overweight horse. An overweight horse will need to start with low-intensity work and spend longer in this type of work to prevent overstressing their body. A horse carrying extra weight will have more strain on their joints and tendons.

Facilities. Dependent on the facilities available to you, if the ground becomes very hard or it is very wet and becomes slippery and you are unable to do canter work you may need to use alternative methods of working towards fitness. In such a situation some canter work can be replaced by hill work; working up hills increases the intensity of the work without the need to increase the speed.

Fitness programme

Horses are 'flight' animals and so have an in-built instinct to flee from danger; this means even an unfit horse will have a reasonable capacity for short sprint exercise. However, the aim of a fitness programme is to condition a horse for the work they are required to do so they will be able to perform at their best and to reduce the risk of injury. During a fitness programme, work will need to be increased gradually over time. If work is increased too rapidly there is a greater risk of injury.

The principle of a fitness programme is to increase the horse's workload gradually by increasing either the duration or the intensity of the work — but not both together. The horse's body will adapt in response to the type of work they are asked to do — however, the work needs to be repeated for these adaptations to occur. The same type of work should be repeated during exercise sessions and then increased on a two-weekly basis. Horses are usually worked for five or six days per week, which is adequate for improving fitness. Working horses only at the weekend is not an effective way of improving fitness.

> **Fitness principle**
>
> *The principle of a fitness programme is to increase the horse's workload gradually. Work should be increased first in duration, then in intensity, but not both at the same time.*
>
> ***Duration***: *length of time.*
>
> ***Intensity***: *the higher the intensity the harder the work (for example, walk> trot > canter).*

Stages

A fitness programme can be split into three stages:

1. *Long slow distance work* — low-intensity work built up gradually in duration.

2. *Strength work* — work to improve strength and stamina and basic fitness.

3. *Fast work* — work to prepare the horse for cross-country type events.

Long slow distance work

If a horse has been out of work, the first part of their fitness programme will be long slow distance work. This is low-intensity exercise, consisting of work in walk initially with the duration of the work being gradually increased, before beginning to introduce periods of trotting. Although low-intensity, this type of work will begin to condition the muscles and cardiovascular system of a horse who has been out of work. The first part of a programme would usually consist of around three weeks of this type of work. A horse who has been out of work would usually start with 30 minutes of walking on a level surface for approximately two weeks, with the duration increasing towards the end of the second week. Some people may choose to cover some of this work on a walker.

Even with low-intensity exercise, for example hacking in walk, always make sure that the horse is working actively.

Initial work in the school should start in walk and trot, using large circles.

It can also be useful to introduce a variety of surfaces in this early part of the programme. It is likely that some of the initial work will be carried out on the road, as short amounts of work (five minutes a day) on a hard surface in walk can be beneficial to the horse as the concussive force of walking on the road increases bone strength. However, the amount of trotting on the road should be limited, as too much trotting can cause damage to joints (five minutes of trot is sufficient). Previously it was thought that this type of work also hardened tendons and ligaments — however, there is no evidence to suggest that this is the case. In addition to work on the road, work on bridleways and in fields while hacking is beneficial; the horse will also benefit from starting some basic work in the school. This will begin to prepare them for work later in the programme on these types of surfaces although, when schooling, circles should be kept large and work is likely to be limited initially to walk and short periods of trot. This could be combined with hacking, so the horse starts with ten minutes in the school then hacks for twenty minutes afterwards. As this is low-intensity work the horse may work up to seven days a week. Although this type of work will not contribute to increasing the horse's fitness after this initial stage, it is likely that it will be included throughout a fitness programme, because it is useful in providing variety within a work programme and is good for the horse's mental well-being.

In summary, this stage could consist of:

WEEK 1.   30 minutes of walking on a level surface.

WEEK 2.   30–50 minutes of walking on a level surface.

WEEK 3.   1 hour of walking, which may include some hills; may introduce short periods of trot on a level surface (ideally not roads).

Strength work

In this stage the intensity of the work will be increased. This type of work will begin to build the horse's muscles and condition their cardiovascular system. The long slow distance work will continue but will be cut back to fewer sessions each week. Specific skill training sessions will be introduced; these are likely to consist mainly of schooling sessions and will be geared towards the discipline at which the horse will compete. Lungeing may also be introduced. As an example, a weekly programme may include two to three hacking sessions, two schooling sessions and a lungeing session. As the intensity of the work is now being increased it is very important to include sufficient warming up and cooling down during these sessions.

Again, any type of work should be introduced gradually. The horse may have already started some basic work in the school; if so this can be gradually increased. If the horse has not done any work in the school up until this point, consideration should be given to the change in surface. If the school surface is softer or deeper than what they previously been ridden on, this will be harder work for them, and this must be taken into account. Initial work should start

As well as strengthening the horse's hindquarters, going uphill requires much more effort from the horse and so raises the heart rate and will begin to work the horse's cardiovascular system.

in walk and trot, using large circles. School work can be increased to include lateral work and some basic pole work and jumping towards the end of the sixth week.

Hill work may be introduced within hacking sessions, remembering that trotting up a hill may be as hard as cantering on the flat. Working up hills develops the horse's hindquarter muscles. When going downhill the horse will need to use the muscles in their forehand around the shoulders, and muscles in the hindquarters, which will have to work against gravity to help balance the horse. Working uphill and downhill is important especially for event horses and endurance horses, as they will have to canter up and down hills during the cross-country phase or during an endurance competition respectively.

In summary, this stage could consist of:

WEEK 4.   Hacking time may increase to 1¼ hours and include some short canters (on the flat). Start to introduce some schooling sessions for 30 minutes, to include basic school exercises, keeping circles large.

WEEK 5.   Hacking time may increase to 1½ hours and include some trotting up hills; schooling work will continue.

WEEK 6.   Schooling time may increase to 40 minutes. Pole work and then jumping may be introduced. Continue with hacking to include work up and down hills, and the amount of canter can be increased.

Pole work and jumping can be introduced during this phase.

Fast work

The inclusion of fast work in a fitness programme is only required for horses who are required to gallop in competition, for example eventers. Horses competing in dressage and showjumping will continue with the work specific to their discipline to further develop their skill and ability to perform at the required level. Many horses competing in lower-level competitions will be sufficiently fit to do so through the canter work included while hacking, and may not require additional specific canter work. However, others competing particularly at higher levels in showjumping and dressage may have some specific canter work included in their programme to help improve their general fitness. During this stage the horse's skill training (school work) will continue, as well as some low-intensity work. The horse is likely to be working five or six days a week, with two or three days of cantering (which may be incorporated into hacks) spaced equally throughout the week during the training period, and two days schooling. On the other days the horse may be lunged or do low-intensity hacking.

There are two methods that can be used when doing canter work; you can use either continuous canters or interval training. For either method the fitness level required will be dependent on the level at which the horse will be competing. For a 90cm ODE the horse will be required to complete a cross-country course at approximately 450mpm over a distance of between 1,600m and 2,800m, so the horse will be cantering for between four and six minutes including jumping efforts. In addition to this the horse will have to complete a dressage test and a showjumping course. For competitions at this level it is usually sufficient to reach the required level of fitness using cantering on hacks, by gradually increasing the length of canters at or slightly above the normal cross-country speed. However, if there is not sufficient space to do this while hacking it may be necessary to do canter work in a field or on an all-weather gallop.

Continuous canters. When using continuous canters, you carry out canter work both of a longer duration but a slower speed, and of a shorter duration at a higher speed, than the horse will be required to do in competition. For example, for a horse preparing for a 90cm ODE, your canter work could be built up to consist of a canter at 400mpm for seven minutes, and a canter of one minute at 550mpm. These may be carried out on the same or separate days; in the latter case the one minute canter can be added on to the end of a slower session.

Interval training is a method whereby you canter for a set number of minutes, then the horse rests so they are allowed to partially recover before cantering again. You would usually have three canters of a set duration, with 2–3 minute rest periods in between. Using the example above for a horse preparing to compete in a 90cm ODE, your canter work could be built up to consist of three 2½ minute canters at 450mpm with two minute rest periods in between. This is an example of what could be used, but there is plenty of flexibility in how interval training can be carried out and programmes can vary by increasing speed, distance, duration, number of repetitions or by decreasing the duration of the rest period. Whatever method is chosen, increases in work should be gradual and increases to distance or duration should be made before increasing the speed of the canter.

Both methods above are suitable for improving a horse's fitness. The choice as to which to use is down to personal preference and the temperament of the horse, and can also depend on the facilities available. For instance, sometimes it may be difficult to find an area where you can canter

Canter work in a field.

a longer distance in one go, so the continuous method is not always practical. There is an opinion that interval training reduces the risk of injury to the horse, as they are allowed periods of recovery, whereas during continuous canters they are likely to experience fatigue to a greater degree. However, there is no specific evidence to prove this.

In summary, this stage could consist of:

WEEK 7.   Build up length of time cantering on hacks and introduce some canter up and down hills, or introduce sessions for canter work (continuous or interval training).

WEEK 8–9.   Continue with work in the school; during canter work include some faster work (forward canter or controlled gallop).

An event horse is likely to be doing two canter sessions a week. The duration and speed of the canters should be increased gradually until they are capable of completing what would be required on the day of the competition. An advanced eventer would usually require around six weeks to reach the required fitness (so, in total, a twelve-week fitness programme). A horse due to compete in a 90cm one day event (ODE) should reach the required level of fitness within three weeks of starting fast work (a nine-week fitness programme in total). However, it is useful to allow more time to account for any setbacks during the programme, which may include minor injuries or poor weather.

During this phase the horse will also do some cross-country schooling; these sessions will count as a canter session.

Tapering

Tapering refers to a method whereby the horse's workload is reduced before a competition; usually in the week before competition. This allows the horse's muscles to recover from the stress of training and maximises the horse's energy stores. Tapering is carried out by gradually reducing the duration (time) a horse trains each day, but keeping the intensity the same.

Assessing a horse's fitness level

Although, at the start of this chapter, we discussed the possibility of bringing a horse who had been out of work up to fitness from scratch, it is more likely that, when you start a fitness programme with a horse, they will already be in work and you will be improving their level of fitness for a competition. In this case, start by noting the amount of work the horse is doing currently and then identify the level of fitness required. From this point you should be able to develop a plan to increase the horse's fitness to the level required.

When starting your fitness plan it is important to assess how the horse is coping with the work, as this provides a baseline for comparison later in the programme and ensures that the horse is not overly stressed by the work. Observations should include:

- The horse should perform well during training sessions and find work easier to perform as training progresses — you may notice that the horse starts to take more of a hold when cantering.

- After work (specifically cantering or galloping), the horse should stop blowing after approximately two minutes (although this can be affected by external elements, for example, in hot weather the horse may take longer to recover).

- After a training session, when the horse has been cooled down correctly, they should return to a resting breathing rate and heart rate and show normal behaviour, for example eating (hay) and drinking normally.

- The horse should not dramatically gain or lose weight during the programme.

> *Remember to make sure that the horse has their tack checked to ensure it still fits comfortably. As a horse increases in fitness, they may change shape because of the development of muscle, particularly if they were overweight or underweight initially.*

Heart rate monitors

Heart rate monitors can also be used to monitor fitness. They can provide readings to show how quickly the horse recovers after work, but can also provide readings to show how hard the horse is working during a session. The higher the heart rate the harder the horse is working; as a horse becomes fitter you should notice that their heart rate is lower than previous readings while doing the same type of work. Also, as a horse becomes fitter their heart rate will drop more quickly after the same type of work than when they were less fit. The best time to assess heart rate recovery is around 1 minute after exercise.

The following examples show the range of horse's heartbeat at different gaits, in beats per minute:

Resting:	28–44 bpm
Walk:	60–90 bpm
Trot:	70–120 bpm
Canter: (may also include jumping):	120–180 bpm
Gallop:	180–220 bpm

While these ranges provide a measure, it is important to note that others factors such as excitement or pain can influence heart rate. A horse's heart rate will increase if they are excited, so the heart rate of a particularly excitable horse may not always give a true reflection of how hard they are working. Since a horse's heart rate will also increase if they are in pain, if you are monitoring a horse's heart and it seems to be much higher than normal in a given type of exercise, this may indicate that something is wrong. The horse's heart rate within a gait will also be affected by the weight of the rider and whether the exercise is slow or fast, flat or uphill, or on a hard or soft surface.

Maintaining fitness and soundness

Throughout the fitness programme the horse should be monitored to ensure that they are on track to be fit enough for the competition date, using both general performance and recovery rates as indicators. The other important consideration — essential to ensure this — is maintaining fitness and soundness.

Using the example above of a horse competing at a 90cm ODE, once the horse has reached the level of fitness required, no further increases in workload are needed and to do so may develop a horse who is much fitter than required and/or increase the risk of injury. Instead, the horse can continue with the same type of work covered in the last two weeks of the programme, as horses maintain fitness very well the level of work can even be reduced by around 20–30 per cent. The week before each scheduled competition the horse may have their work reduced (the tapering process mentioned earlier).

Mature horses competing at top level are often only brought to peak fitness on the lead up to a competition and, after the competition, they may be let down and then kept ticking over at a lower level of fitness. This reduces the risk of injury to the horse and reduces the risk of the horse becoming 'sour' and losing interest in their work. Younger horses may be kept in work so they can continue to develop and improve the skills required for competition.

A horse's weekly exercise plan should, then, contain a variety of work including work on different surfaces, as well as ensuring the horse does not become bored in their work, this also helps to maintain soundness. By working the horse on different surfaces, over varying terrain and up and down hills, the horse's coordination will improve and they should be able to adjust their balance appropriately, which will contribute to preventing injuries.

Caring for a horse after strenuous exercise

This type of care should minimise the possibility of the horse feeling stiff and sore the next day and reduce the risk of illness such as colic or respiratory disease (often as a result of dehydration). Immediately after a horse has done some fast work, and where they have sweated and are blowing, they should be cooled down. Fast work may include the canter/gallop work described earlier or, more probably, be after the cross-country section of an event. The horse will need to be walked until their breathing rate has returned to normal and they are no longer blowing. If out hacking the horse will usually be ridden home in walk; if at a competition the rider will usually dismount and walk the horse back to the trailer or lorry. At a competition it is unlikely that the horse will have recovered sufficiently after walking to the lorry or stable, so at this point they can be untacked, washed off and then walked in hand until they have cooled down. If the weather is hot the horse may need to be cooled down more actively, and will benefit from being washed down several times with liberal amounts of water and walked in between. Walking in the shade will also help the horse to cool down on hot, sunny days. The combination of washing off and walking will be most effective at cooling the horse as the walking promotes blood flow to the skin and the movement of air aids evaporation of water and sweat. If your horse is hot to touch and has an elevated respiratory rate you should continue to cool them.

The horse may be offered water immediately after exercise then, once recovered, should be allowed as much water as they want. Electrolytes may be added to the water, to replace salts lost through sweat; however, the horse will need to have been introduced to these at home, as they may be reluctant to drink if the water tastes different from normal. Plain water should always be available. When at a competition it is often not possible to provide the horse with constant access to water, so you will need to offer the horse water at regular intervals.

Once recovered the horse should be given access to their usual forage and should be rugged appropriately for the weather. After cross-country the horse may also have their legs cooled. This may be with ice boots or wraps, but can include a variety of treatments. However, the

When the horse arrives back at the trailer after cross-country they should be untacked and washed off before being walked to cool down.

application of any types of cooling ointments or liquids directly to the legs is not recommended in case the horse has scratched themselves while going cross-country. Once cooled, the legs may be bandaged overnight to provide some extra support and reduce the risk of filling.

Summary

- If a horse has been out of work it is a good idea to have their tack checked before commencing work. If they have been living out, they will need to be acclimatised to being stabled again if this is to be part of their new routine.

- The length and content of a fitness programme will vary, depending on the individual horse. Factors to consider include the type of horse (for example, Thoroughbred, cob, native breed), the horse's age and experience, any previous injuries, the horse's body

7 | Fitness Training

condition and the facilities available.

- A fitness programme can be split into three broad sections; long slow distance work, strength/stamina work, and fast work.

- During a fitness programme and while maintaining fitness it is important to monitor the horse. Monitor the horse's recovery rate (how quickly they recover after exercise) and be observant of how they are feeling while working.

- Once a horse is fit for the work they are doing, they will maintain fitness with a steady or even slightly reduced level of work and will not require their work to be increased or maintained as it was during the fitness programme. Exercise plans should include a variety of types of work; this will help to maintain soundness and prevent the horse from becoming bored.

- After strenuous exercise the horse will need to be cooled down and cared for so that they can recover from the exertion. This type of care should minimise the possibility of the horse feeling stiff and sore the next day, and prevent dehydration.

TRAINING TIPS

1. During your work, hopefully you will be involved with the process of getting horses fit for competition or any other activity. Try to note the type of work done with each horse and the length of time taken to get the horses fit for the work they are required to do; this may be for a competition or it could be for lessons in a riding school. Also note how programmes may vary for different types of horse.

2. If you have the opportunity to groom at a ODE or another type of competition involving strenuous work (for example, endurance, polo), this would be of great benefit to your understanding of the aftercare required.

3. For more information on fittening please visit the BHS website.

Chapter 8

Travelling Horses

Vehicle checks

Compliance with the law when travelling

Loading and unloading

Summary

Travelling Horses

A growing number of horses are transported using public roads. The types and temperaments of horses will vary significantly, as will the reason for travel (for example, mare and foal returning from stud, event horse travelling to a competition, children's pony travelling to the local show). The aim is to transport all horses to their destination with minimal stress and maximum safety. Although the welfare of the horses will be the most important concern, it is also important to consider carefully the condition of the vehicle, because even minor issues can impact on the comfort of the journey, while major ones could jeopardise horses, attendants and possibly other road users.

Vehicle checks

Regular monitoring and checks of the vehicle will help keep both horses and human passengers safe — and may prevent stressed, late arrival at a show because 'the box wouldn't start'! If left unchecked and untreated, seemingly minor problems could easily escalate and cause safety issues and serious consequences. Regardless of the type of vehicle there are various checks that should be done before every journey. To save time and potential stress on the day, some of these checks could be done earlier (for example, tax, insurance, state of partition), while others (such as testing the light connection on a trailer) will be carried out on the day.

Towing/transporting vehicle checks

Engine checks — oil, water and windscreen washer should be full and have no obvious leaks.

Tyre checks — the wheel nuts should be secure, the air pressure, condition and the tread depth sufficient (the legal minimum tread depth is 1.6mm for vehicles under 3,500kg and 1.0mm for vehicles over 3,500kg). As of February 2021, tyres aged 10 years or older will be prohibited from use on the front axles of HGVs (vehicles with a maximum gross weight of 3,500kg). This includes horseboxes.

Lights check — all the lights should be working. If using a trailer, the electrical connection should be in good condition and the cable long enough between the trailer and towing vehicle so it does not become taut or snag when the vehicle is turning.

Brake checks — regular use will help to keep the brakes working efficiently and avoid them seizing, but they need to be checked on a regular basis to ensure they are doing their job. Brakes failing (or even not working quite as efficiently as normal) could have disastrous consequences.

Vehicle Excise Duty (VED) — tax discs are no longer issued for display, so you may need to refer to the owner's paperwork to ensure tax is current. The vehicle number plate can be used to check this online.

Insurance — needs to be appropriate for the vehicle and the person driving, and provide sufficient cover (the legal minimum is third party liability). *A trailer may require additional insurance as this may not be covered on the towing vehicle's policy.*

MOT/Plating — done annually to make sure the vehicle remains safe to drive. Plating is the annual MOT for vehicles or trailers over 3,500kg. The MOT needs to be current for the vehicle to be driven legally on public roads and for the insurance to be valid.

Servicing — it is just as important for trailers to be regularly serviced as it is for towing vehicles and horseboxes. This should be done every 6–12 months depending on the use/mileage.

Trailer checks

Breakaway cable — must be securely fixed to the towing vehicle and of an appropriate length to avoid snagging or becoming taut when in use.

Jockey wheel — should be securely in the 'up' position.

Correct number plate — should be displayed securely on the trailer.

Check whether towing mirrors are required — for adequate visibility (this will depend on the width of the vehicle compared to the width of the trailer).

Checks on the vehicle interior

Areas to check on a horsebox or trailer before travelling.

Compliance with the law when travelling

This section relates to qualification to drive certain vehicles, licensing, adherence to legal limits of hours driven and compliance with laws relating to carrying/towing capacity of the vehicle, as well as the requirement to travel a horse with their passport.

The passport must be kept with the horse at all times, including when travelling. Failure to produce a horse's passport if requested by a Local Authority Enforcement Officer could result in an unlimited fine!

Licences and certificates

In most cases when transporting horses, especially where larger vehicles and professional transportation are involved, drivers must be aware of and compliant with the following.

Forms of licence

Driver's licence — the driver of the vehicle must hold the relevant licence required to drive the vehicle.

An operator's licence is required by anyone who uses a vehicle of more than 3,500kg gross weight for transporting horses on a business basis (that is where there is hire, reward or financial gain). The operator's licence should be held by the vehicle user, who is the person who owns or hires the vehicle, or employs the driver. People who transport horses for leisure purposes only (not for financial gain) do not need an operator's licence. A towing vehicle that can be classed as dual-purpose (this means they are constructed to carry passengers as well as goods) and any trailer towed by it is exempt from this licensing. Therefore, for a 4x4 vehicle towing a horse trailer, an operator's licence is not required.

Certification

Certificate of competence for the handling and transportation of horses — applies to people who transport horses over 40 miles in connection with a business (applies to both the driver and the attendants). There are two different assessments — for journeys up to eight hours and journeys over eight hours.

Certificate of professional competence (CPC) — driver CPC applies to drivers of vehicles over 3,500kg used for business purposes. The driver must also complete ongoing training (35 hours every five years) in order to keep this qualification.

Conforming with other legal requirements

Driver hours and tachographs

A tachograph is an instrument that records the number of hours driven, breaks and rest periods, the speed of the vehicle and the distance travelled. The rules for these apply to all drivers of vehicles over 7,500kg gross weight, regardless of whether for business or leisure use. The rules do not apply to horseboxes (or vehicle and trailer combinations) between 3,500kg and 7,500kg used for personal leisure use only.

Weight implications

Vehicle weight — all horsebox drivers must be aware of the maximum vehicle weight (which includes the load). It is sometimes very easy to overload a horsebox, especially if it is carrying the maximum number of horses, all their equipment and enough water for the journey.

Towing weight — the driver must be aware of the weight that their vehicle can tow. The combined actual weight of the vehicle and trailer (including load) must never exceed the gross 'train' weight — also called the maximum authorised mass (MAM) — of the vehicle. This information can be found in the vehicle manual or on a metal plate attached to the vehicle.

Equipment checklist

With all these other aspects of travelling horses to consider, it is all too easy to forget something basic but important at the last minute. The overall equipment needed when travelling horses will depend on the reason for the journey, but a useful checklist usually includes:

- *Tack and equipment needed at the destination.*

- *Feed — haynet for the journey and bucket feed if the journey is long or if there will be an overnight stay.*

- *Water and water buckets.*

- *Any rugs required.*

- *Spare headcollar and lead rope.*

- *First aid kit — for horse and human.*

- *Emergency phone numbers — breakdown service, vet, farrier.*

Loading and unloading

Loading a reluctant horse

One of the most important things to remember when loading a reluctant horse is to allow plenty of time. If you are short of time, it can mean things get rushed and this can give the horse a bad experience, which will most probably result in them being even worse to load or travel the next time. It may be that you need to spend time retraining the horse, when there is no pressure or time constraints and you can work with them over time to make loading a positive experience for both parties. The happier and more confident the horse is about loading, the safer and easier it will be for everyone involved.

At one time or another you will probably come across a horse who is reluctant to load. The key to managing the situation is to try to understand why the horse does not want to load. There are various reasons that may explain their reluctance:

- Fear.
- Previous bad experience.
- Learnt behaviour.
- Poor previous training.
- Uncomfortable ride provided by the vehicle or driver.
- Positioning in the vehicle (for example, facing backwards, facing forwards, herringbone).
- Pain, difficulty balancing or difficulty walking up the ramp because of injury or an existing condition such as arthritic hocks or lameness.

Once you have considered why the horse may be reluctant, it is easier to try to resolve the problem, or at least minimise its effect. There are various ways in which you can help to encourage the horse to load, but regardless of the method it is important to keep the safety of yourself and others, and the welfare of the horse, as the priority. Some horses can become stressed about loading and it is at times like these that the horse's behaviour may change significantly and accidents can happen.

The positioning of the vehicle can be used to help encourage a reluctant horse to load. Ensure it is parked on flat ground and if possible position the vehicle next to a high wall on one side. This will create a guide to help keep the horse straight and limit potential escape routes. However, you need to be careful that the space between the vehicle and the wall is not too big so that the horse might consider squeezing through it. By parking with plenty of space for the horse to approach the ramp in a straight line, you can get the horse walking freely forwards before reaching the ramp and, by keeping them straight, you can minimise the risk of slipping or tripping, which may discourage the horse from stepping on the ramp.

If a loading ramp (see photo) is available, this may help to encourage the horse by making the ramp flatter and providing 'wings' to encourage them to keep straight. Regardless of the positioning you should make sure that the ramp is stable on the ground, as any movement when the horse puts their weight on the ramp could again discourage them. The use of lunge lines attached to the sides of the vehicle may help to limit the horse's sideways movement, and crossing the lunge lines behind the horse can provide gentle pressure to encourage them to move forwards, as well as preventing them from moving backwards. However, if too much pressure is applied, this can sometimes panic the horse and cause them to rear up and over, so care should be taken.

A loading ramp.

When a horse is worried or scared, you can try to reassure them by loading another horse first, to provide them with the confidence that the horsebox is a safe place. If loading into a trailer you could open the front ramp and move the back section of the partition across (although this cannot be done in all trailers) as this will make the space look bigger, lighter and more inviting. Some horses can be encouraged by using food as a positive reinforcement, every time the horse takes a step forward they are rewarded with food (some may be encouraged by a packet of mints, while others may be better with a bucket of food). You can try moving the horse's legs one at a time to encourage them to walk up the ramp, but this can have safety implications and it will not be appropriate for all horses.

It is important to stay in control while loading the horse. Use the LIMA principle when deciding which method is required as it will be different for every horse. You may decide to use a bridle or Chifney, and a lunge line can be used instead of the lead rope. However, if you use a lunge line you need to be careful that you do not end up in a dangerous position if the horse is able to get further away from you. The use of a 'pressure and release headcollar' can be useful in training a horse to load. It makes use of the horse's natural instinct to avoid pressure, but needs to be used correctly so that the pressure and the release are at the appropriate moments, rewarding and encouraging the desired behaviour and ensuring the horse is not forced.

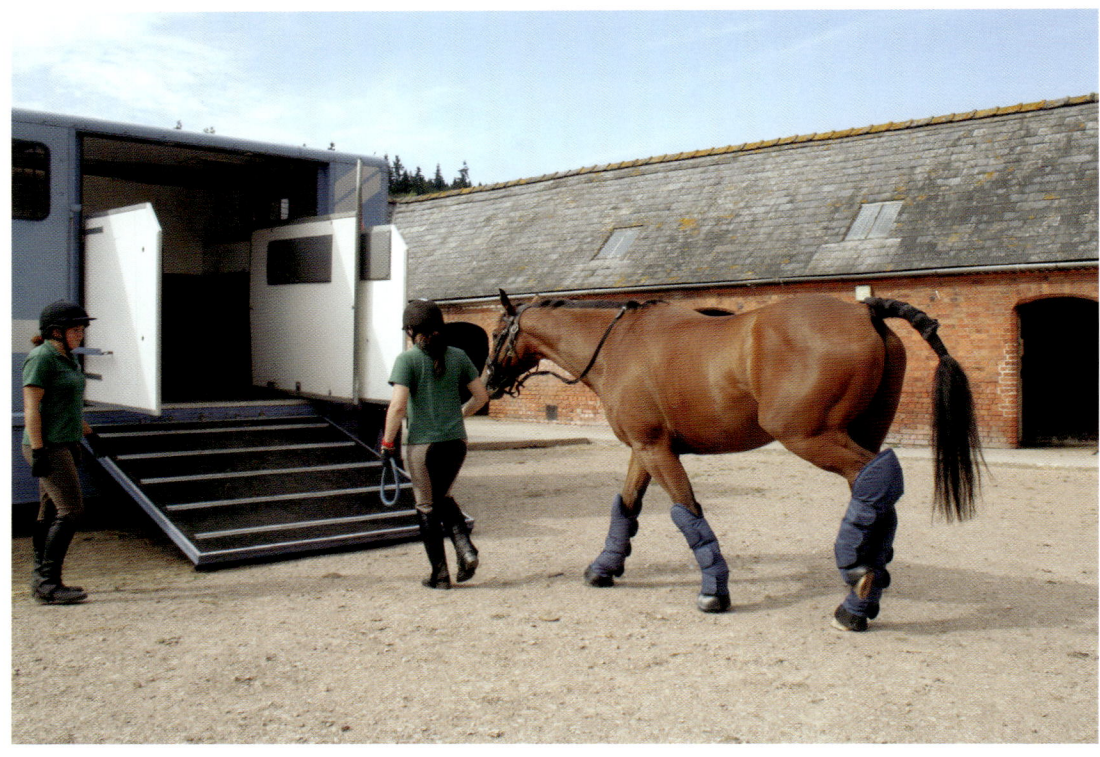

The leader and assistants should all be wearing hat, gloves and suitable footwear, but they also need to maintain safe positioning and communication throughout, allowing everyone to know where the others are and what they are doing at all times.

If the horse has had a bad experience with an uncomfortable ride, you may need to speak to the driver and anyone else involved to make sure that the vehicle is driven more carefully to allow the horse a more comfortable journey. If a horse experiences a more comfortable journey on each future occasion, they will become more confident and will hopefully start to load more easily.

Unloading safely

Unloading a horse can be as dangerous as loading a difficult horse, so care needs to be taken to keep yourself and others as safe as possible. The vehicle should be parked in a safe place with firm, level footing. Sometimes a horse may rush or jump off the ramp, so a non-slip unloading surface is preferable because it provides more grip (the horse is less likely to slip on dry, level grass than concrete, and grass may be safer if there's a problem). There should also be plenty of room for the horse to be able to step off the ramp completely before being asked to turn. Any adjacent gates should really be closed, in case the horse becomes loose, as this could stop them getting out on to a road. In practice, this is not always easy, particularly at a large event where vehicles are constantly coming in and out, but every effort should be made to unload into an enclosed area. As when loading, hat, gloves and suitable footwear are a must for both the leader and any assistants.

Before opening the partitions, you should make sure that you have sufficient control of the horse. You may need to use a bridle, Chifney or lunge line to ensure you can lead the horse safely. In certain situations, for example, when arriving at an event, some horses may become excited and behave differently to normal, so it is always best to be prepared and, if in doubt, use additional methods.

The partitions should be secured back, allowing plenty of room for the horse to exit without any risk of the partition banging into the horse. Particularly when using the front ramp of a trailer, the narrower exit means that there is a distinct possibility of a horse banging a hip, so care needs to be taken to try to avoid this happening.

Before unloading you should make sure that any assistants are standing safely away from the bottom of the ramp. Sometimes, a horse may need time to look at their new surroundings before walking down the ramp, so try not to rush them. Leading the horse from the left-hand side, keep yourself next to their shoulder; do not get in front of the horse, you need to be positioned so that you are able to get out of the way if the horse were to rush or jump off the ramp. If this happens, it is best to try to go with them, so that you don't pull them sideways and conceivably off the side of the ramp. If you suspect a horse might jump from the top of the ramp use a scoop or bucket of feed to encourage them to lower their head and not to leap off but slowly walk down the ramp. Once they are interested in the food use it to help you encourage the horse to take small slow steps down the ramp.

Particularly when using the front ramp of a trailer, you need to be aware of the horse's position and behaviour as you unload, as you will end up slightly ahead of them because of the width of the ramp. Keeping an eye on the horse may give you an early warning if they are going to rush down the ramp or end up directly behind you (from where they could trample on you). If the horse is likely to rush out when unloading from a trailer, it may be safer to unload them by reversing them out of the back ramp. However, many horses do not like to reverse out of a trailer as they cannot see where they are going, so this may require some training at home.

The key things to remember about loading and unloading are being aware of the horse, allowing plenty of time and keeping yourself and others safe. By considering the reasoning behind a problem, you can quite often find a solution a lot more quickly and easily, making travelling less stressful for both yourself and the horse.

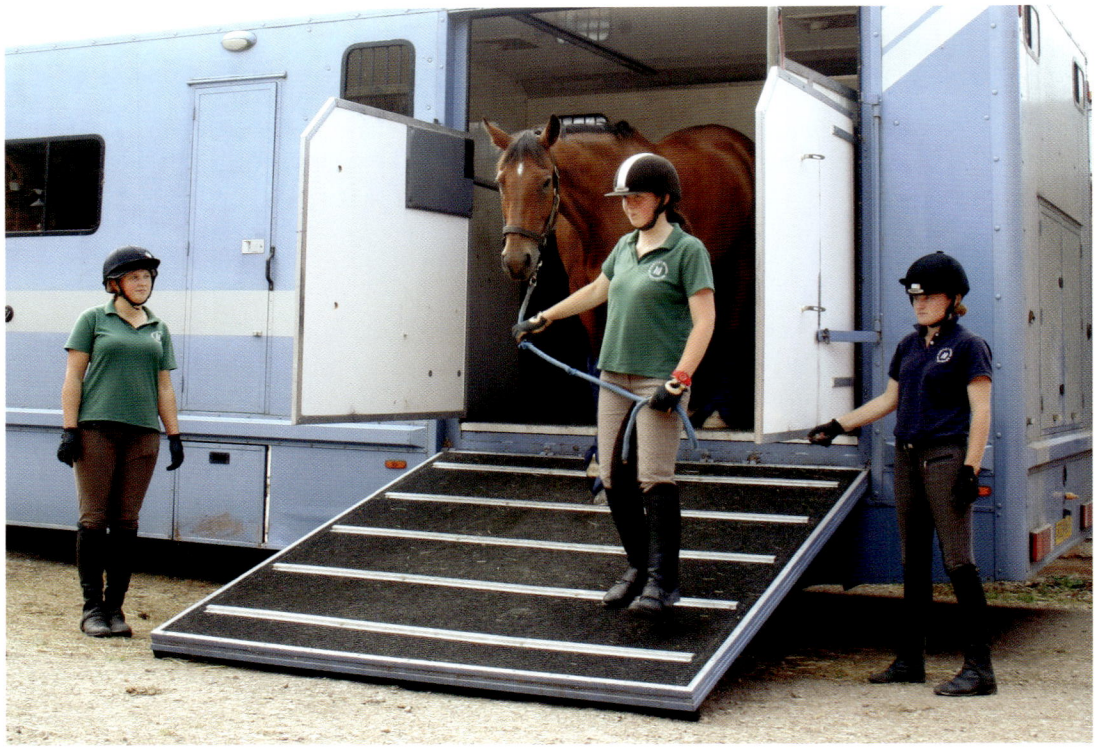

The leader and assistants should maintain safe positioning while unloading.

Summary

- Ensure that you make thorough vehicle checks before travelling.

- Ensure that you have the correct documentation required.

- A horse may be reluctant to load and travel due to fear, bad experience, learnt behaviour, poor training, uncomfortable ride, position in vehicle, pain or difficulty balancing,

- There are several methods you can use to encourage a reluctant loader. These may include using a control headcollar, using food as a reward, parking next to a wall or using lunge lines to guide the horse.

- When unloading, park in a safe place, secure the partitions and make sure you, and any assistants, are safely positioned.

8 | Travelling Horses

TRAINING TIPS

1. Check out a variety of vehicles and consider whether you would be happy to travel a horse in them.

2. Look on the UK Government website to find out more about driving regulations and check what type of vehicles you are entitled to tow or drive. www.gov.uk/driving

3. Observe or offer to assist with loading horses where possible.

4. For more information on transporting horses visit the BHS website.

Chapter 9

Grassland Management

Stocking level

Management practices

A seasonal guide to pasture management

Summary

Grassland Management

In addition to providing a source of food, pasture offers the opportunity for horses to self-exercise and socialise with others and exhibit natural behaviours. Therefore it is important to look after the pasture both in terms of optimising grazing and in providing horses with a suitable environment while turned out. Effective management of pasture is essential, and this can be done in a number of ways.

Stocking level

The recommended stocking level is 0.4–0.6 hectares (1–1.5 acres) of permanent grazing land per horse. However, when considering land for suitability it is necessary to consider the quality of the grass, the time of year, the amount of turnout (few hours daily or full time), the horses' nutritional requirements and the type of soil (for example, clay/sandy), as these factors will influence the amount of grazing the horses require. If a field is over-grazed or under-grazed, it is likely to need a lot more maintenance.

Management practices

The following management practices all contribute to the maintenance of healthy, productive pasture that provides a safe environment for horses. As you will see, they often have an interactive role, with one practice complementing the key aim of another.

Harrowing

Harrowing pulls the dead grass from the soil and leaves more room for healthy grass to grow. It aerates the soil, allowing more air to reach plant roots and encouraging growth. As any weeds with shallow roots will also be pulled up by harrowing, it can be useful in helping with weed control. Uneven or poached ground will be levelled out.

Pasture should be harrowed at least twice a year and preferably more often through

Harrows are available in many different designs and sizes.

the spring and summer months. Although if sycamore seeds surround the fields avoid harrowing in the spring and autumn, as this can spread the seeds and seedlings across the pasture. Ideally, they should be harrowed before the field is rested (ideally for six weeks) to allow maximum grass re-growth.

When harrowing, the ground needs to be hard enough so that the soil is not ripped up by the vehicle or the harrow, but if it is too hard the harrow will be ineffective and just skim over the surface.

Rolling

Rolling can be used to level out uneven or poached pasture once it has dried out enough for the vehicle not to cut up the ground. The grass roots are pressed into the soil and the new shoots are gently crushed, which encourages tillering (the growth of secondary shoots, which increases the density of the grass). Firmly packed soil can encourage grass to grow and, at the same time, discourage weeds, which usually prefer loose soil. However, rolling when the ground is too dry can compact the soil too much, which is detrimental to both grass growth and drainage. Rolling on certain soils, for example, clay, can also result in the ground becoming too compacted, so these areas should only be rolled if it is essential to do so.

Rollers come in different sizes, weights and styles and, depending on their size and weight, can be towed either by a tractor or a quad bike. A lightly ribbed Cambridge roller is often used when rolling pasture, although occasionally a spike or knife roller may be used to aerate the soil when it has become very compacted and the grass growth and drainage have been restricted.

A roller.

Fertilising and reseeding

Fertilising can be done in spring and autumn, but is often only necessary where the soil is deficient in one or more of the key nutrients (nitrogen, phosphorous and potassium). To identify whether any nutrients are needed a soil sample can be taken in late winter (February time) and analysed to determine which type of fertiliser is required. Over-fertilising can result in lush grass, which is not good for horses as it can cause problems such as laminitis, colic and obesity. Therefore it is advisable to seek expert advice before fertilising a pasture. The pasture must not be grazed until the fertiliser has been washed or dissolved into the soil by the rain. Under ideal circumstances, it is best to leave horses off the pasture for at least 2–3 weeks after fertilising to allow time for the grass to re-grow.

Reseeding may be needed where the pasture has been heavily poached or where there are bare patches. It is best carried out in early spring when the weather is improving and will encourage good growth. It could be carried out in the autumn months instead so that the grass will thrive and the field will be ready for the following spring. A suitable grass seed mix should be used, so seeking expert advice is advisable. Rolling the pasture after reseeding will help push the seeds into the soil and encourage germination and root formation.

Removal of poisonous plants

There are many plants and trees that are poisonous to horses, and it is important to be able to recognise them. Those most likely to be found on or around horse pasture are ragwort, foxglove, yew, oak, sycamore, laburnum and deadly nightshade. They all vary in degree of toxicity and palatability to horses, and different plants or trees will only present an issue at certain times of year. It is important that all horse pasture and the immediately surrounding area such as fence lines or bordering hedges are checked regularly for poisonous plants. Many poisonous plants become more palatable when they are cut and have wilted so they need to be removed and then destroyed, usually by burning, to prevent the spread of the seeds. It is best to dig them up manually instead of topping or strimming them, as then the roots will also be removed. Unfortunately, it may not always be possible or practical to dig up poisonous trees or larger plants, in which case these should be fenced off so the horses cannot reach them. However, fencing off a tree will not stop the leaves or seeds from being blown on to the pasture.

Removal of weeds

Weeds such as docks and nettles reduce the quality and diversity of the grazing available and can be an ongoing problem if they start to take over the field. If weeds are present in small numbers, it is best to either pull or dig them up by hand or spot-spray them with a herbicide (weed-killer) before they go to seed. If weeds are more abundant, removal by hand will not be practical, so they will have to be strimmed, topped or sprayed. Weeds around the fence line that will not be reached by machine should be removed by hand or sprayed. Manual removal needs to be done during the growing season before the weeds drop their seeds. The time of year at which spraying should be done will vary depending on the variety of weed, so it is best to get expert advice on when to spray and what to spray with. It is important to remember that anyone who applies pesticides or weed-killer products that have been authorised for professional use, using either a tractor or a knapsack sprayer, must hold a special training certificate. The storage of these chemicals on site also needs to be considered. If they are stored on site the storage area must be secure and the chemicals stored according to COSHH (Control of Substances Hazardous to Health) guidelines. Horses will need to be kept off the sprayed area for at least 14 days but preferably until the weeds have disintegrated. Any wilted remains will need to be collected and burned so that the horses cannot eat them.

Topping

Topping can be used to help keep weeds under control and also to encourage a more even, dense grass growth, which also prevents the long grasses from taking over. It is advisable to top the pasture at least once a year during the spring or summer. Topping too frequently could damage the rooting system and have a negative effect on the quality of grazing. Any cut grass needs to be removed or completely dried out before allowing horses to graze the area.

Cross-grazing

There are a number of benefits to grazing sheep or cattle on horse pasture. Cross-grazing can be used as part of a worm control programme, because the sheep or cattle are not affected by equine parasites, but will ingest them on the grass and stop them from completing their life-cycle. Unlike horses, sheep and cattle are not selective grazers and will eat long or rough areas of grass as well as some weeds. They will also be able to 'top' more lush pasture and reduce the amount of grass available, making the pasture better for grazing horses. However, if it is intended to graze sheep or cattle on horse pasture, it is necessary to ensure that the fencing around the field is suitable to keep sheep in and strong enough to stop cattle destroying it.

Removal of droppings

Regularly removing droppings from the pasture will help with worm control and avoid latrine areas developing. Depending on the size of the pasture, droppings can be removed by hand or by using a machine.

There are many machines available that can be towed by a tractor or a quad bike. Sweeper machines have rotating brushes that 'sweep' the droppings from the ground into the collection box. Vacuum machines 'suck' the droppings up through a tube from where they are collected in a box. The sweeper machine has the added advantage of 'sweeping' debris such as dead grass off the pasture, which then helps to improve the grazing, whereas the vacuum machine will only clean the area on which it is placed. Also, when operating a vacuum machine it is necessary to stop next to each pile or area of droppings, whereas with the sweeper machine you are able to keep moving, so it can be more time-efficient.

An example of a paddock sweeper.

Rotational grazing

An effective rotation system will help to keep the worm burden controlled and the pasture healthy. A larger field can, potentially, be divided into at least three smaller paddocks, so that, at any one time, one paddock can be grazed by horses, one paddock can be grazed by sheep or cattle and one paddock can be rested.

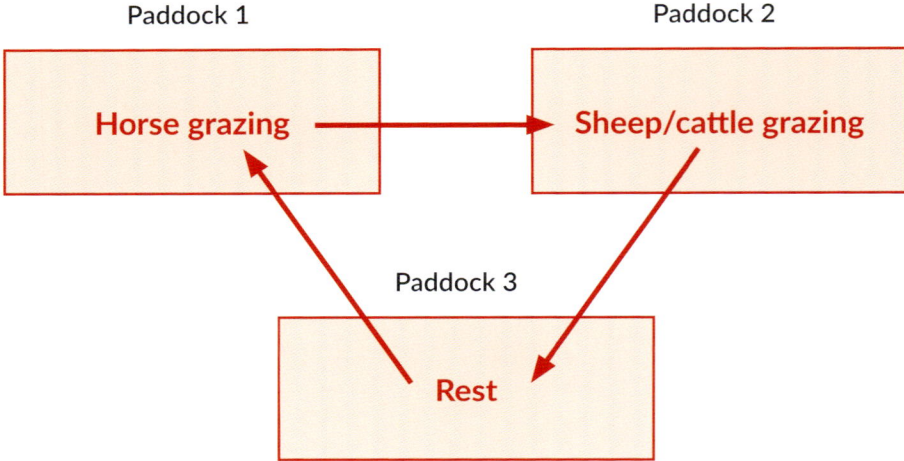

An example of a rotation system for three fields.

The period of rest will allow the paddock to recover while also allowing time for any ongoing maintenance to be done. Rotating grazing every 3–6 weeks will allow more productive grazing and help to keep opportunistic weeds under control.

A seasonal-based rotation system could also be used, whereby certain paddocks are rested over the winter for use in the spring and summer, and other paddocks are 'sacrificed' for winter turnout and then repaired and rested in the spring.

Alternative grazing

Grass is a major contributor of calories in a horse's diet so managing its intake is fundamental in maintaining good health and welfare. Consideration must be given to the changes in grass growth throughout the year, especially where your horse's diet may need restricting.

Using alternative grazing systems such as track systems, Equicentral systems or, where possible, the use of moorland or woodland can be of great benefit in managing horse's grass intake. They encourage the horse to interact more with their environment and other horses in their herd, promoting natural foraging and social behaviours while also increasing the horse's movement.

A seasonal guide to pasture management

Winter

- Allocate a 'sacrifice' paddock or have several paddocks in rotation if spare pasture is available. Winter grazing paddocks should ideally be the paddocks with the best drainage.

- In more poached areas (such as gateways or around water troughs), damage can be minimised by laying woodchip, gravel or grass matting. Having more than one gateway will also help to minimise damage.

- Do a soil test in late winter to identify which, if any, nutrients are lacking and whether (and what type of) fertiliser will be needed in the spring.

Spring

- Check for weeds and poisonous plants, and remove.

- Harrow the pasture once the ground is dry enough to drive on without causing damage.

- Fertilise if necessary, based on the results of the soil test.

- Reseed any bare patches if necessary.

- Roll the pasture.

- Close off any pasture being used for hay-making.

Summer

- Continue weed control and poisonous plant removal.

- Top the pasture.

- Use a rotation system, so paddocks can be rested in between grazing.

- Any pasture kept for hay-making can be cut and baled.

Autumn

- Continue weed control and poisonous plant removal.

- Complete any maintenance required before winter arrives, such as insulation of water pipes, placing hard standing around gateways and water troughs and checking fencing.

Summary

- Horses ideally require a minimum of 0.4–0.6 hectares (1–1.5 acres) of grazing each.

- Harrowing pulls the dead grass from the soil, and evens out the ground.

- Rolling levels uneven or poached ground, encourages tillering, firms the soil and discourages weeds.

- Fertilising can be done in the spring or autumn.

- Pasture should be checked regularly for poisonous plants.

- Weeds can be removed by pulling or digging up, strimming, topping or spraying.

- Topping encourages a more even and dense grass growth.

- Droppings should be removed regularly to help with worm control.

TRAINING TIPS

1. Speak to different yard managers (preferably in different areas of the country) about how they manage their grazing.

2. If you get the chance to visit an agricultural show, look at the different equipment available for grassland management and speak to the salesperson about the equipment and its uses.

3. Investigate different types of alternative grazing systems and enrichment ideas for turn out areas.

4. For more information on grassland management visit the BHS website.

Chapter 10
Tack and Equipment

Bridles

Bits

Saddles

Leg protection

Summary

Tack and Equipment

The range of tack and equipment available is continually evolving as more is learnt about horse anatomy and conformation, and the range of materials available increases. When working at home you can use any combination of tack suitable for the horse, however, competition rules vary throughout the disciplines so it is important to have an awareness of what is and is not allowed.

Bridles

Fitting a bridle

It is important that you are able to put on and fit a variety of bridles as you may find yourself having to select and fit a bridle to a new horse on the yard, or choose a bridle from a selection of work bridles that are used for several different horses.

Bridles come in pony, cob, full and extra-full sizes, so start by choosing one that you think suits the size of the horse's head and then check it for safety and that the runners and keepers are attached.

Check the approximate length of the bridle against the horse's head, remembering to untie the lead rope in case the horse takes exception to the bridle being held up to their head. If the bridle is obviously too big or too small, either adjust the length of the cheekpieces if possible or select another bridle that is a better fit. The cheekpieces should ideally fasten on to one of the middle holes to allow for any further adjustment.

Undo the runners and keepers before you put the bridle on so the height of the bit can be adjusted quickly if required. Once the bridle has been put on, check that the bit is sitting level and there are one or two wrinkles at the corners of the mouth. A bit that sits too low will bang on the horse's teeth; one that sits too high will pull the corners of the lips back and may bang on the molar teeth at the back of the mouth. As well as sitting at the correct height the bit should be the correct width for the horse. As a guide, if you can fit a finger in either side between the mouth and the bit ring it should be wide enough. If the bit has a loose ring you may want to leave slightly more than a finger's width as there is a danger of the bit ring pinching. Generally a bit that is too wide will slide through the horse's mouth as the rein is used, and one that is too narrow will pinch.

Once you have adjusted the bit, do up the throatlash and noseband and check the rest of the bridle. Check the browband and headpiece for signs of pinching around the horse's ears and make sure the noseband is sitting level and adjust it depending on its type. In order to work in a relaxed manner a horse needs to be comfortable and soft through their jaw and able to relax their facial muscles, and they cannot do this with a very tight noseband. All nosebands should be fitted to allow room for the horse to open their mouth enough to be comfortable and to relax their jaw. The noseband should not be tight enough to interfere with the horse's breathing or exert pressure on the cheeks, nasal bones or sensitive facial tissues.

Noseband action

A cavesson noseband has little action and its main purpose is for aesthetic reasons. It should allow free movement of the mouth and jaw but the horse may feel a small amount of pressure around the nose if they make exaggerated movements with their mouth.

A crank noseband is a type of cavesson noseband and should be fitted in the same way. This type of noseband has a lever fastening which can help keep the noseband in a more secure position. However, the lever fastening makes it easier to overtighten. If a noseband is too tight this can cause discomfort or pain as it pushes the horse's cheeks in towards the teeth. Always double check you can fit two fingers between the noseband and the top of the horse's nose after fastening.

The cavesson part of the **flash noseband** reduces the ability of the horse to cross their jaw and the lower strap prevents them from opening their mouth wide enough to evade the contact reducing the amount of control the rider has. Pressure is placed on the top of the nose and in the chin groove when the mouth is opened.

The drop noseband also prevents the horse from opening their mouth wide enough to evade the contact. It places less pressure on the nose than a flash noseband. The pressure is focused on the top of the nose and the chin groove, which can have a lowering effect on the horse's head.

The grackle noseband prevents the horse from crossing their jaw and from opening their mouth wide enough to avoid the contact. Pressure is placed on the crossover point in the centre of the nose as well as on the straps around the horse's face.

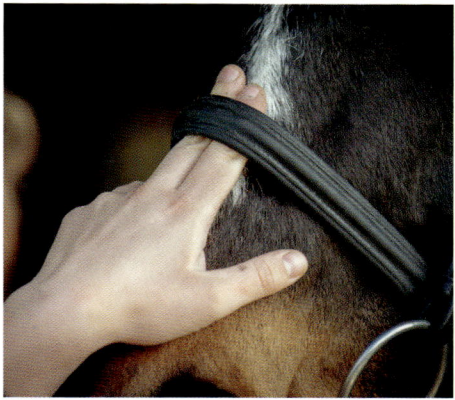

You should be able to fit two fingers between the noseband and the top of the horse's nose.

An International Society for Equitation Science (ISES) taper guage can be used to check the tightness of a noseband.

The double bridle

The double bridle can be used in competition from Elementary level dressage and above. It can also be seen in use across all the disciplines.

The double bridle has two bits — the bridoon, which looks like a smaller version of a simple snaffle and has a similar head-raising action and the curb bit, which influences the positioning of the head. The two bits are used together to refine the aids from the rider and increase the horse's balance and control. The rein attaching to the curb bit is thinner than the bridoon rein to help the rider differentiate between the two.

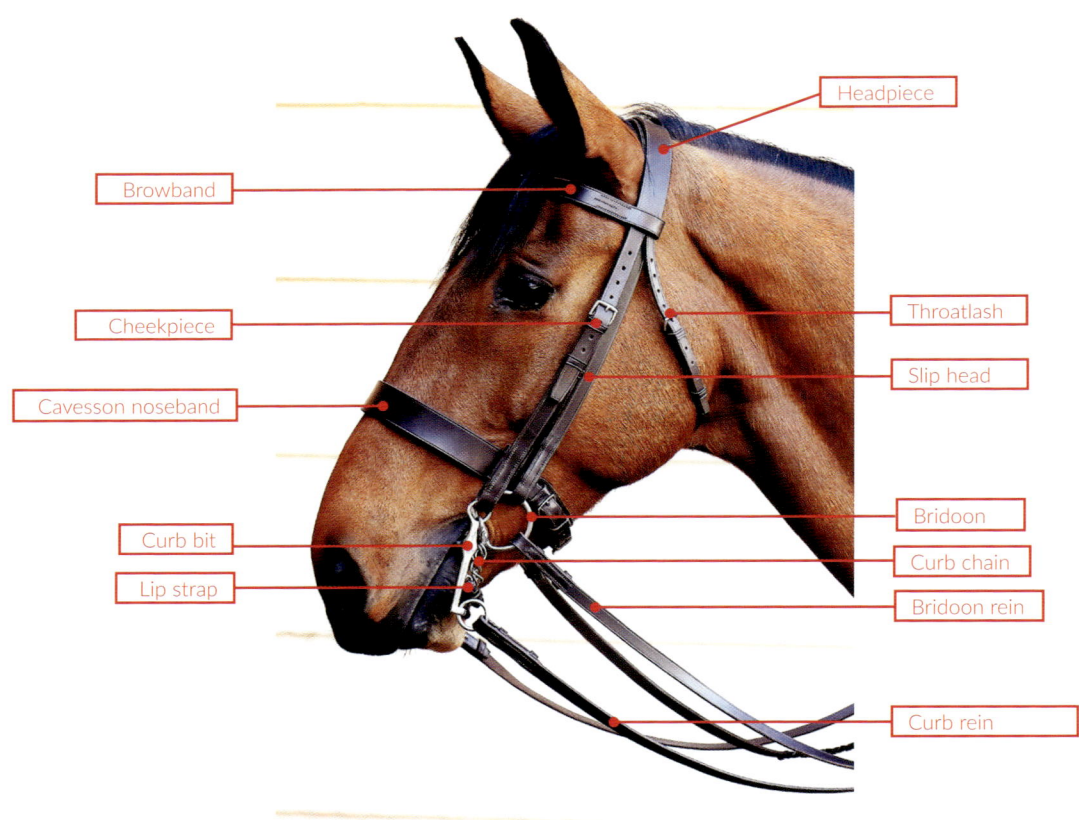

Double bridle.
Photo supplied by The Society of Master Saddlers.

A double bridle is put on in the same way as a normal bridle, but make sure you allow the horse time to open their mouth wide enough to put the two bits in. When in the horse's mouth the bridoon should sit behind the curb in a slightly higher position than a normal snaffle (generally verging towards two wrinkles in the corners of the lips) and the curb should sit roughly a finger's width below the bridoon. Putting the bridoon on top of the curb before you put the two in the horse's mouth will help you to get them in the correct position. Once the bits are in and the horse is comfortable check inside the mouth to make sure that the bits are sitting correctly and also to check that neither bit is touching the horse's teeth.

The bridoon is attached to a slip head, which fastens on the offside, to reduce the number of buckles on the nearside. It should ideally sit level with the buckles on the nearside.

A cavesson noseband is the only type of noseband that should be used with a double bridle. The cavesson should sit two finger's width underneath the projecting cheekbone and be fastened with room to fit two fingers all the way around between the horse's nose and the noseband.

Place the bridoon over the curb before putting the bits in the horse's mouth to ensure that they sit correctly.

A crank cavesson noseband is commonly used with a double bridle. It is usually padded across the nose and under the jaw and differs from a normal cavesson as it is fastened with a strap under the chin that runs between rings on either side and buckles in the centre. This allows the noseband to be fastened without pinching under the jaw. It is easy to over-tighten these types of noseband so great care should be taken to check the fit.

The curb bit should have a curb chain and a lip strap attached to it. Curb chains can be single- or double-link or made from elastic or a leather strap. There are various covers such as rubber, leather or gel pads that can be attached to provide cushioning under the chin.

The curb chain should be fixed on to the offside of the bit and hook on at the nearside. The hook should be facing outwards and sitting between the curb and the bridoon. The curb chain should only come into action when the curb is at 45 degrees to the mouth. To fit the curb chain, turn it clockwise so the links fit into each other and it lies flat against the chin groove then, fasten the link on to the nearside hook. There should be a small fly link at the bottom of the chain for the lip strap to pass through. The lip strap keeps the curb chain flat and buckles directly on to the bit.

As with any bridle, the headpiece and the browband should be checked for signs of pinching at the horse's ears, and the browband should be the correct size for the horse's forehead.

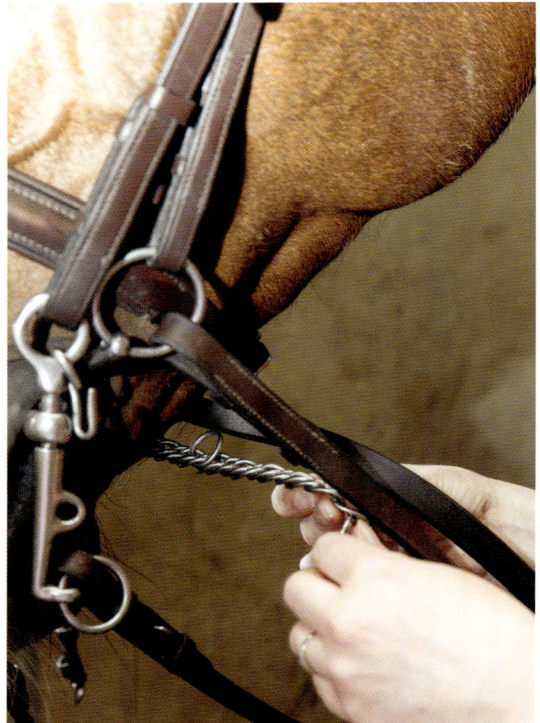

Untwist the curb chain so that it lies flat when it is fastened.

Anatomical bridles

Anatomical, or ergonomic bridles have been designed with the horse's facial anatomy in mind. Anatomical bridles look different to a traditional bridle as they are shaped to follow the contours of the horse's head avoiding the sensitive areas of the face and poll and improving the horse's comfort.

There are several different styles available, but their main features can include a wider or padded headpiece, which is cut back to allow more room around the base of the ears and poll reducing the risk of pinching and discomfort. Shaped cheek pieces that fit around the projecting cheekbones and nosebands that are contoured to reduce pressure across the sensitive facial nerves, nasal bones and teeth making them more comfortable for the horse.

Some anatomical bridles can be worn (with a legal bit) in dressage, showjumping and eventing but some configurations are not allowed in competition so always check the most recent discipline rule book.

10 | Tack and Equipment

An example of an anatomical bridle is shown in the picture above.

The Micklem bridle was one of the first anatomical bridles designed.

Bitless bridles

Bitless bridles have no actual bit within the horse's mouth, but instead place pressure or leverage on the side of the horse's face, jaw, poll, nose and/or chin groove depending on the style.

Great care should be taken when choosing, fitting and using a bitless bridle as it is still possible to cause damage to the gums or cheeks of the horse if the pressure placement is incorrect.

This is a Blair's pattern hackamore. The shanks place leverage on the nose when pressure is applied to the reins. The longer the shanks the more pressure is exerted.

Bits

As more research is done bits continue to evolve, with many variations of the same bit existing. All bits will act on one or more areas of the horse's mouth and head: the corners of the lips, the bars, the tongue, the roof of the mouth, the chin groove, the side of the face, the poll, and the nose, depending on their design. You don't have to know the name of every bit but it should be possible to work out the action of a bit based on the design.

Mouthpieces and bit rings

Mouthpieces

Mouthpieces come in a variety of shapes and sizes. Bits are measured based on the length of the mouthpiece, from each point just inside the bit rings, with the mouthpiece held straight. They range from 9–15cm (3½–6in) and vary in width, with a thicker mouthpiece being milder in action than a thin mouthpiece. The mouthpiece can be made from a variety of different metals, ranging from stainless steel to a variety of composite metals designed to encourage the horse to salivate and increase the acceptance of the bit. Mouthpieces are also available in various types of rubber, vulcanite, plastic and nylon, although the rings of the bit are usually metal. It is important to remember that each horse is different and what suits one horse may not suit another.

Common designs of mouthpiece are as follows.

Single-jointed — has a single V-shaped joint in the centre, which has a nutcracker action across the tongue. Acts on the corners, tongue and bars, producing a head-raising effect.

Double-jointed — these can have a link, lozenge, roller or similar in the centre of the mouthpiece, which modifies the nutcracker action, producing a U-shaped action instead. The angle at which the link is set may vary, putting more or less pressure on the tongue.

Hollow-mouth — the mouthpiece is hollow, making it very light. These bits often have a thicker than normal mouth piece and are considered to have a mild action because of this.

Mullen-mouth — is a single bar slightly curved forward, which sits straight across the mouth and acts on the tongue and the bars of the mouth. Considered a mild bit.

Port — a single bar with a raised curve in the middle to accommodate the tongue; it can have an effect on the roof of the mouth if the port is large enough. Acts on the tongue, lips, roof and bars of the mouth.

10 | Tack and Equipment

Bit rings

As with mouthpieces, these have various designs and actions.

Fixed-ring — holds the bit still in the mouth; no risk of pinching.

Loose-ring — allows the bit to move in the horse's mouth. Some horses prefer the more flexible feeling of the loose ring. These bits can be useful on horses who have a tendency to lean on the bit, and can help to prevent this.

Hanging-cheek — has separate small rings on the top of the bit rings to which attach the cheekpieces. This lifts the bit up off of the tongue. There is some debate over whether a hanging cheek bit applies pressure to the poll; the general consensus is that the poll action is minimal.

Full/fixed-cheek — prevents the bit from sliding through the horse's mouth. Puts pressure on the side of the face when turning.

Shanks — supplementary to bit rings, these act as levers and put pressure on the poll; the longer the shank, the greater the pressure. They can be fixed, or slide up and down. Any construction whereby the rein can be moved lower than the horse's mouth will act as a lever and put pressure on the poll.

Families of bits

Bits are traditionally grouped into families based upon their common features.

Snaffles

Snaffles have a slight head-raising action and have an effect on the corners of the mouth, the tongue and the bars.

Loose-ring with a lozenge.

Hanging snaffle with single joint.

Fixed-ring French link snaffle.

Full-cheek snaffle.

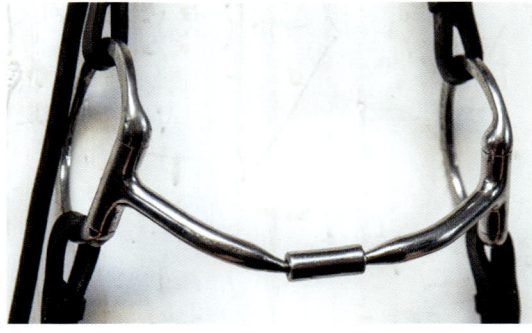

Snaffle with roller.

Snaffle bits.

The double bridle

The double bridle has two bits — the bridoon which acts as a snaffle and the curb. The curb puts pressure on the poll and the chin groove as well as the bars, tongue and corners of the mouth, encouraging lowering of the head.

Double bridle bits. The left-hand bridle has a fixed mullen-mouth curb with a shaped double-jointed bridoon. The right-hand bridle has a sliding-arm curb with a port and a double-jointed bridoon.

The pelham

The pelham is a combination bit that is designed to combine the action of the two double bridle bits into one. It has shanks, which put pressure on the poll, encouraging the horse to bring their head down, and a curb chain, which puts pressure on the chin groove. The pelham acts on the bars, tongue, chin groove, poll and corners. If the bit has a port, the roof of mouth will also be affected.

Single-jointed pelham with roundings.

Gag bits

The gag has a lifting action with the aim of keeping the horse in a controllable outline. The size of the bit rings influences the amount of the leverage the bit has, specifically with a running gag; the larger the bit rings the greater the leverage. With three- or two-ringed gags the lower the ring the greater leverage, and with American gags the greater the length of the shanks, the greater the leverage. Running gags are severe bits and should only be used by experienced riders; using two reins is advisable, with one attached as a snaffle rein and the other to the bottom ring, in this way the gag rein can be used only when required.

Running gag.

Three-ring Continental gag with link.

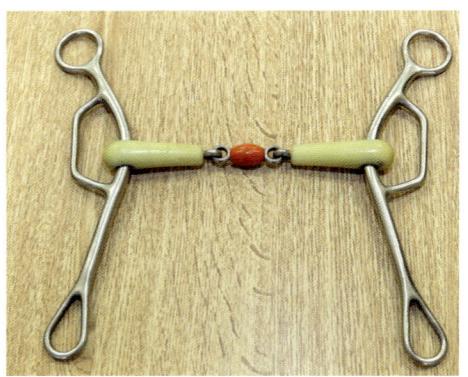

Plastic mouthpiece American gag with double joint.

Saddles

Fitting a saddle

Saddles should be checked at least twice a year by a qualified saddle fitter, who is able to assess the saddle to ensure it is the best possible fit for the horse. Saddle fitters are also able to make adjustments to the saddle such as reflocking, as the flock (stuffing) can become compacted over time, altering the shape and fit of the saddle. There are many factors that can influence the fit of a saddle — the most common one is the time of the year and quality of grazing; a horse who is not fit and has been turned out at grass will have gained weight, resulting in the saddle becoming too tight, especially if it was initially fitted when the horse was fit and in work. Overweight horses will gradually lose weight once back in work (hopefully) and the shape of their back can change as the muscles start to tone up. A young horse who is still growing will also change shape as their muscles develop, and can outgrow a saddle surprisingly quickly. Having the saddle checked at least every six months by a qualified saddle fitter will help the horse stay comfortable and allow them to work and develop muscle correctly and without pain or discomfort.

There may be occasions when you might need to fit a saddle to a horse temporarily until you can book the saddle fitter to visit. There are several things to consider when selecting a saddle for a horse. First, consider the shape of the horse's back. Generally, cobs will have flatter, rounder withers and broader backs whereas Thoroughbreds tend to have narrower, more prominent withers and this will affect the width of saddle required.

Saddle trees come in different widths and lengths. The width is classified as narrow, medium and wide, with stages in between such as medium/wide. The length of a saddle is measured from the stud on the skirt to the centre of the cantle. The majority of saddles for horses will

This is what a saddle tree looks like on the horse's back before the saddle is built around it.

measure between 16 and 18 inches but there are smaller sizes suited to ponies. The saddle should be long enough to accommodate the rider but not too long for the horse. The panels should not sit past the eighteenth rib, where it would place pressure on the horse's loins. Ideally the panels should follow the contours of the horse's back.

Throughout the whole saddle fitting process the horse should be observed for signs of discomfort, pain or resistance that may indicate the saddle is not comfortable. This includes body language and facial expressions, which can be very subtle. An uncomfortable horse may be reluctant to go forward when ridden, alter their stride length or not be willing to work in their normal manner. Extreme reactions may include bucking or rearing, snatching the head forwards or refusing to move.

The saddle should be checked for safety, to include the stitching and general condition of the leather before placing it on the horse's back. To give you the best idea of how the saddle fits, put it on without a saddle cloth or girth (making sure you keep hold of it while you make these checks), as this will let you see how the saddle follows the contours of the horse's back.

The front of the saddle should allow room for the withers.

Check the following:

- The saddle should be the correct length for the horse and the panels should not sit past the eighteenth rib. This rib is roughly a hand span from the point of hip — you should be able to feel the end of the ribcage and gently follow it up towards the spine.

- There should be room for at least three fingers between the front of the saddle and the withers. Because of the design with some cut-back saddles there may be slightly less room, but any saddle that sits on the horse's withers without a rider is too low at the front.

- There should be room to fit a finger between the side of the withers and the front of the saddle.

- You should be able to see daylight through the gullet when you look from the back.

- The panels should not be pressing on the horse's spine.

- There should be clearance for three fingers between the spine and the gullet at the back of the saddle.

- There should be no tight spots when a flat hand is run down the length of the panel from the withers down the shoulder.

- There should be no 'bridging' when a flat hand is run under the saddle from the front along the panel to the back. If a saddle in bridging there will be increased pressure at the front (withers) and back of the saddle and the contact between the panels and the back will not be continuous.

- The saddle should sit level when viewed from the side and the back.

If the saddle seems like a good fit, attach the girth and check that the fit of the saddle hasn't been altered.

Once the saddle has been fitted in the stable the next step is to carefully mount the rider and re-check the fit.

- The weight of the rider will push the saddle down slightly but there should still be room for two–three fingers between the front of the saddle and the withers, room for one finger at each side of the withers and three fingers between the spine and the gullet at the back of the saddle.

- The saddle and rider should be sitting level when viewed from each side and from the back.

10 | Tack and Equipment

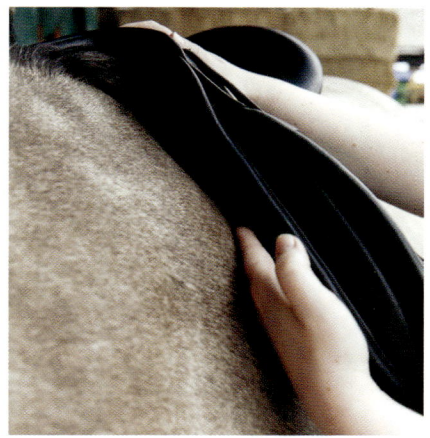

Start at the top of the panel and run your hand down, checking for any tight spots.

The saddle should sit flat on the horse's back.

- The panels of the saddle should be in contact with the horse's back but not pressing on the loins.

The horse and rider should then be observed first in walk and then in trot and canter if the horse seems comfortable. Watch the saddle for any excessive or unusual movement, such as the back of the saddle rising up and down, or the saddle sliding to the side. If at any point the horse is uncomfortable, stop and reassess the fit. Even if the saddle appears to fit perfectly it may just be that this particular style of saddle does not suit that horse. Ask for feedback from the rider as to how they felt the horse went and how comfortable they found the saddle. If they are to be the regular rider it is important that the saddle fits them as well as the horse. When a saddle fitter comes out to check or fit a saddle they will follow a similar, but more detailed, process including taking templates on the horse's back. A list of qualified saddle fitters can be found on the Society of Master Saddlers' website.

Types of saddle

General-purpose

A general-purpose (GP) saddle is designed to be used for both low-level dressage and jumping, allowing one saddle to be used across several disciplines, and is also most suitable for general hacking/pleasure riding. The seat is deep enough to allow the rider to sit in a 'dressage' position but the saddle flaps are forward cut to allow for the rider shortening their stirrup leathers for jumping. Some GP saddles are slightly more biased towards dressage or showing and have slightly straighter saddle flaps to allow the rider to have a straighter leg. These are often referred to as VSD GP saddles.

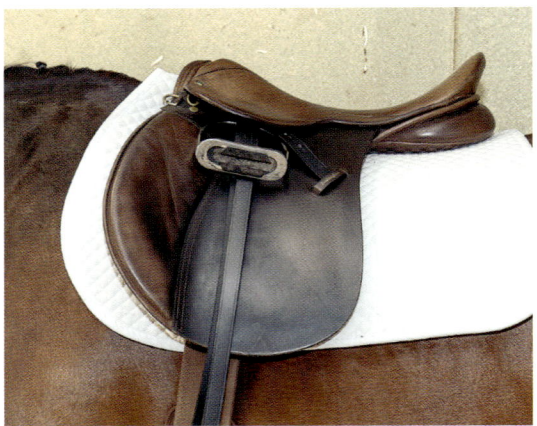

General-purpose saddle.

Dressage

Compared to a GP saddle a dressage saddle has a deeper seat and straight-cut saddle flaps that allow the horse freer movement of their shoulders. The girth straps are long and sit below the saddle flaps, allowing closer contact of the rider's legs with the horse's sides. The straight-cut saddle flap allows the rider to ride with longer stirrup leathers and the stirrup bars tend to be situated further back than a GP to allow the rider's legs to lie underneath them in a classical dressage position.

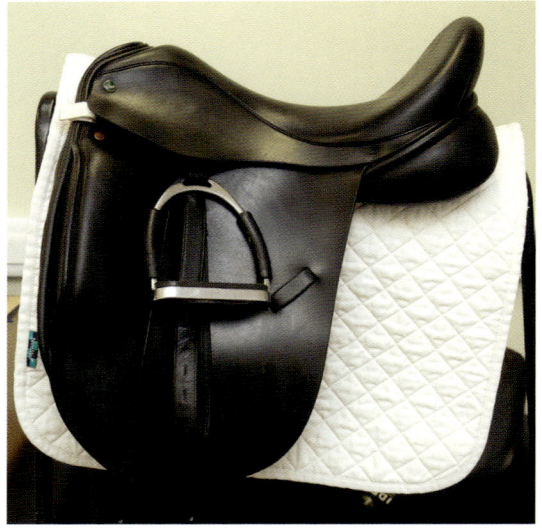

Dressage saddle.

Jumping saddle

A jumping saddle has more forward-cut knee rolls and longer saddle flaps than a GP saddle to accommodate the rider's leg position when riding with jumping length stirrup leathers. The cantle is lower and the seat can be flatter to allow the rider the freedom to fold over a fence.

Jumping saddle.

Saddle cloths and pads

There is a huge variety of saddle cloths (square-shaped), numnahs (saddle-shaped) and riser pads available on the market today, each with its own merit. When choosing what to put under the saddle it is important to consider what effect it might have on the fit of the saddle and the comfort of the horse. Whatever you put under the saddle should be longer than the saddle panels to avoid creating a pressure point and should be pulled up into the gullet of the saddle to ensure that no pressure is placed on the spine.

As dressage saddles have straight-cut knee rolls they require a longer length of saddle cloth with straight edges to fit underneath the saddle.

Forward-cut jumping saddles will require a cloth that follows the shape of the saddle. There are many types of saddle cloth and numnah available on the market. A variety is shown below and overleaf.

Dressage square — *longer, straighter cut to accommodate the shape of a dressage saddle. The sheepskin lining and shaping over the withers provides cushioning and reduces the risk of rubbing.*

Sheepskin-lined GP numnah — *the sheepskin helps to distribute pressure under the saddle and the wool absorbs any moisture and compresses under the saddle so it doesn't alter the fit.*

Thin cotton jumping cloth — *the cloth is shaped at the front to sit high over the withers, removing the risk of creating a pressure point. It is shaped to the forward cut of a jumping saddle.*

Airflow — *made from porous materials or mesh and designed to encourage airflow under the saddle to help keep the horse cool. Good for cross-country or hot weather for keeping the horse's back cooler.*

Non-slip — *made from gel or similar material and designed to help to keep the saddle in place, as well as absorbing concussion.*

A padded dressage square — *the gel pads are incorporated into the numnah and sit under the saddle to reduce the impact of the rider and disperse pressure evenly across the horse's back. The pads can also reduce movement of the saddle.*

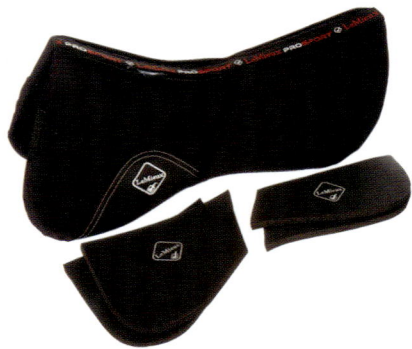

Riser pads *can be made from a variety of materials such as foam, gel or sheepskin and are placed between the saddle and the numnah/cloth to help absorb the impact and disperse the pressure from the rider. They can also be used as a short-term method of adjusting the fit of a saddle. Some have removable shims (pictured) that can be positioned in pockets to target specific areas of the saddle — for example, lift the front of the saddle up off the withers for a horse with muscle wastage.*

Breastplates

A breastplate is used to prevent the saddle from sliding backwards when the horse is working, which can happen even with a correctly fitting saddle when the horse is galloping and jumping. All breastplates should be fitted to allow room for the horse to move their shoulders freely. If the breastplate is too tight it can pull the saddle forward on to the withers, but if fitted too loose it will not stop the saddle from slipping.

The breastplate straps should attach to the D-rings under the skirt of the saddle near the stirrup bars as these are fixed directly to the tree, and not to the rings held on by leather at the front of the saddle, since these can break. Once fitted there should be enough room to fit a fist between the horse's chest and the central ring of the breastplate.

A five-point breastplate attaches to the saddle at five points: the D-rings, the girth under the saddle flaps on each side and to the girth between the horse's forelegs, making the breastplate secure with little chance of the saddle sliding back.

The straps are elasticated, which allows them to move with the horse's shoulders. The rings have fleece under them, which lifts them off the shoulders, reducing the risk of rubbing. The ring at the chest should sit centrally and can be used for a martingale attachment.

Five-point breastplate with a martingale attachment.

A hunting breastplate attaches to the saddle at the D-rings and between the horse's forelegs to the girth. The straps can be made from leather or elastic and can be a fixed length or have buckles to make them adjustable. As with the five-point breastplate, the ring at the chest should sit centrally and can be used for a martingale attachment.

With both these breastplates a removable martingale attachment can be fitted to the ring at the front of the chest. The rings of the martingale should reach just under the horse's throat when the ring is held in the centre of the chest.

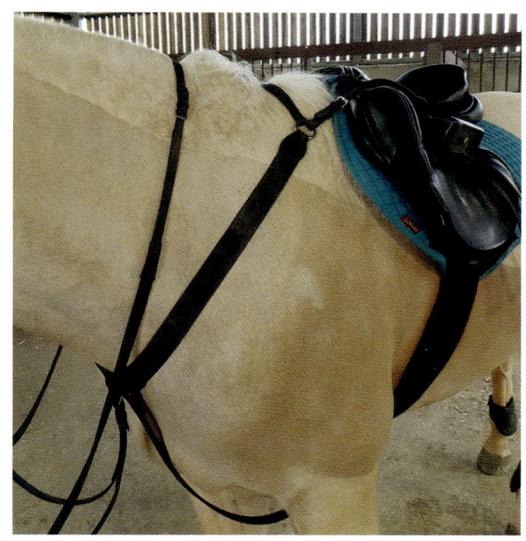

Hunting breastplate with a martingale attachment.

Although breastplates are permitted in all disciplines, martingales or martingale attachments are not permitted for use in dressage competitions.

A racing breastplate is an elasticated or leather band that attaches to the girth straps under the saddle flaps and has a neckstrap to hold it in position. It is usually fully adjustable with buckles on the neckstrap and across the chest. There is no strap that goes between the horse's forelegs.

The martingale straps should be long enough for the rings to reach under the throat when they are straightened.

A breastgirth is an elasticated band that sits around the horse's chest and attaches to the D-rings of the saddle. It should be fitted with space for a fist in between the band and the horse's neck.

Racing breastplate.

Leg protection

Boots or bandages?

It comes down to personal choice whether to use boots or bandages; each has its own advantages and disadvantages. Bandages mould around the horse's leg making it harder for dirt or arena surface material to get stuck in between the bandage and the leg, which can cause rubs or irritation to the horse. However, they do not offer the same level of protection from knocks or brushing that the strike pad of a boot provides. Bandages take more time to put on correctly compared to boots and there is a risk of pressure rubs if they are not put on correctly.

Bandages can be fitted to the correct length for the horse's legs, whereas boots come in specific lengths, which can make finding the correct length for a horse with particularly long or short cannon bones difficult.

Some bandage material can cause the leg to heat up, which could potentially increase the risk of injury to the tendons. Boots can have mesh inserts or perforations in them to allow a flow of air, keeping the legs cooler while the horse is working.

Bandages are soft and will flex and move as the horse bends and straightens their legs whereas, because of their design, some boots can have rigid outer shells, which are not flexible and can rub or press on the horse's legs.

Further details about specific types of leg support and protection are given below.

Schooling bandages

Schooling bandages can be used to provide support and protection to the tendons and ligaments of the lower leg. They are made from fleece, are not elasticated and can be fitted with or without padding underneath.

If padding is used it should be wrapped around the leg from front to back and the overlap should not sit where the tendons pass underneath. Any wrinkles that could create pressure points when the bandage is applied over the top should be smoothed out. Ideally the bandage should fasten on the outside of the leg with the Velcro facing backwards.

Complete Equestrian Volume 3

i. The flat side of the bandage is placed against the leg and the bandage should be unrolled from the front to the back of the leg.

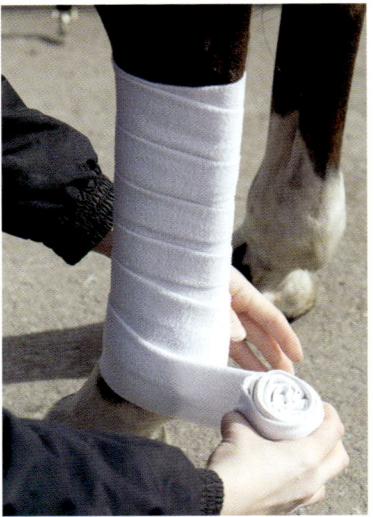

ii. Each turn should be equally spaced and the bandage firm enough that you can fit a finger comfortably inside the top. The tension should be the same the whole way down the leg. A very tight bandage will affect circulation and a very loose bandage can slip down.

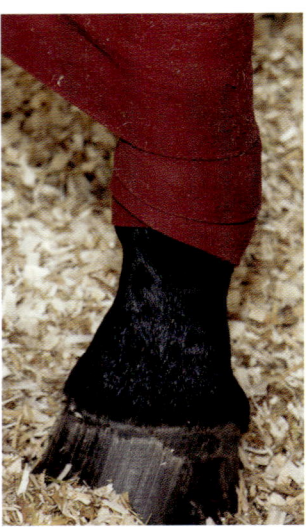

iii. The bandage can be slightly angled to cover the ergot at the back of the fetlock and create an upside-down V-shape at the front.

Sports medicine boots

Sports medicine boots offer a quicker and easier alternative to putting on a bandage. They are anatomically designed to wrap around the horse's lower leg encompassing the fetlock and are said to offer tendon and ligament support. They are made from neoprene or similar material, which allows them to mould around the leg. They are held in place by three Velcro straps: two fasten on the outside of the leg facing backwards and the third wraps under the fetlock at an angle of 45 degrees and fastens at the front.

Tendon and fetlock boots

Open-fronted tendon boots differ from brushing boots as they provide protection to the back and sides of the horse's lower leg but leave the front of the leg exposed. They are popular for showjumping where injuries may be caused by a hind foot striking into the back of a foreleg when landing

Sports medicine boots.

after a fence, as the back of the leg is protected but the front of the boot is open, allowing the horse to feel if they knock a fence.

Tendon boots often have a tough outer shell, but can also be made from leather or other materials. They are fastened across the front of the leg with elasticated straps that allow for the flexion of the limb, the fastening being either with Velcro, buckles or billets depending on the material the boots are made from.

The boots should sit below the projecting bones of the knees to prevent rubbing, and provide support around the fetlocks. They should be fastened to a tightness that allows a finger to fit comfortably inside the top of the boot. Some tendon boots are lined with sheepskin or fleece for extra padding; these liners are often removable to allow for cleaning and brushing off any dirt or sand that may irritate the horse's leg.

Fetlock boots are used on the hind limbs and are usually paired with tendon boots. They sit around the hind fetlocks and offer protection to the fetlocks from brushing or from being struck by the opposite leg, without restricting the movement of the hind limb.

Cross-country boots

Cross-country boots are designed to offer all-round protection to the limb as well as being lightweight, breathable and water resistant. They are more substantial than normal brushing boots, with tough strike pads that wrap around the leg offering protection from impact as well as shock-absorption.

Tendon boots.

Fetlock boots.

They often have vents or mesh to allow airflow through them keeping the horse's legs and the tendons cooler, which is thought to reduce the risk of tendon injuries.

Overreach boots

Overreach boots sit around the front hooves, covering the bottom of the pastern over the coronary band and down the length of the hoof, protecting the bulbs of the heel and the coronet band from injury. The boot should be fitted with one–two fingers width between the pastern and the top of the boot and should be long enough so that the bottom edge sits just above the ground when the horse's foot is flat on the ground.

Depending on their design, overreach boots can be pulled on over the hoof, or secured with a single fastening. Some are shaped to fit the hoof and are lower at the back than the front; these tend to have cushions that sit in the horse's heel to prevent the boot from turning round the hoof.

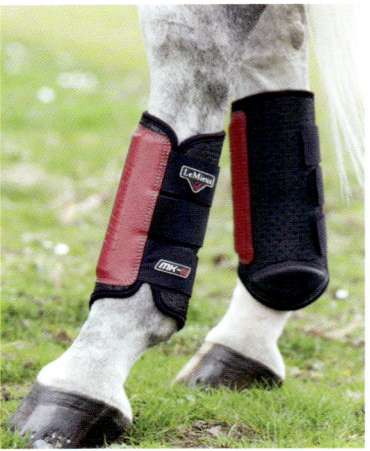

Cross-country boots.

Overreach boots.

Studs

Studs can be fitted to the shoes to give the horse more traction and reduce the risk of slipping and possibly sustaining strain injuries, or even falling, when working on grass. Stud holes are drilled into the shoes near the heel by the farrier, who should be able to offer advice as to what might suit an individual horse, in terms of whether it would be better to have one or two stud holes per shoe, and whether to fit them all round or just in the hind shoes. If there is to be just one stud hole per shoe it should be positioned on the outside of the shoe to reduce the risk of injury to the horse if they strike into themselves with the opposite leg. (Horses should always wear boots when being ridden in studs as there is a big risk of them striking into themselves with the opposite foot in this way. A stud girth can also be used to protect the horse from striking themselves in the chest when tucking up their forelegs over a fence.)

Plugging the stud holes as soon as they have been put in, and after each use, using cotton wool soaked in oil or a plug will help keep the holes clear of dirt and grit and make them easier to clean out when it is necessary to fit the studs.

The dirt and grit can be picked out of the hole, but when doing so, be very careful that you don't dig down too deep into the foot. Once the hole is clear you can use a T-tap to rethread it. Hold the horse's leg as if you were removing a shoe so you have both hands free. Line up

10 | Tack and Equipment

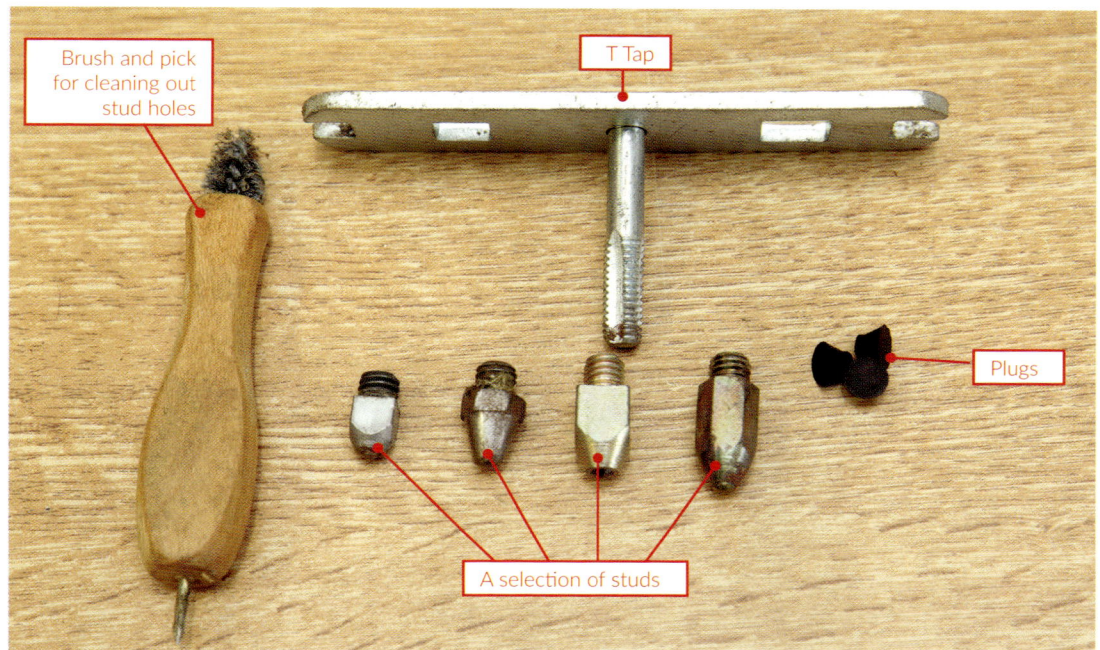

Stud kit.

the T-tap with the thread and screw it into the hole, stopping when it starts to resist, and then unscrew it. You need to be careful not to 'cross the thread' (screw the tap in crooked) as this will make it impossible to screw in the stud.

It is best to clean and rethread the stud holes the day before you want to use them and then repack them with cotton wool or plugs to keep them clean, to make things easier on the day of the competition.

To put the stud in, unplug the hole and carefully line up the threads then start to screw it in by hand; as it starts to tighten use a spanner to tighten it further. Be careful not to over-tighten the stud as it can be difficult to remove them later. However, if you leave them too loose they are likely to fall off. If you are putting studs in on grass it is useful to have a magnetic armband or dish that you can put the studs in so you don't lose them in the grass. To store the studs, clean any mud or grass off them and then spray them in oil to prevent them from rusting.

As studs are designed to sink into the ground they should not be used on any surface where this cannot happen, for example, tarmac or concrete. Also, the horse should not be travelled in studs as this will alter the balance of the hooves by raising the heels thus putting extra strain on the horse's legs. There are studs available for all types of ground conditions. It is normal practice to put smaller studs in the front shoes than the hind shoes. Generally, for very soft ground you would use big, chunky studs and for harder ground pointed studs, but you should always aim to put in the smallest studs that will do the job.

Summary

- A double bridle is used to refine the aids given by the rider.

- Bits are grouped into families called: snaffle, double bridle, pelham, and gag and there are also bitless bridles.

- Saddles can be classed as general-purpose, dressage or jumping.

- There are various types of saddle cloths, numnahs and pads available to go under the saddle.

- Bandages or boots can be used to protect the horse's legs.

- Studs are used to increase the amount of grip when working on hard or slippery ground.

TRAINING TIPS

1. Practise putting double bridles on horses who are used to wearing one.

2. Go and watch higher level affiliated competitions to see riders using double bridles and how they influence the horse.

3. The warm-up arenas at affiliated events are a good place to observe lots of different tack combinations in action.

4. Have a look around tack shops or online at the variety of leg protection, tack and bits available. See if you can work out the action of the bits.

5. Find out if anyone on your yard uses studs and ask to observe or help when they clean out the stud holes. Ask questions about what types of studs they use for different ground conditions.

6. Speak to farriers about the use of studs and stud holes and watch how they are put in the shoe.

7. Observe a registered saddle fitter during a saddle fitting. Speak to them about different types of saddles and bridles.

Chapter 11

Lungeing

Purpose of lungeing

Tack

Safety considerations

Lungeing technique

Notes on working a horse on the lunge

Summary

Purpose of lungeing

Lungeing is a useful way of providing variety in a horse's exercise programme and can also be used when time is tight as the horse can be exercised within a shorter timescale. In addition, there are advantages to lungeing in relation to exercising and training the horse. The following are some of the benefits of lungeing:

- In some situations lungeing can be used to exercise a horse when they cannot be ridden, for example if the rider is ill but the horse still has to be worked, or the saddle has gone to be adjusted by a saddler. This means the horse can be kept fit, or at least exercised.

- Lungeing is used throughout the process of training the horse. It is used when the horse is being backed, when the horse learns to respond to voice aids while being lunged. These voice aids can then be used when a rider is introduced to help the horse understand the leg and rein aids. It is also used later in training and provides an opportunity to work and strengthen the horse without interference from a rider.

- Correct lungeing will help to develop a horse's suppleness.

- Careful use of the side-reins when lungeing can improve the contact your horse gives you when ridden. Lungeing in side-reins allows the horse to build the strength and coordination of working in a correct outline without the weight and interference from a rider.

- Lungeing enables you to see the horse working from the ground.

Tack

Before lungeing, the horse's tack will need to be checked to make sure it is fitted correctly and securely and that it is in good working order. This is to ensure that the tack is safe to use and the horse is comfortable. It is good practice to lunge from a cavesson as this eliminates the risk of an uneven and opposing contact, which can occur when lungeing directly from the bit with the side-reins attached. Ideally, the horse should wear brushing boots, as they are on a continual circle and the risk of brushing is higher. It is also advisable to use overreach boots for horses who are excitable on the lunge. It will be necessary to check that the side-reins are even and have been adjusted to approximately the correct length for the horse. The side-reins should reach no less than a fist's distance away from the bit (see photo) although you may want to start the horse off with slightly longer side-reins and shorten them as the horse warms up.

11 | Lungeing

One method of measuring the approximate length of side-reins, is to measure the clip to a distance of a fist away from the bit.

Safety considerations

The following safety points should be borne in mind.

- The lungeing surface should be level with good footing (ideally an all-weather surface), and the area should be enclosed. If a surface is deep or slippery the horse will be in danger of injuring themselves. On a practical note, lungeing continuously in one area of the school is not good for the surface, so ideally you should alternate the areas where you lunge within a school and make sure that the surface is harrowed regularly. Some centres choose to have a lungeing pen to avoid damage to school surface.

- Ideally you should not lunge in school while others are riding because, if the horse became loose, this would cause significant risk to the person(s) riding. In addition to this, horses often let off steam at the start of a lunge session, which could be unsettling to other horses.

Horses often let off steam when being lunged; ideally horses should not be lunged in areas where others are being ridden.

- Caution should be exercised when initially letting a horse out on the lunge, since an excited horse can jump forward and might kick out. Therefore, when starting a horse out on the lunge you should always make sure you are positioned safely and ready to move out of the way if necessary. For this reason, when lungeing, horses should always be encouraged to walk quietly away from the handler. Ensure that you have your lunge line coiled correctly and ready to let out, if the horse does move off quickly you need to be ready to let the lunge line out and move the horse onto a bigger circle to reduce the risk of injury.

This horse is walking quietly out on to the circle.

- Irrespective of how experienced you are, you should always wear suitable footwear, a riding hat and gloves when lungeing.

- Moving on a continuous circle is hard work for the horse. A lunge session need not be longer than 30 minutes. If a horse is worked too hard they will be at greater risk of sustaining an injury. Lungeing on too small a circle will also put strain on the horse's joints and should be avoided; 18–20m is recommended as a suitable size for a circle. If the length of the line doesn't allow this with you standing stationary, you should be prepared to walk a small circle yourself.

Lungeing technique

To be able to work a horse effectively on the lunge you should have developed competence in handling the lungeing equipment so that you are safe and efficient. This takes practice, so the more you lunge the easier it will become. It is important to be strict with yourself while handling lungeing equipment, so that you do not fall into bad habits. It is easy to become complacent, especially when lungeing well-behaved horses who you know. You should also have perfected the use of your body language, in order that you can give clear signals to the horse. This is also developed through practice, particularly through lungeing different types of horses.

You should be able to lunge laid-back horses in a way that will encourage them to go forwards. With a laid-back horse you should be clear and positive with your voice aids. Try to use the same principles as when you are riding — the horse should respond to your aids promptly. If the horse does not respond, you should repeat the aid and you can back-up your voice aid with the whip. The whip is to be used to influence the horse as your leg would when riding. When pointed towards the horse's shoulder you can use it to position the horse on the circle as your inside leg would when riding. The whip pointed towards the hindquarters encourages the horse to move forwards. Practise your control of the whip so that you can make small aids and adjustments such as flicking the lash of the whip towards the horse's hindquarters. If you need to contact the horse with the whip to reinforce your aids then this should be done between the point of buttock and the hock, this is only to be done to back up your other aids and not to reprimand the horse. Body language and positioning are often overlooked as aids when lungeing, but if you watch horses interact with each other this is their main form of communication. When lungeing if you position yourself facing more towards their hindquarters you will encourage them to go forwards, whereas positioning yourself facing towards their shoulder will encourage them to slow down. Try to keep your shoulders square on towards the horse rather than turning and leading them around on the circle and be ready to take a step towards them if you need to move them away from you on the circle.

You should be able to lunge more forward-going and sensitive horses and be able to adjust your body language and lungeing technique to keep them calm. Standing slightly in front of the horse's shoulder can help to steady the horse. For sensitive horses, make sure you use your aids steadily and calmly; also handle the whip with care and try not to make sudden movements. Moving the whip further away from the quarters or lowering the whip will take the pressure off the horse. Be aware of your body language and make your movements smooth and quiet.

Some horses, especially if fresh, need to be worked forward fairly early on and be directed in their work with transitions to keep them attentive. However, other horses, if particularly sensitive, may benefit from time in walk, with short trots initially to settle them into their work. With all horses you should be able to build up a rapport and show clear communication with them.

With practice, you should be able to work a horse on the lunge to a level similar to the level of their ridden work. This is a particularly valuable asset when, for some reason, they cannot be ridden. Ideally, the horse should be warmed up without side-reins in walk, trot and canter on both reins. If a horse is not established in the canter and cantering causes them to lose balance, warming up in trot is sufficient. Similarly, if the horse is fresh or becomes excitable in the canter, cantering may be avoided until they have settled. In situations where a horse is particularly fresh you may attach the side-reins earlier; this is a good way of maintaining control and focusing the horse's energy. At the end of the lunge session the horse should be allowed to walk without the side-reins attached to cool down.

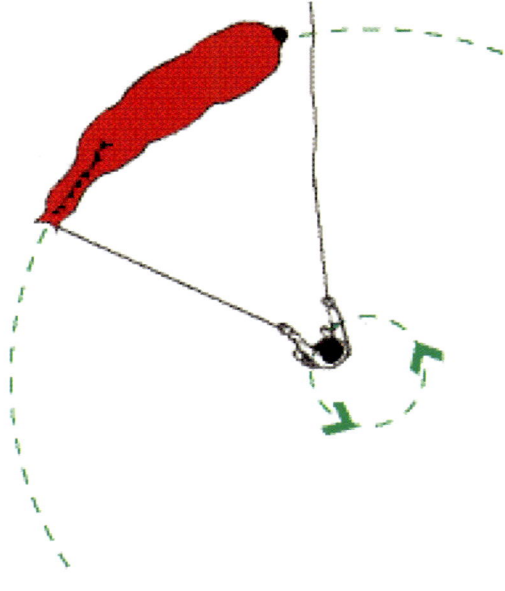

Walking a small circle allows you to position yourself closer to the horse without reducing the size of the circle the horse is on.

Notes on working a horse on the lunge

Gaits and transitions

Walk. The horse should be allowed to walk freely using their head and neck. For this reason, the amount of walk while side-reins are attached should be limited. The horse should walk actively and show good overtracking (hind feet stepping over and in front of the prints the forefeet have made).

Trot. The horse should be active and tracking up (hind feet stepping into the prints the forefeet have made). The trot should have an even two-beat rhythm.

Warming up the horse without side-reins.

Canter. This should be in an even three-beat rhythm; the horse should not be rushing or losing balance. Some horses find it hard to balance in canter on the lunge, so it should be used in short periods on large circles while the horse is developing their balance. If a horse picks up the incorrect canter lead or goes disunited in the canter they should be returned to trot, rebalanced and then asked to canter again. The difference in a horse's ability to canter/retain canter on different reins can be a clue to one-sidedness.

Start with short canters if the horse is still developing their balance on the lunge. This handler is walking with the horse in the canter, with a steady connection through the lunge line.

Transitions. Using transitions will help encourage the horse to work from behind and, in doing so, will improve their activity. Transitions can be used frequently between walk and trot and trot and canter. Make sure that the horse works obediently off your aids and steps under with their hind legs. The more transitions you do the harder the horse will be working. It can be

A horse working actively in trot.

helpful to use frequent transitions to improve activity, then afterwards allow the horse to work and carry themselves with fewer transitions.

Rhythm, tempo and balance

Rhythm is the regularity of the horse's footfalls within each gait and tempo is the speed of the footfalls. Good rhythm, tempo and balance work together; you cannot have one without the other. When working a horse on the lunge, you should be able to recognise obvious signs that they are not balanced; they may speed up and then slow down, and find it difficult to work in a regular rhythm. The best way to work to achieve a good rhythm is to use your voice and body language backed up with the whip where required to encourage a laid-back horse to maintain forwardness and activity within the gait, and to use your voice and body language to steady a lively horse. Be consistent with your aids so the horse is encouraged to maintain rhythm in each gait consistently. It is also very important to ensure the size of the circle is big enough. A horse will struggle to maintain activity for longer periods on too small a circle and is much more likely to lose balance.

Suppleness

This includes both longitudinal suppleness (over the top of the back from poll to dock) and lateral suppleness (from left to right). While working on the lunge the horse should round over their back and there should be freedom within their movement. They should appear mentally relaxed in their work and be working without resistance. On the lunge, the horse's body should follow the line of the circle. However, if they are unbalanced, a horse will often look or tilt to the outside when working on a circle; horses who lack suppleness or find bending in a particular direction more difficult will also do this. If a horse does this, first check that they are working in a steady, regular rhythm. Then you can subtly encourage them to look to the inside by using the contact on the lunge line to guide their head gently to the inside and then release the pressure.

Contact

The side-reins provide a contact for the horse to work into in a similar way as the reins do when the horse is ridden. In addition to side-reins there are numerous training aids available on the market that can be used while lungeing the horse. The same principles will apply in relation to the horse's way of going irrespective of which training aid you are using. When side-reins or any other training aids are fitted they should not pull the horse so the nose is behind the vertical, or restrict movement in any way.

Once the side-reins are attached the way the horse is working will offer clues as to whether they are in balance. If a horse is working actively in balance they should be able to maintain a consistent outline. If the horse goes too fast they will lose balance and will not be able to maintain the outline and is likely to come above the bit. Similarly, if a horse is not working forward and actively in a consistent manner they will not be able to maintain their outline as a result of inconsistent balance. Some horses may come behind the bit if they are not working actively enough. Horses who are not yet established in their way of going may be inconsistent in their outline; they should be encouraged to work in a regular rhythm while they begin to develop the strength to maintain this.

In most cases the aim is for the horse to work with the front of their face on or slightly in front of the vertical, with the poll as the highest point. If a horse drops their face behind the vertical they may not be going forwards enough, or the side-reins may be too short. If the horse's face is too far in front of the vertical the side-reins may be too long, or the horse may be out of balance.

Impulsion

As mentioned earlier, the horse should be working actively, overtracking in the walk, tracking up in the trot and taking energetic steps. Transitions are a useful exercise to help the horse engage their hind legs underneath them and propel them forwards, using their hindquarters while remaining in balance.

Summary

- There are numerous benefits of lungeing the horse both for exercise and training. Lungeing provides an opportunity to see how the horse works and provides a situation whereby the horse can work and develop without the weight of a rider.

- It is important to consider all the safety implications of lungeing for both the handler and the horse. Consideration must be paid to the area for lungeing, others in the vicinity, the welfare of the horse and the safety of the handler.

- Lungeing technique should be developed so that you are able to handle the equipment almost automatically so that your sole focus can be on the horse. You should be able to apply the relevant technique to different types of horses — in other words, be proficient at lungeing both forward-going and laid-back horses.

- Learn what to look for to encourage the horse to work correctly. This includes rhythm and balance, suppleness, contact and impulsion in all three gaits. You should also know how to work towards achieving these qualities on the lunge.

TRAINING TIPS

1. Try to gain experience lungeing lots of different types of horses.

2. Watch more experienced people lungeing and ask questions about the horse's way of going, with the aim of being able to recognise when a horse is going well.

3. Watching young horses being lunged, or even helping with the process of starting young horses on the lunge can be a useful experience. Pay particular attention to the commands the handler gives the horse and where they position themselves.

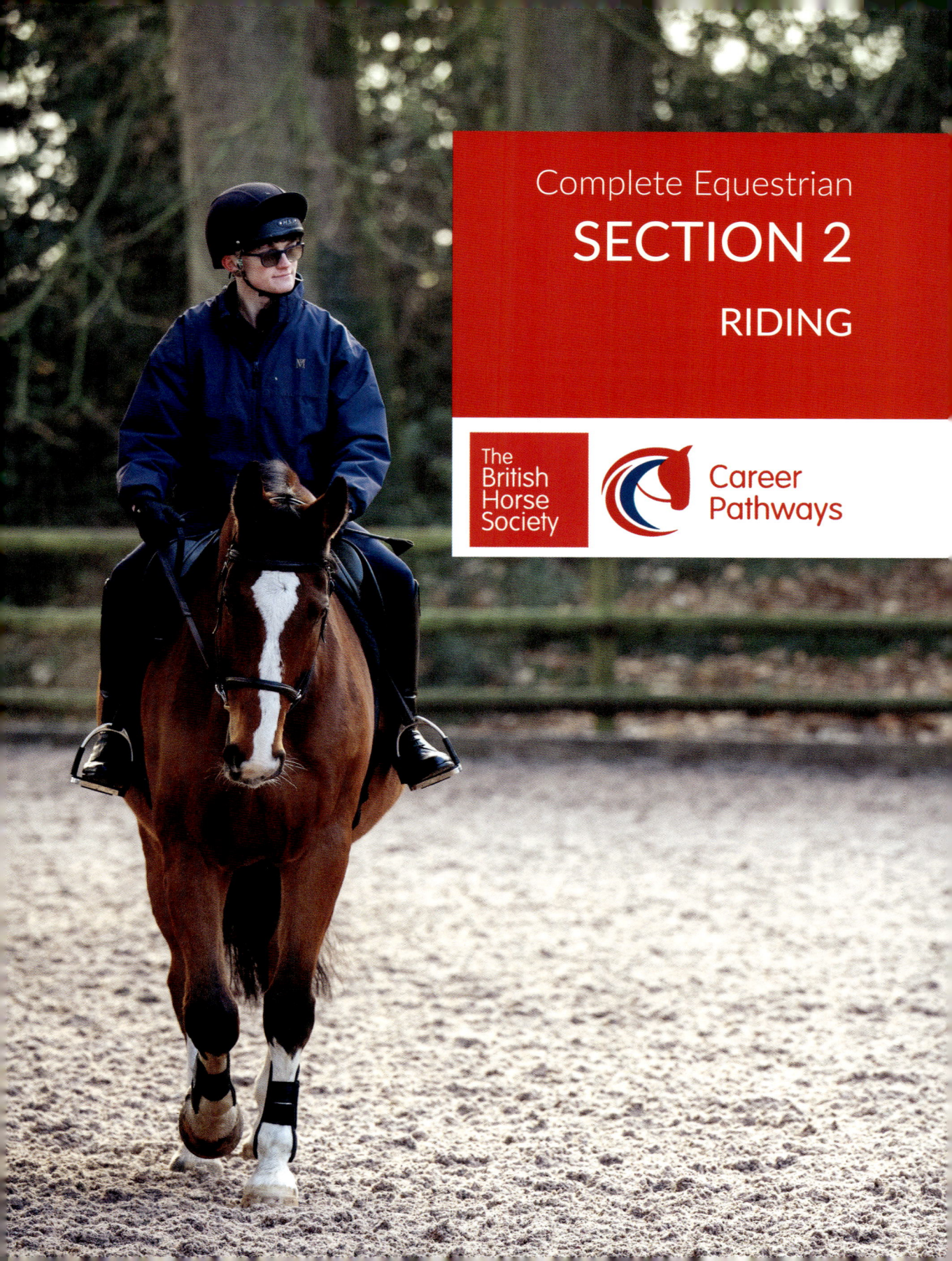

Chapter 12

Flatwork and Jumping

Developing your flatwork

Jumping

Summary

Developing your flatwork

In your riding so far you will have been working on developing a more independent and balanced position and beginning to have a greater influence over how the horse is going. To progress further you now need to focus not only on continuing to develop your seat but also to build on your knowledge and understanding on the horse's way of going and how to apply more refined aids in order to ride lateral work and work towards riding medium gaits. You will also start to develop the skills necessary to be able to assess the horse you are riding and select appropriate exercises to help maintain their level of schooling.

Developing these skills is a gradual process and the skills you will be focusing on are:

1. Maintaining a correct, balanced position and secure seat with and without stirrups in walk, trot and canter and being able to apply quiet and effective aids on a variety of different horses.

2. Being able to assess and create a work plan for the horse you are riding.

3. Understanding how to ask a horse to work in the correct outline and what exercises to use to encourage this.

4. How to ride lengthened strides in trot and canter.

5. Introducing lateral work such as leg-yielding.

6. Maintaining the standard of training of the horses ridden.

To develop these skills it is important that you ride a variety of horses of all types and levels of training so that you will be able to make comparisons and develop your feel and understanding for the correct way of going. By riding different horses you soon become aware of whether a horse has a longer or shorter trot stride, a balanced canter, or an elastic or heavier contact compared with others. Your appreciation and feel for the strengths and weaknesses of each horse will develop.

An independent seat

Your seat can be described as 'independent' when you are not reliant on the reins. For example, you can maintain a correct position on the lunge in canter on a quiet horse without stirrups or reins. Some of the horses you ride will have bigger movement than others, so you will need a greater degree of suppleness and strength through your core to be able to absorb this movement and, at the same time, keep your hands and legs steady enough to apply clear and consistent aids. Lunge lessons are a good way of developing greater core stability and a more secure seat as they allow you to concentrate solely on your position. Be disciplined and ride without your stirrups regularly to lengthen your legs. Key points to remember when riding without stirrups are to allow your lower back and hips to swing with the rhythm of the horse's back, relax and open your knees and keep your heels down. Try to stretch your legs down, keeping your lower legs relaxed lightly by the horse's side. Your back should be supple and upright, your elbows bent and your hands still. If you feel that you are bouncing, put the reins in the outside hand and hold the pommel of the saddle with your inside hand to stabilise yourself. Feel your seat start to swing with the horse's back and stride: you can test this by dropping your inside hand behind your thigh and feeling whether you can maintain your security and suppleness. If not, put your hand back on the pommel and try again. It will take perseverance to develop a supple and secure seat. Working without stirrups in canter encourages your pelvis to relax and go with the horse.

A secure balanced position.

The Training Scale

You will have previously touched on the Training Scale and how you might start to apply it to your riding. It is a useful method of assessing a horse's basic way of going as you can measure the horse's ability against each heading. Each of these headings is interconnected. For example, a horse who lacks suppleness will find it difficult to maintain a rhythm and accept the contact consistently. One who lacks energy will find it more difficult to stay straight. By using the Training Scale you have a clear method for assessing any horse you are riding and this will help you to select work for the remainder of the session.

Use the Training Scale as a measure to help you to assess and compare the horses you ride.

The elements of the Training Scale in terms of their basic progression is as follows.

1. **Rhythm**

This is the regularity of the gait and includes correctness of the gait. For instance, the walk should show a clear four-time beat, trot should be two-time and canter three-time. The tempo is the speed of the rhythm and should not be too quick or too slow. It should remain consistent throughout the work if it is not consistent then it is not possible for the horse to maintain a rhythm.

The walk should be relaxed and regular, with good overtracking. In trot the horse should go freely forward, covering the ground, tracking up. The trot should not feel 'stuffy' or lack suspension — the moment when all four legs are off the ground briefly. The canter beat should be three-time and is incorrect if it is four-time. A four-time canter is when the second or diagonal beat is split. If the horse is not moving in the correct sequence of footfalls in each gait it is likely that the correct rhythm and tempo will be affected.

2. **Suppleness**

Consider whether your horse works with a supple, swinging back in each gait to allow the energy from the hind legs to flow through the body into the rein. This is longitudinal (lengthways) suppleness. A horse who is supple and finds it easy to bend should be relatively easy to keep on the line of a circle. If a horse lacks suppleness they may fall in to the inside of the circle with their shoulder, evade your inside leg or swing their quarters either out or inwards. It may be markedly worse on one rein than the other and it is important to identify your horse's better rein. A horse who lacks suppleness will find it difficult to bend laterally is unlikely to be able to keep a consistent rhythm and tempo, particularly on turns and circles.

3. **Contact**

A horse lacking suppleness will also find it more difficult to offer the rider a soft, elastic contact and work with a rounded topline, when ridden forward into an asking hand. The horse should not hollow their topline and evade the contact by raising and stiffening their head and neck. The correct outline or frame in which we should like the horse working is where the hind legs are active and elastic, stepping well under the body, with the back swinging and supple. The horse flexes at the poll, which is at the highest point and has their head either on or slightly in front of the vertical with their jaw relaxed. In this way you can hold or contain the energy the hind legs generate. The contact should not be unyielding and heavy, with the forehand loaded.

A horse who tilts their head to one side may be doing this to avoid the rein contact or to avoid pain or discomfort on one side of the mouth. Such a horse may be very heavy on one rein and more difficult to turn in that direction. All these are contact issues to note and should be investigated further to rule out pain as the cause.

4. Impulsion

It is more difficult for an unsupple, hollow, horse to work with impulsion (controlled energy). Without enough impulsion your flatwork will be more laboured and your horse less able to react quickly to your aids. This is likely to have a detrimental effect on the horse's balance (correct weight distribution). Do not confuse energy with speed. Assess whether the horses you ride work with sufficient energy to perform their work easily, maintaining their balance and rhythm.

5. Straightness

When a horse finds their work difficult, they are likely to evade by swinging their quarters in or out. In canter, horses will sometimes put their quarters in on the long side of the arena. This can be as a result of riding on the track too much where, because the horse's quarters are wider than their shoulders, if they 'lean on the wall' so that their outside shoulders and quarters are parallel to the wall, the effect is that the quarters are moved inwards. However, some horses also do this to ease the strain on their hind legs. In leg-yielding, a horse will often try to lead with their shoulder to avoid the weight on the limbs when moving laterally. When riding smaller circles the horse's quarters are more likely to drift out to avoid the bend. Working on an inside track is a good way of assessing the horse's straightness. When you do this, some horses may try to fall out through the shoulder back towards the track, so you need to make sure that you use your outside aids to control the outside of the horse.

6. Collection

This refers to the horse taking more weight on the hind limbs and lightening the forehand. For the level of work requested at this stage the horse is not required to have a great degree of collection. You should, however, be aware if the horse is heavy on their forehand and be able to ride and suggest exercises to help encourage the horse to begin to take more weight behind.

A riding session

If you are to work with horses it is likely that, either occasionally or frequently, you will be asked to exercise or school horses you may not be familiar with, and also horses you may not have ridden for some time. Developing the ability to assess horses effectively and to ride them in a thoughtful, productive way will not only benefit the horses, but will add considerably to your own skills and experience.

Initial checks

Tack and equipment. Always check the tack of the horse you are about to ride for safety, correct fit and comfort. You cannot expect a horse to go well in incorrectly fitting or uncomfortable tack. If the saddle presses down on the horse's withers, or pinches, this is likely to result in a hollow outline and incorrect muscle development if not rectified promptly. Check that the numnah is pulled up into the gullet of the saddle and is not pressing down on the withers. The bit should fit correctly and comfortably in the horse's mouth. A bit that is too high or too low is likely to be uncomfortable for the horse and affect your contact. Ensure that all the bridle's runners and keepers are tucked in, so they don't flap. Check that the noseband is sitting level across the horse's face and that it is fitted correctly with room for two fingers between the noseband and the nose. If the horse is wearing boots, check that they are fitted correctly and haven't slipped down.

The horse. When you ride a horse for the first time, you should quickly assess their type and conformation before you get on. Developing your assessment and observational skills will help improve and develop your riding. The way the horse is put together should give you an indication of how they may move. For example, a horse who is croup-high with a neck set on low may well be on the forehand. Have a look at the horse's muscular development — are they well muscled in the correct places? All this will give you valuable clues about what the horse might be like to ride and the work they have been doing.

Warming up

Before you begin working a horse you need to warm up both them and yourself. The aims of this are:

1. To calm and settle the horse.

2. To supple the horse and rider.

3. To gradually increase the blood supply to the horse's muscles.

4. To increase the heart rate gradually.

5. To reduce the risk of injury to muscles, tendons and ligaments through sudden activity before the horse's systems are ready.

6. To increase confidence and concentration in the horse to assist them to work at their best.

Generally a warm-up will take between ten and twenty minutes, but the length of time depends on the horse you are riding and the conditions you are riding in. An older horse may need more time to become free and supple than a younger horse; they may be losing their topline musculature and be dropping their back, needing more forward, active work and stretching before they can give their best. A fresher horse may take longer than most to settle and may benefit from moving into trot more quickly than you might do normally. Horses may also take longer to settle in windy conditions, at competitions or in a new environment. A less active horse may need more variety of work initially and may benefit from movements in quicker succession to motivate them, such as direct transitions, where the next gait up or down is missed (for example, halt to trot, walk to canter). In contrast, more excitable, tense horses will need calmer, slower work. Your feel is important, along with your ability to plan an effective, progressive way to warm up an individual horse. You should be working towards improving your influence over the horse and focusing on what you can feel happening underneath you. Therefore, your warm-up should be logical and progressive; have a basic plan in your mind that you intend to follow to ensure that you have warmed up the horse on both reins — but be prepared to adapt the plan if you need to.

Start by asking the horse to walk forward freely, with a long, active, swinging stride. This will give you an idea of how responsive the horse is to your leg aids, but also how forward-going they are. Some horses may need a few minutes of walking gently to free up before they can really walk forward actively. You want to feel the horse swinging through their back and allow your pelvis to go with this movement. To encourage the horse to use their hind legs actively, apply your leg aid, alternately to encourage the hind leg on that side to step forward.

It is useful to ride circles and changes of direction to begin to assess the horse's suppleness and responsiveness to the aids. Pay attention to how easily the horse bends around your inside leg on circles and through turns, as this will give you an indication of how supple they are. Riding transitions between walk and halt will allow you to assess the horse's responsiveness to your leg and rein aids. Use your legs before your rein aids in the transitions to encourage the horse to keep their hind legs stepping under in the transitions, and to keep swinging through their back. If the horse doesn't respond to light leg aids to walk forwards from the halt, repeat the aid firmly to obtain a better response. By keeping your legs on and encouraging the horse to step forward into the halt, it is more likely that the halt will be square, with fore and hind legs together.

After a few minutes in walk to warm up the horse and assess them you can begin to work in rising trot. It is easier if you start on the rein the horse finds easier. Start to move the horse around the school using figures such as circles of varying sizes, shallow loops, three-loop serpentines and tear drops (half-circle and return to the track). This will vary the work, help focus the horse's attention on you, and allow you to assess the horse's suppleness, contact and straightness in trot.

At this stage you can start asking the horse to stretch down and work over their back to further free them up and encourage them to draw forward into the contact.

Once you have settled the horse in trot, move on to the canter work. It is useful to remember that some horses work better in trot after some cantering, so don't wait too long before trying canter. Do so on both reins, as one may be considerably better than the other. It is easier to adjust the canter on a circle than on a straight line and variations in the canter (such as moving between working and lengthened strides) may activate a less forward horse. With an excitable

Encourage the horse to stretch and work over their back.

horse you may just want to concentrate on achieving a suitable rhythm and tempo. Assess the quality of the canter: is it elastic and springy or is it flat, fast or unbalanced?

Having tried the three gaits, gauge how to complete your warm-up. You may decide it is better to work for the remainder of the warm-up mainly on either trot or canter. Don't forget to allow the horse to stretch on a long rein at the end of the warm-up before beginning your theme for the remainder of the session.

During the warm-up you should have identified any areas of weakness, such as lack of suppleness, and you may now decide to focus on a particular exercise, movement or theme for the rest of your session that will help improve the horse's way of going. This might entail, for example, direct transitions, smaller circles, improving rhythm and straightness. Think about what you felt happen underneath you. Did the horse change rhythm every time you changed the rein or did they find it harder to bend on one rein compared to the other? These are areas you could focus on during the main part of your session.

12 | Flatwork and Jumping

If you felt that the horse relaxed and worked better in one gait compared to another then you can carry out more work in that gait before moving on to the gaits the horse finds harder.

How correct are your horse's working gaits? Are they free with sufficient ground cover? How consistent is the rhythm? Problems here should be given priority. For example, to improve ground cover, work on lengthening the stride in trot and canter may be beneficial, while direct transitions in quick succession may activate the horse and encourage them to open their stride.

School figures

Once the horse has warmed up, and you have carried out an assessment of the sort of work that is likely to be beneficial, you can move on to riding more specific movements and exercises. When riding any school movement, focus on finding the correct rhythm and tempo and maintaining these qualities throughout the movement.

As well as the school figures you have previously used, reverse half-circles and satellite circles are two useful exercises to further test your horse's bend and your coordination.

When riding a reversed half-circle, for example on the right rein, you could ride diagonally from M to X, changing your horse's bend from right to left as you do so. At X, you would then ride a 10m half-circle to B, and continue round the school on the left rein. This movement requires an accurate half-circle to be ridden from the centre line to the track.

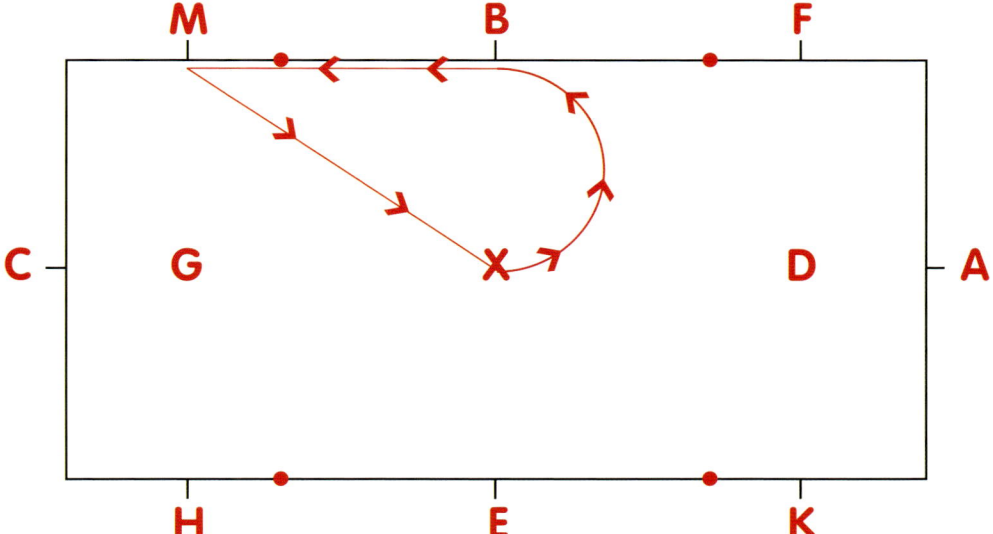

A reverse half-circle.

235

For a satellite circle ride, for example, a 20m circle on the left rein from B. Each time you cross the centre line ride a 10m circle right and then continue on the 20m circle left until crossing the centre line again. This necessitates careful preparation for the changes of bend from one circle to another. This is a useful exercise to improve horse and rider accuracy and coordination.

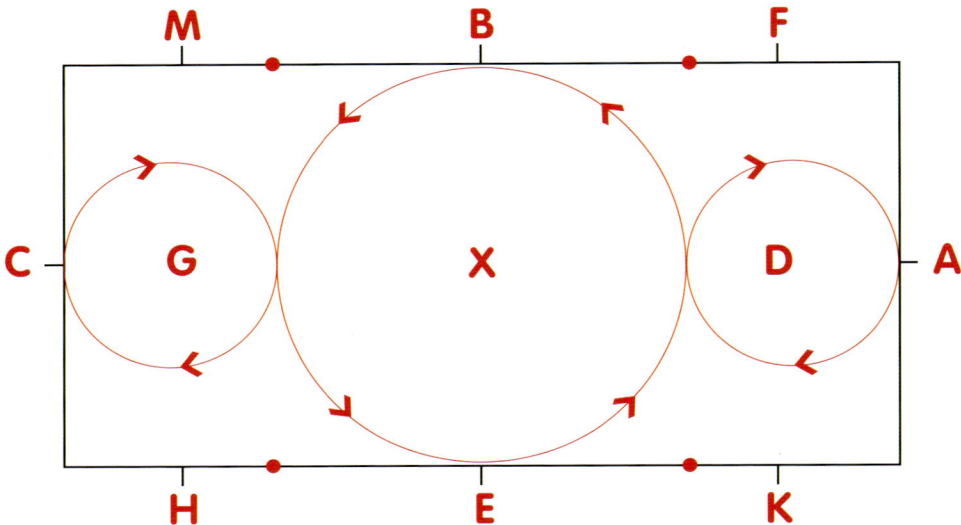

A 20m circle at B on the left rein with satellite circles to the right over the centre lines.

Transitions

Transitions are especially useful to help establish a horse's obedience to and concentration on your aids. They can both encourage horses to listen and make them more active and responsive. Good transitions from one gait to another and within the gait (for example, lengthened strides) will be smooth and flowing, with the horse maintaining contact and balance. The horse should not hollow, tighten over the back, drop on to the forehand or lose their straightness. The key to successful transitions is preparing in time and riding leg to hand, particularly in downward transitions. When working on the transitions, seek to develop the horse's response in the half-halt. This is where you combine back, seat, leg and hand almost simultaneously to energise your horse, rebalance them and bring them to attention, thus preparing them for a movement to come, such as riding a corner or transition. Basically you request more energy, hold it briefly and then release it. Perhaps a good way to think about it is as a 'half-forward' rather than a half-halt. The combination of leg, seat and back sends the horse forward into a quiet rein contact which, after a moment, releases the gathered energy. You will know when the half halt is successful if your horse moves forward out of it with increased energy. Being able to ride half-halts correctly develops your ability to communicate more subtly with your horse.

12 | Flatwork and Jumping

Lengthened strides in trot

When the trot strides are lengthened, the horse's hind feet should overtrack the imprints of the forefoot on the same side. The tempo should not quicken but the horse's frame should open or lengthen. To ask the horse to lengthen their stride, increase the pressure from your legs to ask the horse to bring their hind legs further underneath them and maintain the contact down the rein to prevent the horse from 'running' rather than lengthening. Ask for the transition over several strides; if the horse starts to quicken their tempo rather than lengthening, use half-halts to rebalance them and then ask again.

Lengthened strides can be ridden on the long side, down the quarter line or centre line, across diagonals and on circles. It is easier to practise transitions within the gait on a circle rather than on a straight line because it is easier to control the horse's outside shoulder and they are less likely to hollow or lose balance and quicken the steps instead of lengthening the stride. After riding lengthened strides encourage the horse to go forwards into the working trot with sufficient leg support to ensure that their hind legs continue to step under their body in the transition.

With some horses, using lengthened trot strides as part of their warm-up can encourage them to go forwards and help to open their stride. However, lengthened strides will not be beneficial in the warm-up for every horse. Be guided by your feel, which becomes increasingly important as your riding develops. Through feeling what the horse is doing underneath you, you adapt your riding to obtain the best way of going.

Initial work in canter

A useful exercise to develop your horse's canter is to ride half-circles across the arena, cantering as you leave the track and trotting as you reach the opposite side. The curve of the half-circle helps to control the canter and the transitions improve the horse's response to your aids and develop your ability to apply accurate, clear and concise aids. To prepare for the transitions use half-halts to rebalance the horse and check that they are listening to you. If riding your half-circle from E to B, begin your preparation in trot between K and F to ensure that the horse is forward, positioned and attentive. Sit to prepare for the trot-canter transition, making sure you stay supple through your back and move with the horse. Apply the canter aids and sit up tall just before you leave the track at E.

On the circle, the horse should be bending around your inside leg. You may need to start preparing for the trot even before crossing the centre line to ensure that the transition happens as you touch the track. Using your inside leg as the horse's inside hind comes forward to send the horse into an even contact. The aim is that the horse becomes more responsive in transitions, cantering 'on the aids' when you ask with the legs, and flowing smoothly from canter into a balanced trot.

Cantering half-circles across the school.

Gradually the preparation time should decrease as your horse's response improves. The transitions at the beginning and end of the half-circle will help to contain the canter and improve its quality. It can also help produce more energy in the trot afterwards.

Changing the canter lead through trot

Another test of the quality of the canter and transitions is changing the canter lead through a few strides of trot, either on a diagonal line or going from one circle to another. Prepare early enough for the canter to trot transition by lifting your sternum and opening your shoulder-blades as you ride forward from your legs into holding hands to balance the canter before asking for the transition with a clear aid. With a responsive horse you would ride two strides of sitting trot, changing the aids and bend before asking for the strike-off on the new canter lead. With a less responsive horse, stay in trot for more strides until the horse is positioned correctly, balanced and ready to be asked for the new canter lead.

Lengthened strides in canter

Riding transitions within the canter can further develop the horse's obedience, responsiveness and balance. The horse's topline should lengthen or open, but the tempo should not quicken.

Working on lengthened strides in canter will encourage the horse to respond more readily to your leg aids and go freely forward in canter when asked to do so.

Be aware of the horse hollowing in the transitions into lengthening, or pushing the hindquarters in or out, losing straightness. The transition down from lengthened strides to the working canter should be clear. Make sure you prepare early enough and ride quietly with the legs at each stride into an elastic rein contact. To begin with it may take you several strides to return from lengthened strides to working canter in order to keep the horse in balance and the transition smooth.

Cantering on diagonal lines across the school also tests the quality of the canter, and transitions to trot can be ridden anywhere on the long diagonals. However, it is better to establish the responsiveness and roundness in canter-trot transitions first on the circle, as the horse is more likely to rush and hollow on the diagonal than when following the bend of the circle.

Improving the contact

Asking the horse to work 'long and low' or to stretch down in each gait will encourage the back to lift and aid acceptance of the contact. Taking the weight out of the saddle may free the horse's back and encourage a more elastic contact. If the horse is inclined to fall out on a circle and escape through the outside shoulder, working with outside bend (or counter-flexion or contra-bend) with the horse slightly bent around your outside leg may be beneficial. If your horse is less supple on the left rein, try working with counter-flexion to the left on the right rein to soften the left side.

Generally, acceptance of the contact comes first in walk, then trot and finally in canter, but each horse is an individual and there is no hard and fast rule — for instance, a horse who frees up after canter work may then accept the contact more readily in trot.

Leg-yielding

As it requires no collection from the horse, leg-yielding is one of the first lateral movements a horse can be taught. It has considerable benefit as a suppling exercise and improving the coordination and feel of the rider.

In the leg-yield the horse crosses their inside legs in front of the outside legs, so they are moving forwards and sideways at the same time. The horse's body should be straight, with a slight flexion at the poll away from the direction of movement. Riding leg-yield initially in walk will give you more time to coordinate your aids and feel how the horse reacts to them.

When riding lateral work the terms 'inside' and 'outside' refer to the inside and outside of the flexion or bend of the horse, for example, for a horse in right bend your inside leg would be your right leg and the outside leg the left, which may be different from the direction in which the horse is moving around the arena.

One of the simplest ways to ride a leg-yield is from the quarter line towards the track. Starting by making sure you are sitting in balance and are straight in the saddle, make a turn on to the quarter line and ride the horse straight for a few strides. To ask for leg-yield, use your inside leg slightly back behind the girth to ask the horse to step sideways and forwards. (If you are on the left rein, the inside leg will be your left leg, asking the horse to step towards the track to your right.) Your outside leg and outside rein are used to control the horse's outside shoulder and to keep them moving forwards and straight.

In this exercise, the horse should stay parallel to the school wall and move the same amount sideways as forwards so the steps are even. Common issues you might come across are the horse leading with the shoulders (so the shoulders are ahead of the quarters and the horse is not parallel to the wall), or the horse bending through the neck and falling through the outside shoulder back towards the track. If this happens, ride the horse straight and forward out of the movement before asking for leg-yield again. Check that you are not lifting your outside hand and rein up, thereby losing control of the outside shoulder, or that you are using too much inside rein and pulling the horse's neck to the inside.

When leg-yielding in walk is going well you can move into trot. Start by going from the quarter line to the track and, if the horse finds this easy, you could change the exercise so that you leg-yield from the outside track to the quarter line. This is more difficult, as horses are generally less keen to leave the outside track than to return to it. Other exercises to try are leg-yielding

Leg-yielding to the right; the horse is moving away from the rider's left leg.

from the centre line out towards the quarter lines or the track, and it can also be used on circles as a way of moving from a smaller circle to a larger one. On the circle the horse remains bent around the rider's inside leg, and the shoulders and quarters should still be in line.

Turn on/about the forehand

In a turn on or about the forehand the horse's quarters move around their forehand in a small circle, away from the direction of bend.

Turn on the forehand is ridden from a square halt with the horse picking up and putting down the inside forefoot on the same spot. Turn about the forehand is ridden from walk with the horse walking a small circle with their forelegs.

To introduce turn about the forehand it is easier to ride it from a slightly shortened walk, instead of halt, this allows you to keep the forward movement and reduce the risk of the horse stepping back. Ask for a slight inside bend, remembering that the horse's quarters are moving away from the direction of bend, so if you are moving the quarters to the right the horse should be bent to the left and your left leg will be your inside leg. Apply pressure with your inside leg just behind the girth to ask the horse to step sideways away from this pressure with their hind legs. Your outside leg moves back slightly, where it can be used to control the amount of sideways movement if required. Your outside rein is used to prevent the horse from moving forward and to prevent them from bending too much through the neck. The horse should not step back or rush through the movement. Some horses may find this movement easier on one rein than the other, especially if they are less supple on one side. Start by asking for a step or two and then gradually progressing towards quarter-turns and then half-turns before attempting full turns when the horse is ready. At the end of the movement make sure you ride the horse forwards in a straight line.

Give and retake the reins

Giving and retaking one or both reins is a test of the horse's relaxation, rhythm and balance in trot or canter. You need to sit up tall but release the contact down the reins by moving your arms forward quietly for two or three strides, maintaining the bend in your elbows and then smoothly retaking the contact. If the horse is in balance the rhythm, outline and tempo should not change. Persevere with this exercise until your horse maintains their rhythm and is able to maintain their outline in the give and retake.

In the give and retake the horse should maintain their outline and balance as you push the rein forward.

Common problems and possible solutions

Some common issues that may arise throughout ridden sessions and some suggested solutions to try are given below.

Problem	Possible solutions to try
With any problem it is crucial to ensure the horse is first examined for any areas of pain or discomfort. This should include saddle/tack checks, musculoskeletal checks, lameness and dental checks from qualified professionals.	
Not forward	Direct transitions, transitions in quick succession, lengthened strides in trot and canter, variety of work
Tense	Walk on long rein, school figures in trot to settle, stretching down, trot-walk-trot transitions, use voice

12 | Flatwork and Jumping

Problem	Possible solutions to try
Lack of suppleness	Turn on forehand and leg-yielding can be used to encourage the horse to move away from the inside leg, leg-yield on a circle, a variety of circles with changes of direction, for example, satellite circles
Hollow	Establish forwardness and bend, encourage stretching down, ride with your weight off the horse's back, counter-flexion or bend
Not straight	Make sure you are sitting straight, use poles as tramlines, work to improve suppleness, ride centre lines and down the quarter lines
Hollow in transitions	Earlier preparation, ensure horse is active enough, better half-halts, ride forward from leg to hand
Shoulders lead in leg-yield	Outside rein against neck, ride straight, push quarters in line with shoulders, ride leg-yield from the track inwards towards the centre line
Hollow in give and retake	Practise on a circle, release slowly and quietly
Not working over the back	Stretch down in rising trot and canter in light seat, free walk on a long rein, open frame, longer in neck
On the forehand	More active varied work, improved half-halts, lengthened strides in trot and canter, direct transitions, for example, trot to halt
'Downhill' transitions	Improve the quality of the gait, prepare earlier, keep your shoulders back, lift your hands, ask off a circle approaching the long side

Self-evaluation

Much of what has been discussed in assessing the horse's way of going and carrying out the work described gives you the evidence and information needed to evaluate a horse's performance. However, to continue to develop your own performance and skill you should also be assessing objectively how you rode. Everyone has positional faults and you should be aware of what yours are at present and how they can affect the horse. For instance, did you feel that your seat was independent and secure? Were you able to offer the horse a secure and steady contact, or were your hands unsteady? In terms of what you did in the session, particularly if your plan went wrong or you didn't achieve what you had hoped for, would you do anything differently with the same horse next time?

Referring to the principles of training

As mentioned earlier, the Training Scale provides the foundation of training and the main elements have already been discussed in detail. The aim behind them is that, through a series of progressive exercises, the horse's musculature is strengthened and they are able to transfer weight to the hindquarters and lighten the forehand. Clearly, this weight transference leads on to collection, the final step on the Training Scale, which is the next step to progress your riding on to. At the current level you should be concentrating on the initial stages of training, whereby the horse learns to go forward freely, working without tension throughout their body, bends correctly on curved lines and accepts the rein contact willingly (rhythm, suppleness and contact). When these three foundation blocks are in place, it is possible to develop a more energetic way of going (impulsion) as energy cannot be truly contained and released without elastic contact. Increased energy develops the horse's athleticism and the scope of the movements and exercises you can perform together. When a horse is energetic, it is easier for them to be straight. Straightness means that the power from the horse's hind legs is channelled more efficiently through their body without asymmetry or uneven muscular development. It is all about laying a sound foundation upon which to build later work. However, none of this can be achieved without a supple rider with a secure and independent seat, who is able to absorb the horse's movement through their joints and muscles. Hence, training the rider comes before training the horse.

Free walk on a long rein is a way of letting the horse relax and have a break during a schooling session.

Analysing and responding to schooling issues

If a horse is not going as you would expect, start by examining your own riding and whether this may be the cause. Did you apply the aids clearly? Did you shift your weight and unbalance the horse? Are your legs, hands and seat steady? Recheck your position and reapply the aids more clearly and see what happens.

The first principle with regard to the horse is to ensure that they are going forward freely and is responsive to your aids. It is difficult for a horse to make good transitions if they are inactive. For instance, many incorrect canter leads are the result of inactivity in the trot. If this happens, you may need to establish a better reaction to your leg aids.

If a horse is becoming upset and not understanding what you want, try walking on a long rein and letting them relax. A stressed horse cannot learn. Think about whether they have already worked hard enough in the training session and are becoming tired. Alternatively, they may not be as advanced as you thought they were in their training, and not yet ready to cope with what you are asking of them. Therefore, they may need further suppling and strengthening work before they are ready to understand and cope with these new demands. In this case, re-establish mutual understanding by working on something the horse does better to rebuild their confidence and refocus them. Stretching in trot and canter is useful for relaxing the horse. For a problem with leg-yielding, improving response to the leg by focusing on turns on the forehand may help. If you are having a problem with the contact in trot, returning to the walk and establishing a softer, more elastic contact in walk may help. Do not be afraid to go back to basics if things are going wrong, and rebuild the exercise step by step. Patience and calmness are important traits to have as a rider and, as your experience develops, you will become more adept and resourceful at analysing problems.

How you finish a working session is important. Stretching down in trot and walk is excellent for relaxing the horse's musculature as well as developing it simultaneously. It is good practice, after any faster or harder work, to walk your horse for at least ten minutes until their breathing is almost back to resting rates and the horse, if previously hot, is cooler. During this time ask the horse to walk actively, stretching their back and neck. It is a chance for you to reflect on the session and what you will work on next time.

Use of the whip

A whip can be used for an appropriate reason, at an appropriate time, on the correct area of the horse and with the appropriate level of response.

An appropriate reason to use the whip would be as an aid to support your natural aids (leg, seat) when asking the horse to go forwards, or to help you keep the horse straight (for example on the approach to a fence). The whip should never be used to vent your temper or used hard enough to leave a mark on the horse's skin.

A schooling whip can be used behind your lower leg as encouragement to respond to a leg aid. A short whip can be used down the shoulder or behind the leg (in this case the whip hand should be taken off the rein to prevent pulling back).

> *There are strict rules regarding the use of a whip in competition. Always make sure you refer to the most recent version of the relevant discipline rule book for guidance.*
>
> **Using a schooling whip to support your leg aid**
>
> *If your horse does not respond to a light leg aid, start by repeating the aid more firmly. If the response is still insufficient, support your leg with the whip.*
>
> *Tap the whip immediately behind your lower leg after giving your leg aid, so the horse learns to associate the whip with the leg, and then immediately allow the horse to move forward. Always start with the light leg aid and reward the horse with your voice when they go forward. You may have to repeat the aid once or twice for the horse to understand what is required, but the whip must not be used continually to keep the horse forward. If the horse does not understand and respond to the leg aid you may need to go back to basics with your schooling with the help of an experienced coach. Be strict with yourself and make sure you are consistent and clear with your aids and not restricting the horse's ability to move forward with your position.*

Jumping

Previously you will have learnt about riding in a forward light seat and jumping small courses. Now the aim is to develop this further by riding showjumping courses and grids up to 1m (3ft 3in) in height and riding cross-country fences up to 90cm (3ft) in height at a suitable cross-country speed.

A sound understanding of the theory underpinning practical jumping training helps you and the horses you ride to develop progressively and steadily, gaining the confidence and skills to jump bigger tracks. Important principles to help achieve this are:

1. The development of a secure seat and position.

2. The better the flatwork training, the easier a horse will be to jump.

3. The Training Scale applies just as much to jumping as to flatwork.

4. As with flatwork, always ensure your horse is in front of the leg.

12 | Flatwork and Jumping

Work over poles encourages the horse to lift their feet and bend their joints.

5. Good quality and rhythm in the canter are essential.

6. Don't ask too much too soon and destroy your horse's confidence.

7. Build safe, inviting fences.

These principles will be emphasised throughout this chapter to reinforce the link between theory and practice.

How to introduce a horse to jumping

Correct, unhurried introductory work will lay a sound foundation for jumping from which to progress, building confidence for both horse and rider.

Pole work

Work over poles encourages the horse to be calm, to develop rhythm, to swing through their back, to use their neck as a balancing agent, to bend their joints and to become more athletic and agile. Ideally, before introducing a horse to jumping, they should go forward willingly, bend round your inside leg on both reins, canter with reasonable balance and accept your contact. Therefore, in your warm-up for jumping, ride lots of circles, loops, serpentines and leg-yield, making sure that the horse is bending round your inside leg, not falling in and losing rhythm. If a horse falls in through the turn to a fence, they lose their rhythm and reduce the chances of jumping a fence well. It can be useful to circle round fences in the jumping arena, making the horse concentrate on your bending aids when warming up. Frequent transitions into and out of canter when warming up for jumping, should increase obedience and concentration and also help with the quality of the canter. Changing the flexion slightly and quietly from one side to another will help to soften your rein contact.

You can start by trotting over a single pole. When your horse is trotting calmly over the pole, go on to three poles with 2.74m (9ft) between each. Your horse should take one stride of trot between each pole. Adjust the distance for horses with longer or shorter strides. A helper on the ground able to alter poles and fences is useful! Add more poles to the line of three if you wish. Using weighted or wooden poles will reduce the risk of the pole rolling if the horse knocks it.

When the horse is calm and confident with this exercise, you can place the poles 1.37–1.52m (4ft 6in–5ft) apart so that the horse will go over each pole without taking a trot stride between them. By raising one end of each pole alternately, the horse is encouraged to elevate their trot steps over the poles. Poles can be positioned on quarter, centre or diagonal lines for variety.

Cantering over poles tests the horse's calmness and rhythm. Start with a single pole and progress to three or more poles at 2.74–3.05m apart (9 to 10ft). This exercise will test whether the canter is rhythmical and elastic. Whenever a trot or canter pole is knocked out of place, make sure it is repositioned correctly before riding the exercise again.

The better a horse's gaits are, the easier they are likely to find the initial jumping work. A balanced, rhythmical canter is particularly helpful.

A good exercise to test the quality of the canter is to work over poles on a 20m circle. This can be done first in trot to accustom your horse to the exercise. The ultimate aim is for the horse to sustain their rhythm and take an equal number of trot or canter strides between four poles, placed equal distances apart on the circle. For example, place poles across the track at B and E and over the centre line 10m up and down from X. Start initially with one pole. Add a second pole half a circle away and only introduce third and fourth poles when the horse can keep their rhythm and is safe. This exercise tests your position, control and balance! It is fun counting the number of strides between each pole, it develops your concentration and tests whether you go consistently over the centre of each pole.

Previously you may have used a placing pole 2.44–2.74m (8–9ft) in front of a cross-pole to help you jump out of trot, and this is one method of introducing a horse to jumping. It is important that the initial fences a horse jumps are simple and inviting, for example, cross-poles and uprights with diagonal drop poles. When the horse is ready, introduce small spreads. As the horse's confidence grows, judge when to introduce fillers. When introducing fillers it is best to use two fillers that can be pulled out to the sides of a familiar, inviting fence. Once the horse is happy jumping through the middle of them, the fillers can gradually be pulled inwards until the horse is jumping over the fillers. This may be done progressively over several sessions. When the horse is landing in reasonable balance over one fence, start to link single fences together into short sequences.

Poles are not only a preliminary introduction to jumping but also valuable in helping to improve it. Poles placed as tramlines for the horse to go through approaching a fence help with straightness, and after the fence they encourage you to ride straight and to look ahead.

Placing poles can also be used in front of fences jumped in canter to help you find a more accurate take-off point. The distance in front of the fence for this varies with fence height, design and horse's stride, but the normal range is between 2.74 and 3.66m (9 to 12ft).

Using placing poles when jumping out of trot will assist with controlling the approach and to help you develop a supple fold with your upper body over the fence after the placing pole. If the horse is calm when trotting over a placing pole in front of a fence, move on to a canter approach using a timing rail.

A timing rail is a pole placed 5.9–6.1m (18–20ft) in front of a fence. The horse will go over the timing rail in canter, take one non-jumping stride and then jump the fence. This gives you a more accurate take-off zone. Used consistently, timing rails will help you gauge your distance from the fence and, when the timing rail is removed, you may be better able to take off the correct distance from the fence.

The phases of a jump as a guide to progress

A useful way to think about progress with your jumping is to link it to the phases of the jump. These are: (1) Approach, (2) Take-off, (3) Flight phase, (4) Landing and (5) Get-away.

1. **Approach**

From initially concentrating on riding a straight approach to fences your skills will develop to ride better turns to fences, bending the horse round your inside leg through the turn, and maintaining rhythm and balance without the horse falling in or on to the forehand. To help with this, you can place two parallel poles to ride through where you want to complete your turn, circling through the poles until you can keep your horse in a better balance. As well as using a positive inside leg, your contact needs to be clear and even on both reins to maintain the gait and straightness.

2. Take-off

Here the horse's forehand lifts off the ground and it is important for you to go with this movement, not interfering with the horse's neck or back. When doing this, fold from the hips, not the waist, to keep your back flat. Push your seat back as well as lowering your shoulders to avoid getting in front of the horse's movement.

3. Flight phase

In this phase the horse is over the fence with all four limbs off the ground. Ideally the horse will make a rounded shape or bascule, using their back and neck as they stretch over the fence, bending fore and hind limb joints carefully. Allow the horse maximum freedom by keeping your weight off their back and responding to the stretching forward of their head and neck with your hands, thereby maintaining a light contact with their mouth. This is called the 'following hand'.

4. Landing phase

Here the horse raises their head and neck as the forelimbs unfold and travel towards the ground while the hind legs are still in the air. As the forelimbs unfold, so should your body, to remain in balance and not in front of the movement. Maintain a light, elastic contact with the horse's mouth, looking up and ahead to the next fence.

5. Get-away phase

This is the departure from the fence, which should be balanced and controlled. Adjust your position to how the horse has landed. If they are on the forehand or rushing away, adopt a more upright position; if they are hollowing, lighten your seat, Remember 'back means slow: forward means go'.

Phases of the jump.

Combinations

Once jumping single fences confidently, it is time to think about doubles and trebles. Before jumping an easy double, consider jumping the second element first as an individual fence so that the horse is less likely to spook at it when it is the second element of a double. As you and the horse should be used to jumping cross-poles, it may be encouraging to have a fence of this type as an easy first element. It depends on the horse whether you jump the first element out of trot or canter, with or without a placing pole. The jump out of canter is an extension of the canter stride, whereas jumping the first element out of trot will require more effort but may teach a rushing horse to wait and listen to your aids, focusing more on the fence.

When the horse is accustomed to the idea of jumping very simple doubles, and you start to build up the construction of the elements, it is common practice to have a spread as the first element and an upright out so that, if the horse slides into the second element, there is less danger from falling poles. Having the front part of a spread as a cross-pole helps to keep the horse straight and is more forgiving if they take off closer to the fence. It is also safer to have potentially intimidating fillers as the first element in combinations, rather than the second, to prevent a situation where the horse may back off or refuse the second fence. Equally, it is important not to introduce fillers too soon, and make sure the horse is confident jumping fillers in single fences before introducing them in combinations. Remember to use flat cups for gates and planks for safety.

With one-stride doubles in an arena about 76cm (2ft 6in) in height the distance between the two elements will vary between 6.4 and 6.7m (21 and 22ft). As the fences are raised in height towards 1m (3ft 3in) the distance will be lengthened to 7.32m (24ft) for one non-jumping stride and 10 to 10.4m (33 to 34ft) for two non-jump strides.

Distances will be 15–30cm (6–12in) shorter when the elements are parallels as the horse should take off closer to a parallel than an upright. If you are going too fast from upright to upright, the danger is that the canter will be flatter and the horse less able to jump the upright cleanly. If the horse takes off too far back from a parallel they are more likely to hit the back

It is common to have a spread as the first element of a double and an upright as the second.

rail. Taking off too close to a parallel they are more likely to hit the front rail. When you start jumping trebles, build confidence by jumping one and then two elements before attempting the whole treble.

Poles can also be placed between elements of combinations to make the non-jumping strides in between the fences rounder. However, before doing this, trot the horse diagonally between the combination elements over the poles so that they are not surprised by the poles when jumping the combination.

Raise the heights of fences gradually to build your own confidence and to avoid overfacing horses. Learning to jump little and often (for example, three or four times a week) facilitates progress. As your horse's experience increases, jump less frequently (for example, once or twice a week) to meet training needs.

Gridwork

The benefits of gridwork (three or more fences and/or poles with set distances between them) for horses include variety, improved confidence, quicker reactions, greater agility, adaptability, carefulness, straightness and a rounded bascule. Grids should improve your own folding, suppleness and confidence and quicken your reactions. They should be designed to improve your and the horse's jumping technique.

Approaching a grid, it is important to be straight, to focus on the centre of the final element and then to keep the horse straight through the whole grid between your legs and hands. Your upper body should go with the horse's movement, folding and unfolding at each fence, while your lower legs remain stable and in position. Your hands allow your horse to stretch their head and neck in the air for balance and in order that they can use their back. Control the speed so that the horse neither rushes nor loses impulsion. If the approach is active enough they should keep the same rhythm and tempo through the grid and not rush.

A typical grid might be a placing pole to a cross-pole followed by an upright fence one non-jump stride away, with another fence as the final element, each fence slightly higher than the previous one. Raise the height of the grids you jump gradually, thus building your confidence and that of the horse. By varying whether there are one or two strides between grid elements, you develop your horse's adaptability and quicken their reactions. If there are three or more trotting poles in front of the grid, calmness and athleticism are developed. Cross-poles in grids gradually raised in height can improve bascule and the fold of your horse's fore and hind limbs in the air.

Bounces

Bascule and folding of the horse are further developed by using bounces, which are jumping efforts where the horse takes no strides between fences 2.74 and 3.05m (9 and 10ft) apart

12 | Flatwork and Jumping

A rider working through a grid of bounces.

depending on their height. Bounces are also excellent for developing rider suppleness and folding, but should be introduced carefully. For example, start in trot with a placing pole to a cross-pole with one stride to an upright and then reduce the one stride to a bounce, making sure your horse is confident over this before introducing further bounce elements. As the height of the bounce elements is raised you will feel the horse really folding their limbs and using their body. Therefore, bounces are a beneficial gymnastic exercise. Gymnastic jumping is the use of exercises designed to develop a horse's athleticism and adaptability, with quicker reactions and responses to the rider. It is also good for increasing rider suppleness, flexibility and quickening reactions.

Only when a horse is proficient with bounces as individual constructions should you incorporate them in grids — for example, approach in trot to a placing pole and three bounces with one stride to an upright and two to a spread. More difficult (and only for a confident, capable partnership) would be: placing pole to a cross-pole, one stride to an upright, two strides to three cross-pole bounces and two strides to a parallel, requiring quick and flexible reactions to adapt to the different distances.

Related distances

Whereas combination fences (doubles and trebles) have no more than one or two strides between the elements and are judged, in competition, as 'single' obstacles, related distances refer to layouts where two fences have three to five non-jumping strides between them. These are judged as individual obstacles, but the relatively short distance between them means that how the first is jumped has a significant impact on how the second is approached, hence the term 'related'.

The distances between related fences are based on a non-jumping stride length of 3.66m (12ft). It is easier to jump them well if your horse has a consistent stride pattern and responds readily, if necessary, to lengthen or shorten their stride (see Warming up a horse for showjumping, later in this chapter). Related distances also help to develop your feel for rhythm and striding. For fences between 90cm and 1m (3ft to 3ft 3in), related distances would be built in the ranges below, precise distances being dependent on the actual size of the fences, and the course-builders assessment of conditions and, perhaps, the types of horses in a particular class.

>3-stride related 13.76m (45ft) to 14.63m (48ft)

>4-stride related 17.37m (57ft) to 18.29m (60ft)

>5-stride related 20.57m (67½ft) to 21.95m (72ft)

Doglegs

Doglegs are curved lines from one fence to another to test your control and reactions, and are a particular challenge when they are incorporated into shorter related distances. By looking toward the second fence in the dogleg when jumping the first, you position your shoulders in the direction you want to go and the horse is more likely to land on the correct lead for the dogleg. You can also bring your outside leg back and feel the inside rein to help the horse land on the correct leg. The aim is to have good control and rhythm on landing to take the right number of strides between the two fences, which entails knowing the number of strides between the fences and planning where to turn on to the line for the second fence. To ride a good line, keep your eye firmly focused on the top of the front element of the second fence.

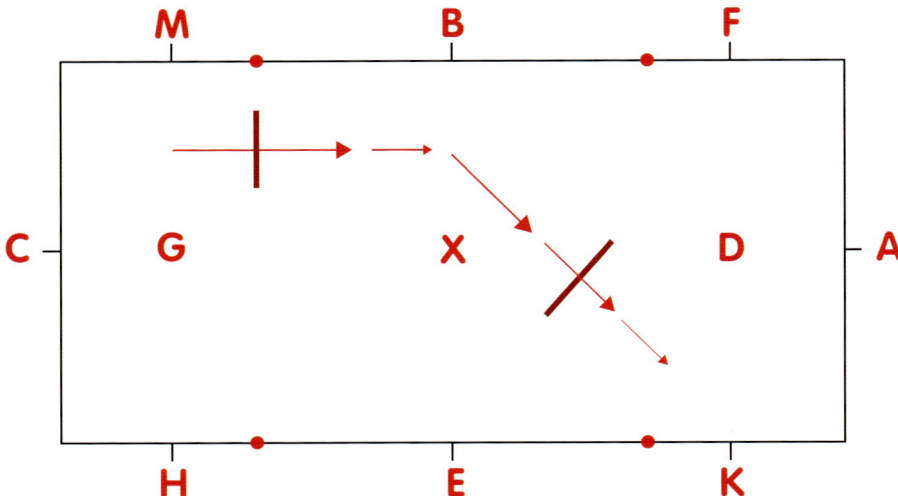

A dogleg

Maintain a good contact with your outside rein and leg to discourage your horse from drifting through the outside shoulder. If this happens, you could practise using poles as tramlines to ride through, or to ride inside.

Walking a showjumping course

Walking a showjumping course carefully will play a significant role in helping you to ride it better.

As well as learning the order of fences to jump, it is essential to assess how to jump each fence and to work out the best lines to and from the fences so that your track is flowing with smooth turns, approaches and changes of direction. When you are walking the course, don't take short cuts or be distracted by other riders; always try to walk the exact line you intend to ride. Turns should be completed so that you are lined up with the centre of the fence with sufficient strides in the approach for the horse to assess the fence and to jump it well. Check where you can use the ends of the arena to allow space and time if needed to rebalance, adjust the canter, steady your horse or get them in front of the leg.

Note the state of the ground or surface; whether it is hard, soft, or slippery and if there are any deep patches. Any slopes up or down affect distances in combinations and take-off zones. If there is a downward slope the horse is likely to cover more ground; going uphill they may cover less ground. Watch for hollows or dips, sunlight, shadow and shade that might distract your horse. Also consider whether there is anything outside or inside the arena at which your horse might spook.

Stepping out the distances in combinations and related distances

Common measurements for combinations and related distances have been given in the previous sections, and these are likely to be used by accredited course-builders. However, you should never make assumptions about distances and you may need to relate them to the jumping characteristics of an individual horse, so you should always pace them out.

If one of your paces is about a 0.9m (a yard) long, a one-stride double would be 8 of your paces from the back of the first element to the front of the second. This allows 2 of your paces for landing, 4 for the horse's non-jumping stride and 2 for take-off. A two-stride double will be 11 or 12 of your paces; a three-stride related distance 15 or 16, four strides 19 or 20 and five strides around 23 or 24. Train yourself to step out these distances accurately on foot at home, using a measuring tape if necessary for accuracy. Remember that distances from upright to upright will be longer than distances from upright to parallel.

There will be collapsible cups on the middle and back elements of spreads for safety and flat cups for any gates and planks. Poles will be dislodged from flatter cups more easily, necessitating cleaner jumping.

Having walked the course, make a mental video tape of how you will ride the track and then check whether you can remember it all. Good luck!

Warming up a horse for showjumping

Much of what applies to warming up on the flat is relevant here, although attuned to the demands of jumping. For riding a course you need the horse to be responsive to your aids; you want them to react immediately to aids to move forward or to steady. After the initial riding-in, use direct transitions such as walk to canter to activate a horse, and downward transitions to establish obedience. In terms of suppleness and balance, cantering circles will help, as will riding figures of eight around the fences in a home setting, although this would not be appropriate in a competition warm-up arena. When warming up for jumping the main emphasis will be on the canter as this is the gait out of which you mainly jump. The jumping canter is more open than a dressage working canter and if your horse is not forward and active in the jumping canter on the flat, they are likely to be less so approaching a sizeable spread or double.

It is also desirable for the horse to be able and willing to lengthen and shorten their canter stride, so focus on this in the warm-up. In fact, while it is useful to be able to shorten and lengthen the stride correctly, if the horse is not yet fully established in this it is still useful to send them more forward and bring them back in the canter, to ensure that they are responding to your aids. When working on varying the stride length it is best to work on shortening before lengthening; the horse will often lengthen better after you have worked on shortening the stride, as they will have more ability to push from their hind legs. It may be easiest to ask the horse to shorten while you are sitting in an upright position; keep a good contact with your legs to prevent the horse from dropping back into trot, then half-halt and slightly control the movement of your seat for a few strides, then allow the horse to move forward into their normal working canter. To encourage the horse to lengthen, apply both legs to send them forward, maintain your rein contact, but allow the horse to travel and cover more ground with their stride. When doing this you can either remain in an upright position or in light seat. If in an upright position allow with your seat; in order for the horse to lengthen their stride in a light seat stay soft through your joints and allow them to lengthen. For both shortening and lengthening it is best to start by asking for a few strides at a time. (Pole work exercises can be incorporated into schooling sessions to develop this work further.)

It is sensible to progress from a pole on the ground, to a cross pole, followed by upright and then spread. Some horses need more warming up than others and you will learn what each horse needs through practice and experimentation.

Riding a showjumping course

All that has been said about walking the showjumping course applies to riding it. Don't approach the first fence until the horse is forward and in the best canter you can obtain. Focus on rhythm and impulsion throughout, looking ahead.

It will help to obtain the correct lead on landing if, in the air, you turn your body subtly towards the next fence (don't throw yourself about, or you will unbalance both yourself and the horse). If, despite this, the horse lands on the left lead when going to the right, return to trot quickly and ask for a right canter lead (unless you are too close to the next fence or the horse understands flying changes). In your preparation, try to practise being able to feel for correct leads rather than looking down. Ride to the ends and sides of the arena, creating more distance between the fences, to give yourself more opportunity to adjust the canter and prepare for the next fence. If you lose control temporarily, or your horse becomes unbalanced, it is better and safer to circle and re-establish control and balance before jumping the next fence. Throughout the course ride the horse between leg and hand, encouraging them to bend through turns using your inside leg and supporting them with your outside aids to prevent them from drifting out.

Make sure you are straight coming into combinations and related fences and jump in the centre of any cross-poles. If the horse is not responding promptly to your leg aids use your whip if necessary behind your lower leg to back up the aid. If the horse refuses and stops in front of the fence, turn them away and re-establish the canter quickly, without moving too far away from the fence. When you re-present the horse to the fence, make sure that your approach is straight, the canter active and you are positive with the use of your legs. If, rather than stopping in front of the fence, the horse runs out, turn them to the opposite direction of the run-out, for example, to the right if they have run out to left and evaded the right rein and left leg. As with a refusal, re-present them with a short, active approach, making sure that they are straight. When dealing with run-outs or refusals be positive with your lower leg aids to let the horse know that you are confident. If the horse runs out or refuses in a combination at a competition, you need to jump the whole combination again, for example, if your horse ran out at 7b, the second element of a double, you need to jump 7a again before jumping 7b. This also gives you a straighter approach rather than coming in from an angle to jump only 7b, so it is wise to do this in training. If you encounter difficulties while schooling at home you can reduce the height and spread to encourage the horse over the problem fence and raise it again gradually after jumping it successfully at the lower height.

Analysing your showjumping round

Reflection after your showjumping round is the key to improvement. If the horse refused, ran out or dislodged a pole, why do you think this happened? Reflecting on your horse's gait and speed, your lines, corners, control and problems or issues with the horse's way of going will enable you to set goals for improvement.

Once more, using the Training Scale provides a comprehensive assessment model. Rhythm includes the quality of canter, balance, suppleness, how the horse turns and uses their back (for example, do they bascule over the fences or do they jump in a hollow outline?) Contact includes control and whether the horse is on the forehand, while impulsion and straightness are self-explanatory.

Also include in your reflection your own flatwork strengths and weaknesses and how these relate to your jumping, for example, lack of suppleness in your back on the flat may mean difficulty with your sitting trot and, when jumping, difficulty with folding, so a main aim would be a plan for you to improve your suppleness.

After your show jump round, try to reflect on your own performance as well as the horse's, in training it is a good idea to discuss each round with your coach to highlight the positives as well as areas for improvement.

Introducing cross-country terrain and obstacles

Training horses for cross-country begins with riding in open fields or hacking out (if available) so that horses learn to balance themselves going on varied terrain up and downhill. Following schoolmasters through puddles and water, over small ditches, or up and down banks in the open is a natural way to accustom horses to these features. For cross-country, horses need to learn to jump a variety of obstacles to include ditches, 'rail, ditch, rails', steps, corners, brushes, water, roll tops, Trakehners, skinnies, offset and angled fences. Many of these obstacles can be schooled over at dimensions to suit you and an individual horse on cross-country courses for hire, where the horse also gains valuable experience in a different location. If a horse is frightened by ditches, a reliable school master can encourage their companion to make that first leap! When the horse is more confident about jumping ditches, approach them with the horse well connected between leg and hand in a positive, forward canter. Unfold quickly to avoid burdening the forehand and unbalancing your landing.

Whether you are hiring one for schooling, or taking part in competitions, it is compulsory to wear a back protector that meets current standards on most cross-country courses.

Using simulated cross-country fences at home is also a valuable method of teaching a horse to jump cross-country fences. For example, using showjumping equipment you can build fences at angles to one another to practise holding your line through them. You can also build offset fences and practise riding your line through them as a rehearsal for the real thing. With shorter poles it is easy to erect skinnies. Gradually reduce the width of the fences, keeping the horse between both legs and reins. To start with, you can use wings if you think the horse might run out at a skinny, then remove the wings when they are more confident. Once a single skinny is jumped confidently, a useful exercise would be to build a double or treble of skinnies, with each fence narrower than the previous one. You can also reduce the number of strides between each skinny until you are jumping three skinnies with one stride between each. Corners can also be practised by using showjumping poles and materials such as blocks. The technique for riding a corner is to draw an imaginary line through the centre of the corner and to aim for it at a right angle.

A water tray can act as a simulated ditch and can be useful as a training aid for introducing cross-country obstacles. Once your horse is jumping the water tray with a rustic pole above it confidently, you are in effect jumping a Trakehner-type fence, a Trakehner being a heavy rustic pole or tree trunk over a ditch. Put a small rustic fence two strides (about 9.9m/32½ft) after the water tray and approach in a bouncy canter, keeping your focus on the middle of the rustic pole. Once this is going well, put another rustic fence two strides in front of the water tray so that you have built up progressively to jumping a simulated rail, ditch, rail combination. Reduce the distances between to one stride when you are confident. Traditionally, rail, ditch, rail combinations on cross-country courses have a slope down after the fence towards the ditch and a slope up to the fence out. When approaching one of these combinations, on a cross-country course, maintain an energetic but bouncy canter. With too fast an approach your horse will be unbalanced on landing. Focus on the fence you jump out so you don't lose your line, and keep your shoulders back on landing to avoid burdening the horse's forehand and losing your balance. Your body and hands should move with the horse's movement over the ditch and you should aim to keep the horse together and balanced on the slope to the fence out.

A water tray can act as a simulated ditch.

Before jumping into or out of water firstly make sure both you and your horse are confident trotting and cantering through water.

Simulated cross-country can, as stated, introduce your horse to different types of cross-country fences but for logs, steps up and down, jumping banks and water complexes you need the real thing.

Cross-country riding is all about bold riding for bigger, wider fences in the open and control and accuracy for other obstacles. If you jump too fast into water, the resistance and spray will unbalance your horse. Approach in a bouncy canter, sitting back on landing to free your horse's forehand. Through the water, press your horse between leg and hand as drag from the water can affect the jump out for an inexperienced horse. However, at this level all that may be required is to trot or canter through water, keeping the horse balanced.

Riding steps uphill, approach in a bouncy, energetic canter. To go with your horse's movement, you need a supple fold and unfold at each step to free the quarters at take-off and the shoulders on landing. Your hands allow the movement of the horse's head and neck. For steps downhill, approach steadily and stay upright in your position while allowing with your hands as the horse lands on each step to maintain your position. If you are too far forward you will burden the horse's forehand and are more likely to make a sudden exit out the front door — so sit and look up.

When jumping down a drop allow with your hands, stay upright in your position and maintain a secure lower leg. Make sure you and the horse are confident going down a single drop before attempting steps.

Walking a cross-country course

If you are to jump a cross-country course, walking it beforehand is essential in order to assess the terrain, going and obstacles so you can make sensible decisions about how to tackle the course. For cross-country schooling it also helps you to plan your training session better.

When walking the course observe closely the terrain (for example, flat, undulating) and the going (muddy, hard, deep patches to avoid). It is useful to give yourself landmarks to aim for that offer the best approaches to and landings after fences. These landmarks might be a tree, post or building and they help you to look up and think forward. For showjumping, you mostly aim for the centre of the fences, but with wider cross-country fences you may select a take-off point away from the centre that is less sloping, offers better going, or a better line on landing.

If you are jumping from light into shade, or vice versa, both your eyes and the horse's will need time to adjust so, if possible, approach in a shorter, bouncier canter.

The way to ride the different cross-country obstacles was discussed in the previous section and you should take all this information into account when deciding how to tackle those on the course. Remember, cross-country is ridden faster overall than showjumping (for example, the optimum time for BE90 cross-country courses is currently 450m per minute).

It is important to practise riding at cross-country speed when schooling and, when walking a course, deciding where it will be safe and sensible to go faster, and where you will need to go more steadily. If there are alternative routes to take at fences, check the layout and decide clearly which alternative you intend to take, but have a back-up plan to use if the horse is not going as expected.

Warming up a horse for cross-country

The differences between cross-country and showjumping are that for cross-country the fences are solid, the horse's balance and adjustability will be tested over more varied terrain and going and, for some fences, you will be jumping at a faster speed than when showjumping. You also need to consider whether the horse will be wearing studs. If the horse is not wearing studs and the going is slippery you will need to ride carefully.

While warming up, make sure that the length of your stirrup leathers feel comfortable. These can be shorter for cross-country than for showjumping to give a more secure lower leg position when riding over uneven terrain and landing down drops. In gallop, shortened leathers will help your weight come off the horse's back. However, your upper body will come upright when asking for a bouncier canter, riding downhill and jumping drops.

When warming up, assess the horse's canter using straight lines, turns, shortening, lengthening and, if possible, going up and down slopes.

As soon as practicable in your warm-up, assess the horse's suppleness, adjustability and contact in a forward light seat canter. Use the full area available to you, making circles and straight lines as big and long as practical. How does your horse respond when lengthening and shortening? What is the balance like up and downhill if you are riding on this terrain? If your horse is on the forehand and difficult to balance downhill, try shortening the canter, sitting up and holding the horse together between leg and hand.

If the horse goes on to the forehand when asked to shorten the canter stride, a useful exercise is to open the canter on a larger circle, then shorten it and immediately riding a smaller circle in a shorter, bouncier canter. When asking your horse to shorten, keep your shoulders back and use your legs to encourage the horse's hind legs to step under their body while your hands discourage the forehand from going down. Then, on the smaller circle, give with both reins to encourage the horse to use their back and hind legs and carry themselves. By giving the rein, it becomes more difficult for the horse to lean on it. Repeat this exercise on both reins until you are happier with the response.

If the horse does not go forward willingly enough, you can use repeated lengthening and shortening on a big circle. Riding walk to canter also sharpens the horse's reactions to your aids.

When warming up for a cross-country competition, you will not always have an array of fences at different heights to use for practice. Therefore, learn to prepare your horse to jump a log or

When jumping the warm-up fence, make sure you are jumping with the red flag on your right. If schooling you can warm up as you move around the course, starting with simple fences such as logs or roll tops.

whatever is available as your first fence. Jump cross-country practice fences at different speeds as well, for example, from a bouncy canter or from a strong, open stride, with the emphasis on your horse listening to you. If confident, jumping the practice fences at an angle tests whether you can hold your line and prepares you and your horse for corners and offset fences.

> *Note the way the practice fences are flagged (red on your right, white on your left) and only jump them in that manner.*

Some horses need more warming up for cross-country than others. Excitable horses may need quieter, slower work to keep them calm and listening, with fewer practice jumps.

However, the warm-up can be more gradual in several respects if you are training on a cross-country course with a wide variety of heights and types of obstacles to use. In this case, start by jumping easier fences with your horse in a confident rhythm before tackling potentially more difficult ones. Leave water complexes until later so that the leg protection on your horse stays dry for longer. (Riding slowly through water is also good for cooling off both horse and rider at the end of an energetic training session.)

Riding a cross-country course

Riding with a clear and steady contact means that your horse can stay working into the bridle and be better balanced. Make sure that the horse is forward and between your hand and leg as you approach the first fence. If the mental plan you formulated when walking the course and when warming up isn't working, take positive action and adapt to the circumstances. The horse may not travel so freely going away from other horses, so you may need to ride more positively. Alternatively, they may be keener than anticipated and you need to sit up, steady them and ride more quietly.

Deal with any refusals, run-outs or spooking as normal. If you feel that the horse is tiring on the course, steady the speed (although keep supporting them between leg and hand) until they gain a second wind. If in any doubt, pull up and walk until the horse's respiration rates drop. In training you may need to work more on fitness.

Hold your horse between hand and leg when you finish, gradually easing them down from cross-country speed to steady canter, trot and finally walk. By keeping your horse balanced after exertion, you reduce the risk of injury. The horse should then be ridden in walk on a long rein while their respiration and heart rates return to normal.

Ride positively with the horse between your leg and hand, keep in mind the plan you formulated when walking the course, but be prepared to adjust your plan according to the horse's performance throughout the course. (This horse has got pretty close to this fence, but horse and rider have adjusted well.)

12 | Flatwork and Jumping

Analysing your cross-country round

In analysing your cross-country performance think about how appropriate your horse's speed was and the lines you rode. Did the course ride as expected? What went well — what was your best jump and why? What problems did you experience? How did the horse go and what are their cross-country strengths and weaknesses? Are they bold or strong, or do they need more confidence and cross-country experience? Was the tack suitable? What type of cross-country obstacles would you need to practise more with them? If aspects of the round could have been better, think about how you would develop a strategy for improvement. Honest self-reflection is the key to better performance and enjoyment of cross-country riding.

Summary

- A supple, secure seat enables you to apply your aids better and increases your effectiveness.

- Forward and lateral response to your leg is the foundation of successful communication.

- Use the Training Scale to assess the quality of your horse's way of going.

- Demonstrate a progressive plan using relevant exercises for the horses you ride.

- Canter quality and its adjustability is a key factor in successful showjumping.

- In grids, a supple folding and focusing on the last fence in order to stay straight are priorities.

- Bounces are excellent for improving folding and agility, but should be introduced carefully.

- When showjumping, ride lines that allow more time to set your horse up for the fences.

- Cross-country combines both bold riding and jumping out of a shortened, energetic stride.

Chapter 13

Towards More Advanced Coaching

Introduction

Developing your own coaching style

Advancing your flatwork coaching

Coaching jumping

Summary — managing and developing your coaching practice

Introduction

As you progress through your career as a riding coach, you will develop skills and competence in a variety of areas. You will be able to demonstrate professionalism and accountability at all times so that you instil confidence in all of your pupils. You will be skilled in first aid and safety procedures as well as improving your equestrian knowledge and technical competence, but most of all you will display commitment to your chosen sport in the satisfaction of having achieved a world-renowned qualification.

It is important that you give a professional impression; the image you give will affect the respect you gain from your riders. This comes from your knowledge and experience, appearance and dress, demeanour and interest in your clients. In the age of social media confidentiality must be respected, as must equity and equal opportunities. Your personal social media pages should stay private from your professional activities; nothing should be displayed without your client's permission. You should never give anyone cause to question your integrity. Your riders should be educated in respecting the well-being of the horse at all times from both a training and care perspective. They should demonstrate acceptable behaviour in training and competition, showing respect for clean sport, for other riders, and for the authority of judges and stewards.

Your role as a coach is to make your sport safe and enjoyable. The training should be rider- and horse-centred rather than coach-centred. Each session should have an agreed goal, decided upon by an assessment of the pupils' needs by both discussion and observation. The session should be interactive, with open questioning to encourage the participants to help solve their own problems, along with feedback from the coach to help them improve. This technique can be used to develop beginners just as much as high-performance competitors. This type of training helps riders to become independent and responsible for their own learning rather than just being reactive to commands.

A smartly dressed coach.

As a coach you have a responsibility to ensure that your sessions are well planned and safe. You should make a risk assessment that ensures the surroundings are safe and that the level of risk for the exercises you choose to use are within the capabilities of your riders. Checking that tack and equipment is safe and fits well is essential. When coaching, it is important to develop a rapport with your riders; this develops out of trust from your riders that you understand their ability and encourage them to stretch themselves enough to progress, while remaining within safe parameters.

You need to have the confidence to coach with authority, enthusiasm and positive body language. You need to show empathy for the riders' needs and a true desire to help them improve. You need to be a good observer and listener, showing respect for people's ambitions, whether it is to ride safely in walk around a field, or compete at Olympic level.

Working as an equestrian coach means that you are:

- Promoting high standards of horse care and welfare.

- Providing a safe and supportive environment.

- Removing unnecessary distractions or interferences.

- Directing a person or group along the path from their present stage of learning and development to their future goal.

- Developing skills and capabilities.

- Developing new strategies that can be applied in multiple situations.

- Providing new information.

- Helping to shape participants' beliefs and values (particularly children).

- Using your experience to encourage your participants to follow the 'best way'.

- Guiding individuals to discover their unconscious competencies and overcome internal resistances and interferences.

- Helping pupils extend their own knowledge.

- Promoting self-esteem and confidence.

Developing your own coaching style

Effective coaches inspire loyalty, trust and confidence. Therefore your coaching style needs to reflect your natural personality. Demonstrating sincerity, commitment to your personal beliefs and individuality are all really important but, above all, you need to be yourself — don't try to be someone you're not. It will be very hard to pretend to have certain qualities over a longer period of time. Your natural style of coaching will attract a particular type of pupil to you and you will have greater success with someone who enjoys your style than if you try to adopt a different style from you own.

Riders value consistency from their coach. It gives them security and a feeling of comfort, so you should try to be consistent in your approach when explaining exercises, correcting problems and giving feedback.

In developing your coaching style, there are various aspects of learning and teaching that you should be familiar with.

Using technology to aid your teaching

There have been many advances in technology over the recent years, which you can utilise to your advantage in your teaching sessions. Your voice is one of your most important assets and you should take care to look after it. If you are doing a lot of teaching you might want to consider using a wireless headset and microphone to allow you to communicate with your rider or riders without having to shout. These have the advantage that riders can hear you no matter where they are in the arena and you shouldn't have to move around to be heard. They tend to be battery operated and can be one-way, whereby the rider can hear you but cannot speak back, or two-way whereby you and the rider can talk to each other.

There are many smartphone Apps that can be downloaded that can help you to plan and track your lessons and allow your clients to keep track of their progress.

Taking short video clips of your riders (with their permission) during the lesson can be helpful for riders to see what was happening during a ridden exercise and relate it to what they felt, for example, the straightness of the horse during leg-yielding or their position over a fence.

Understanding phases of learning

When people learn new skills, they go through four phases of learning. They may not spend equal amounts of time in each phase — and some people can spend weeks or months in one phase and may never get completely to the 'unconscious competence' stage in their riding.

The first phase is called *unconscious incompetence*, or 'blissful ignorance'! At this stage of learning, we are unaware of just how much we need to learn in order to become competent

The second phase is called *conscious incompetence*. This applies whenever a new skill is being learnt and is crucial to skill development and motivation. It's often the stage when confidence dips, so this is the time when you need to be patient and avoid overloading your pupil.

The third phase is called *conscious competence*. Your rider is now able to perform exercises but needs time to practise and embed them. You should try to think of lots of different exercises that enables practice of the same skill in different ways.

The fourth phase is called *unconscious competence*. This is when someone displays skills that appear to be 'automatic'.

As an example of how to relate your coaching to these phases of increasing competence, once a participant has mastered the light/jumping seat on the flat, over poles on the ground and over individual small fences, you should consider introducing a small course of fences. The idea is that the rider will consciously focus on new aspects of riding the course and the jumping posture will become an unconscious skill that is done without thinking about it.

Learning styles

You also need to understand that everyone has a preferred learning style: 'auditory' (they like to be told),' visual' (they would prefer to watch demonstrations, videos), or 'kinaesthetic' (learns by feeling and doing). Although you should try to recognise their preferred style and use it to their advantage it is also essential to develop greater use of their less preferred styles in order to maximise potential.

Everyone has personality traits that also affect their learning. Your riders may be 'activists', 'reflectors', 'theorists' or 'pragmatists'. Recognising your clients (and your own) traits will help you understand the way your riders react to new exercises and ideas, thus helping you adapt your training to suit them. For example, a reflector learns and reacts in a very different way from an activist. These traits are covered in more detail in Volume 2.

Your coaching should always be horse- and rider-focused. In that way, your attitude and commitment will help your riders to achieve their goals and ambitions — on the other hand, coach-led, negative training with a lack of interest in their progress could lead to them giving up riding altogether. A supportive coach, who gives positive feedback, encouraging the rider to think of solutions, will develop confidence and self-belief. Negative feedback, always saying that what someone is doing wrong, will have the opposite affect and can ultimately be destructive.

In some respects, however, the current level of a rider's ability will affect the coaching style you select. Autocratic or 'telling' is necessary when teaching new skills. This could be with a complete beginner or with a more experienced rider learning a new exercise. Once the rider has an understanding of a process you can use a democratic style — 'set-up and stand back'. Now you encourage the rider to work more independently on an exercise, with as little help as necessary. You then ask open questions about how the horse might feel, whether they were easy or difficult. You may well need to remind the rider what aids to use, demonstrate how it should actually be done, explain how their position may affect the effectiveness of their aids, use cones or poles as visual markers. Although they may find it difficult, you should give them room to experiment so they can develop their skills, rather than you reverting back to 'telling'.

With more experienced riders you can use a laissez-faire style. This gives them a goal to achieve, for example 'go and improve the suppleness of your horse' with little guidance from you as to what to do. The feedback from this type of session should give them some pointers as to what to consider and how they might improve the work, but while questioning and empowering the rider you should try to avoid giving them the answers. You want them to feel the affect they have had and recognise the improvement that they have hopefully achieved.

During the warm-down period at the end of a session you should ask riders what they feel they have achieved and help them recognise some aspect of the work that they can take as homework. What you are trying to achieve is to give them responsibility for ownership of their own development.

The coaching process is a continuous cycle, as shown in the diagram.

Planning and carrying out a coaching session

Goal-setting (creating an outline session plan)

Before you begin coaching, it is important that you (and your pupils) select session goals and content (to include warming-up, exercises and cooling down), making sure that your goals match their goals. The goals you set for sessions will thus need to take into account the strengths and weaknesses of your riders. The main issues to consider when preparing your sessions include:

- Identifying your riders' needs and setting goals for the series of sessions.

- The timescales and any potential obstacles involved in achieving the goals.

- Establishing where they are currently in relation to the goals (technically, tactically, mentally, physically and socially).

- A planned route to achieve the goals (an action plan on your part), which includes clear stepping stones to keep riders on track, motivating them so that they remain committed to pursuing their goals, and supporting their self-belief in their ability.

Key considerations during the session

There are a number of key points for you, as coach, to consider during a session. These may be interrelated, but can be broadly grouped as follows.

Observation and feedback. This is your opportunity to update your pupils on your observation of their performance to help them identify areas where they need further development and understand how to use their strengths in order to progress.

Analysis. This means trying to establish the cause of any problems and identify particular strengths. You need to balance how you analyse while you are observing, so that you do not miss the opportunity to observe other strengths and weaknesses. This is your opportunity to:

- Fill any gaps in knowledge.

- Challenge misconceptions.

- Present new knowledge.

Monitoring and evaluation. There are many reasons why you want to monitor progress; some of the key ones are to:

- Identify strengths and areas for development.

- Pinpoint the starting point for individual training programmes.

- Identify the ideal training programme to achieve the goals set.

- Evaluate the effectiveness of the training programme.

- Assess changes in performance.

- Help to motivate your riders.

- Show whether the training programme is being followed.

- Help with selection or inclusion in teams or squads.

It is important to keep records that are helpful to both you and your riders so that you can show them how they have progressed over a period of time.

Feedback and review. Recall is improved when information is reviewed regularly. Unless you review what you have taught, that information is often forgotten almost immediately. Consider how you can build reviews into your coaching sessions. As a coach, you need to consider how you will deliver feedback regarding success/failure to maintain motivation in each individual case.

After the session — self-reflection

This is when you as the coach can look back at either an action within a session or a whole coaching session for future practice or skill development. For example:

- What did I see happen?

- Was this a positive result, or did this achieve the desired effect?

- Was this a negative result; if so, what was the cause?

- What worked well? How will I continue to reinforce this?

- What needs changing? How will I change it?

There are many ways of self-reflecting — the important points are identifying what to keep and what to change. Developing coaches must be encouraged to identify their strengths and not dwell too much on any weaknesses, otherwise self-reflection can be confidence-sapping and de-motivating. This should be a 'tool for growth' not 'paralysis by analysis' for the less experienced coach.

Maintaining confidence and self-motivation

Apart from the riding school environment or training yard, freelance coaching can be a solitary occupation. Maintaining confidence and self-motivation in this context is an important part of a coach's development. The following are various sources of support in achieving this.

Community of practice. This is formed when a group of coaches work together to share ideas and good practice. This would naturally occur in a yard context, but social media (used positively) can help freelance coaches maintain professional contact with their peers/people they have trained with.

Mentors. These can come in various guises, not necessarily being a more highly qualified person. A mentor will be someone to confide in, bounce ideas off and generally be a source of motivation and inspiration for the coach's professional or personal development. Informal mentoring relationships have been proved to be the most successful.

Attending CPD events will help you to develop your coaching skills and technique.

Continuing Professional Development (CPD). This can be either formal or informal. Formal sessions are usually organised coach education courses or days, administered by the national governing body of an equestrian discipline. Informal development may be in the form of networking opportunities at the above, interacting with peers, or observing other coaches at camps or clinics.

Research has shown that the majority of coaches favour being observed in their practice by a senior coach as their CPD of choice. However, this can be a costly business so may not be possible as a sole source of development. As a coach you must constantly seek knowledge and information from a variety of sources to ensure that you remain up to date in your practice.

Advancing your flatwork coaching

Concept

As the rider's ability develops, your coaching strategies and exercises will adapt. At this level, riders should be developing 'feel' and the ability to assess the horse's way of going — your role is to guide them through this development, and to enable them to begin to improve the horses they are riding.

This section will help you to develop your ability to coach more developed flatwork, concentrating on coaching more established riders on possibly more advanced horses, and/or progressing the training of riders on inexperienced horses. It will guide you towards the stage at which you should be able to coach a rider who is working towards developing their horse to include the beginnings of lateral work. For such riders, you should be demonstrating your ability to encourage the development of independent thinking and problem-solving, with a view to assessing the horses they are riding, showing your understanding and suggesting exercises to improve the horse's way of going. This should be following the principles of the Training Scale.

Rider position

At this stage, the rider's basic position should be established, however, development and corrections will still need to be addressed to ensure that the rider maintains good balance and consistency and works in harmony with the horse. The correct position, and subtle movements within, allow the rider to absorb and even enhance the horse's movement.

Developing suppleness and stability of the position is important, in order to maintain correct balanced lines, while being able to ride forward to the contact, deliver subtle aids, and feel how the horse is responding and moving. This position should be demonstrated in all gaits and on a variety of horses.

Working without stirrups regularly during training is key for riders to develop a deeper, more receptive seat. This enhances the ability to feel how the horse is performing and to read the horse's way of going and then, in turn, be able to apply more appropriate, precise and effective aids. This could be done initially on the lunge or horse simulator, to allow you to focus on position, particularly during transitions. As rider ability and confidence develop, time spent without stirrups should increase, and the exercises performed and type of horse ridden should become more advanced.

Work without stirrups can help riders to improve their own position as well as working on the horse's way of going.

In addition to work on the lunge (which could perhaps be suggested to the rider as it may not be possible to do this at the time of the lesson), closely observing the rider working on specific school movements will give you greater insight to their strengths and areas that require further instruction, or reminders. The school movements that are particularly useful for this are asking the rider to ride three-quarter lines away and towards you, circles of various sizes and many transitions, ensuring that you as the coach position yourself in places from which you can observe the rider's position from all angles, such as directly head-on and behind on a straight line, from the outside of the circles and turns. Also watch closely the rider's position during transitions both progressive and direct. These particular movements should give you a very good idea of the rider's working position and you can then advise them from there.

Observe your rider from different positions around the school to check their position and the straightness of both horse and rider.

Common faults to be addressed include:

- Collapsing the upper body forward during transitions.

- Swinging the lower leg forward during transitions (particularly downward).

- Excessive tilting around circles (this may be a subtle shoulder or hip shift).

- Unintentional 'blocking' of the horse by the rider through gripping, weight shift or lack of independent hands.

- As riders develop their feel and understanding, and focus moves towards improving the horse, it is common for the rider's position to be compromised, typically by lowering hands and leaning forwards.

School movements

When coaching the slightly more advanced rider you will be encouraging them to be able to ride more independently, with minimal direction in school movements and transitions. As the coach your aim is to improve the understanding and confidence of the rider to be able to decide what movements to use to help gain increased obedience and suppleness in the horse, as well as starting to improve the overall way of going, with reference to the Training Scale. These movements and transitions should be demonstrated with clear preparation and confident execution.

Direct transitions

Direct transitions are a progression from 'normal' transitions; involving moving up or down the gaits by a factor of two rather than one, for example, from halt directly to trot, or walk directly to canter. The upward transitions tend to be easier for both horse and rider, and so are taught before their downward counterparts.

Successful direct transitions are the result of understanding (on the part of both horse and rider) what is being asked and clear application of the aids, combined with preparation, timing, and contained energy.

In order to prepare for these, the rider should understand and be able to use the half-halt, and be able to assess the quality of the gait before and after transitions.

Regardless of gait, the process for teaching direct transitions will be similar. Ask the rider to ride a series of progressive transitions, decreasing the steps spent in the intermediary gait in each transition. Pay attention to the quality of the gait either side of the transition — the horse should remain balanced, supple and engaged.

The most common mistake is the rider over-applying the aids — you do not want to see a 'big kick' or a harsh pull. The horse should not overreact, or their way of going will be compromised.

Direct transitions help to engage the horse, encourage weight to be taken on the hindquarters and increase attentiveness.

Transitions within the gaits

At this stage the rider should be able to begin to vary the horse's ground coverage and frame within each gait, and move between working and lengthened strides in trot and canter without compromising the rhythm, tempo or quality of the gait. The coach's role is to ensure that the rider understands the variations in gait that are recognised, and how to ride the required type of gait.

While the frame is permitted to be a little longer and lower when the strides are lengthened, the horse should still be in a generally rounded outline. The horse must not be hurried, but should be travelling with forward, clearly lengthened strides, a product of the impulsion from the hindquarters. The horse's nose may be a little more in front of the vertical compared to collected or working gaits, and the horse's head and neck may lower slightly. The rider must be encouraged to ensure that the strides maintain evenness and balance, and are unconstrained;

they should cover the ground with energy and self-carriage. The rhythm and tempo of the gait should not alter.

When first introducing the idea of transitions within the gait, pole work can be a useful exercise to assist with lengthening or shortening ground coverage, while regulating the steps. Start by using ground poles separated at a working distance, then progressively increase the distance to encourage lengthening, with the aim of working eventually towards medium strides, or shortening to work towards collection. Regardless of the actual variation of gait, encourage the rider to think about the preparation for the transition and the poles with a balanced, engaged gait (and turn, if appropriate), with contained energy.

Once the rider understands the concept, you can move on from the pole work. Encourage the rider to work the horse more forward, towards lengthening for a few strides and then contain the strides briefly. Ask for this forwardness and shortening repeatedly, in fairly quick succession; this will encourage forward energy contained by an effective half-halt, encouraging engagement of the hind legs. Ridden correctly, the horse will start to give bigger, ground-covering steps into a positive forward contact with engaged hind legs. This can then be progressed into more steps at one time leading to a clear demonstration of a medium gait.

The rider may need support when learning how much to ride individual horses more forward, and then towards collection, and for how long at a time; talk them through this process as they do it, and reassure and discuss with them the effect it is having on the gait. This will, in turn, develop their feel and understanding for the variations within the gait and how to develop them when training horses.

COMMON MISTAKES

- Tight, short neck when asking for a half-halt, causing tension and hollow outline.

- Giving the rein away, allowing the horse to run on to the forehand.

- Hurrying, losing the quality of the gait.

- Loss of balance, resulting in irregular steps.

- Loss of rider balance in the medium gait, leading to lack of stability for the horse to work to.

Turn on/about the forehand

The turn on or about the forehand is a useful and informative movement for both the horse and rider; it is a good basic movement that can further develop a rider's understanding of, as well as attainment of, the skills and coordination needed to ride with 'independent aids'. In addition, it allows assessment of the horse's understanding of the leg aids; how responsive and educated the horse is about moving away from the leg.

If performed well, the turn on the forehand encourages the horse to step across with their inside hind leg, bringing the quarters more underneath the body, aiding suppleness and engagement. It is important that the rider understands that it can be performed from halt, where the horse moves around the inside foreleg, which should move up and down on the spot as the horse turns, or as a turn about the forehand, performed at walk, where the forelimbs trace a small circle.

The rider must be very clear about the correct application of the aids for this movement, and this is a common source of confusion initially. Ensure that you explain the aids in detail, and clarify the role of the independent aids for the movement, discussing how this will be relevant for further training at this level and beyond.

It is paramount that each attempt at turn about the forehand starts by establishing an attentive, straight walk with balance and energy. When introducing this movement to a horse and rider starting from walk will reduce the risk of the rider using too much rein and the horse losing forward movement and stepping backwards.

A good exercise is to ask the rider to ride a square floor pattern with a quarter-turn in every corner; this way just a few steps are being requested and the rider learns to control the potential swinging out of the quarters by using their outside aids effectively. This exercise also encourages a more forward-thinking approach to the movement, as the rider stays in walk throughout the movement. This can be progressed onto a quarter-turn and then a half-turn about the forehand. Once both horse and rider are well practised this can be progressed to a full turn about the forehand.

COMMON PROBLEMS

- Confusion of the aids and their application, particularly as each hand and leg has to work independently. Ensure you have explained the purpose and application of each aspect of the aids clearly, and be prepared to remind riders of specific aspects as they ride the exercise.

- Horse falls out through outside shoulder — this is often a result of lack of support down the outside rein, and/or overuse of the inside rein aid.

- Horse swings quarters away from inside leg — this is often a result of lack of support from the outside leg, possibly combined with over-enthusiastic use of the inside leg aid.

- Horse steps backwards — outside rein aid may be too strong, and/or inside leg aid too weak.

- Rider position is compromised — in their effort to apply independent aids, the rider neglects their position — often looking down, and/or collapsing over the inside leg.

- Loss of rhythm, balance, clarity.

DISCUSSION POINTS

Help the rider to recognise the reaction of the horse to the individual aspects of the aids. The rider needs to understand the aids, their timing and pressure in order to execute the movement successfully. This is a useful exercise for encouraging the rider to assess the horse; to read the reaction and recognise the effectiveness of the movement in improving the horse's way of going. This is a key foundation for later lateral work, and for developing the ability of the rider to use their hand, leg and seat aids independently of each other.

Leg-yielding

Once the rider is able to use their aids independently, and has an appreciation of the concept of lateral movement, leg-yielding can be introduced. The horse is required to move forwards and laterally, showing clear crossing of the inside legs over the outside, moving away from the rider's inside leg. The rider should understand the value of leg-yielding in increasing suppleness and engagement from the horse, developing elasticity and harmony in the gait. It is typically ridden in walk or trot during training, but is only demonstrated in trot during competition.

The rider should be encouraged to ensure that the horse's way of going is not compromised during lateral movements, therefore, whether ridden in walk or trot, the balance, rhythm and frame of the horse should not change.

To prepare the rider for leg-yielding, explain the purpose of each aid and the overall aim of the exercise. You may need to physically demonstrate on foot what is meant by crossing of the legs. Initially, you want the rider to recognise the feel of the horse moving forwards and sideways. A useful exercise for this is to ride a three-quarter line, and ask the horse to leg-yield towards

Watch the horse and rider from the front in the leg-yield to check for straightness.

the outside track. The rider should maintain speed and control of the horse's shoulders with the outside rein, while applying pressure at the girth with the inside leg. The outside leg controls the quarters, while the inside rein asks for slight flexion. As the coach, you may need to give immediate and frequent feedback, advising on angle and quality of steps, so that the rider is able to distinguish correct steps. This is where the use of arena mirrors can be very useful to the rider — allowing them to self analyse. Be careful, however, that they do not become dependent on seeing the movement — you should encourage them to develop an objective feel.

Once the recognition of feel for correctness is established, the aids and position of the rider can be refined, and the movement developed elsewhere in the arena, and in trot. A useful progression exercise is to spiral a 20m circle down to a 10m circle, then leg-yield out to original circle size.

A successful leg-yield demonstrates the rider's ability to use independent aids, and encourages their ability to assess the horse's suppleness and ability to engage the hindquarters. Discuss with the rider the effect the movement had on the horse's way of going, and whether the horse moves equally off each leg.

COMMON PROBLEMS

- Too much inside flexion, which leads to falling out through the shoulder.

- Quarters in advance of the shoulders.

- Rider collapsing over the inside leg.

- Lack of lateral movement — no crossing of legs.

- Too much lateral movement, loss of forward movement (angle of movement is too steep).

- Quality of gait is compromised, often by losing impulsion or conversely, rushing.

- Over-application of aids resulting in tension and loss of outline.

Assessing the horse's way of going

Riders at this level need to be able to assess the horse's way of going, and suggest a plan for improvement. As the coach you need to encourage the rider to first logically assess the horse's way of going, and then think about what exercises would improve the horse's performance. This is a good habit to establish for each time they ride. You should encourage and develop the rider's ability to give verbal feedback on their assessment of the horse. Initially, this might be done by asking open questions, allowing you to ensure that all aspects have been considered.

As the rider's skill in this area develops, they should be able to give a short summary of the horse without prompts.

In order to assess the horse logically, it is useful to work through a floor plan of progressive exercises on each rein. This should allow both coach and rider to assess many, if not all, aspects of the horse's way of going at that time, as well as quantify the horse's level of education, and their strengths and weaknesses.

This floor plan should also be clear to an onlooker and all movements and transitions should be well-prepared and planned, demonstrating that there is an obvious logical assessment of the horse's way of going occurring.

As well as encouraging your rider to develop their floor plan, they must also be advised to ensure that they are mindful of any other riders who may be in the arena. They need to demonstrate confidence in riding independently in their own space, without interfering with others or compromising the horse's way of going.

The role of the coach is to encourage the rider to have a basic plan to start with, which can then be adapted according to the horse's needs. This would also be very relevant for a competitive rider warming up for a competition in a collecting ring. The following is a suggested floor plan to practise with your rider:

- Relaxed walk figure of eight.

- Transitions, developed on to direct transitions.

- Purposely ridden, clear half-halts.

- Turn on the forehand.

- Various circles from 20m, 15m and 10m equally on both reins.

- Serpentines with various loop sizes depending on arena length.

- Various different ways of changing the rein.

- Transitions within the gait; working and lengthened strides in trot and canter.

- Leg-yield in walk and then in trot if appropriate for the individual horse.

Discuss with the rider what qualities they are assessing, and the information they could gain about the horse, with each exercise, using the Training Scale as a guide. You may want to prompt initial discussions with questions regarding suppleness, quality of gait and obedience.

Initially, you may suggest to the rider the exercises that would aid improvement in the horse's way of going alongside the assessment. As the assessment skills develop, the rider should take more responsibility for suggesting a plan for progression, with feedback from you as coach.

Encourage verbal feedback from your rider throughout the session.

Referring to the Training Scale

Riders at this stage should have an initial awareness of the Training Scale. However, it is now your role to develop this to a deeper appreciation of the Scale, and how it is applicable to assessing and training horses.

Rhythm

Coaching the rider at this stage should involve assessment of their ability to recognise if a true rhythm is being produced in all gaits, as well as their ability to assess the quality of the rhythm. This can be developed by asking the rider to identify the rhythm and any variations of it, you can give feedback to the rider regarding their correctness, and highlight moments where the rhythm is lost or maintained. This can be done as a simple discussion while the rider is moving around you, and you can mirror what the rider is feeling with your observations. A good exercise to help could be to ask the rider to intentionally hurry the gait, and slow the gait, allowing the rider to make a judgement as to what the correct tempo and rhythm feel like and how then to describe it. This is particularly easily recognised on circles or turns: a loss of rhythm often translates to a loss of balance, the importance of which cannot be overemphasised.

Suppleness

The rider should now be able to recognise good suppleness in both themselves and the horse. It is important that you develop their skills in recognising areas where they lack suppleness, and what effect that could be having on the horse's way of going. The rider should also be taught to recognise when a horse lacks suppleness that is inhibiting their performance and future training. This may be as simple as recognising which rein the horse finds a movement 'easier' on — more elastic, fluid, and showing less tension. Your role would be to increase awareness of the rider's own and the horse's suppleness, and encourage the rider to evaluate what may be causing issues. Once the cause has been identified, you can work to suggest appropriate exercises to alleviate it. This may include the rider addressing their fitness off the horse as well as mounted. If an underlying physiological issue is suspected, this may be something warranting further discussion.

Contact

By this stage, the rider should have a fair understanding of what a contact is, and be able to work horses towards the appropriate outline. This feel has to be developed; you should encourage the rider to provide an equal, consistent contact in both reins, with the feeling of elasticity and of riding the horse forwards to the contact. The horse should accept the contact with a quiet mouth, with their poll the highest point and their nose slightly in front of the vertical; frequent feedback may be needed initially so that the rider can learn to recognise the feeling when this is achieved. They can then work to maintain the required frame independently. When first explaining the concept of the contact, it can be useful to demonstrate the sought-after feeling by physically holding the reins and acting as the horse.

Impulsion

Impulsion is energy utilised through the engagement of the hind limbs to drive the horse powerfully forward. Once the principles of rhythm and contact have been established, asking for more energy from the horse while containing this energy with the contact will result in a greater spring in the steps, recognised as greater cadence. This is only achievable with a supple, swinging back, which is one of the key aims of training. You should guide the rider in their appreciation and recognition of the importance of this. As a coach, you should instigate activities that heighten the rider's awareness of increased impulsion, and develop their ability to regulate the impulsion. A useful exercise for this is transitions within the gait, taking particular care to maintain the tempo.

Straightness

Straightness of the horse can be recognised by several key aspects: equal contact; hind limbs following their respective forelimbs on the same track irrespective of straight lines or turns; equal power coming from both hind limbs through the back to the contact. Straightness is closely associated with suppleness; the horse should be able to move equally well on both reins, with equal flexion and bend. Horses are naturally crooked, therefore straightness requires ongoing maintenance. Riders at this level should be able to recognise a lack of straightness, and suggest ways to improve it. Any exercises that improve suppleness, both laterally and longitudinally, will aid straightness, as long as they are executed equally on both reins. The rider should be coached to recognise a loss of straightness, for example, unequal rein contact, through various movements and lateral work.

Collection

Collection is considered to be the most demanding aspect of the Training Scale, and should only be truly attempted when all other aspects of the Scale are established, and the horse is appropriately conditioned. Saying this, riding towards collection is part of the training process. Collection can be recognised by the feeling of the horse taking the weight on to the hindquarters and lightening the forehand, with a higher level of contained energy. You should encourage the rider to appreciate the demands of true collection on the horse, and recognise that it is not a simple shortening or slowing of the gait, in preparation for their later training.

Flatwork exercises

1. **Leg-yielding from the quarter line to the track**

    AIMS AND BENEFITS

    - To move the horse sideways and forwards starting on the quarter line and ending up on the track.

    - Increases coordination of the rider's aids.

    - Improves suppleness of the horse.

    - Teaches the horse to move away from rider's inside leg.

    DESCRIPTION

    - Rider rides a good turn on to the quarter line and rides the horse straight for a few strides.

    - Rider asks the horse to leg-yield over towards the track, keeping the horse parallel to the wall until they reach the track.

    - The steps should be even and not rushed.

    - Can also be ridden from the centre line to the track, or from the track to the quarter or centre line.

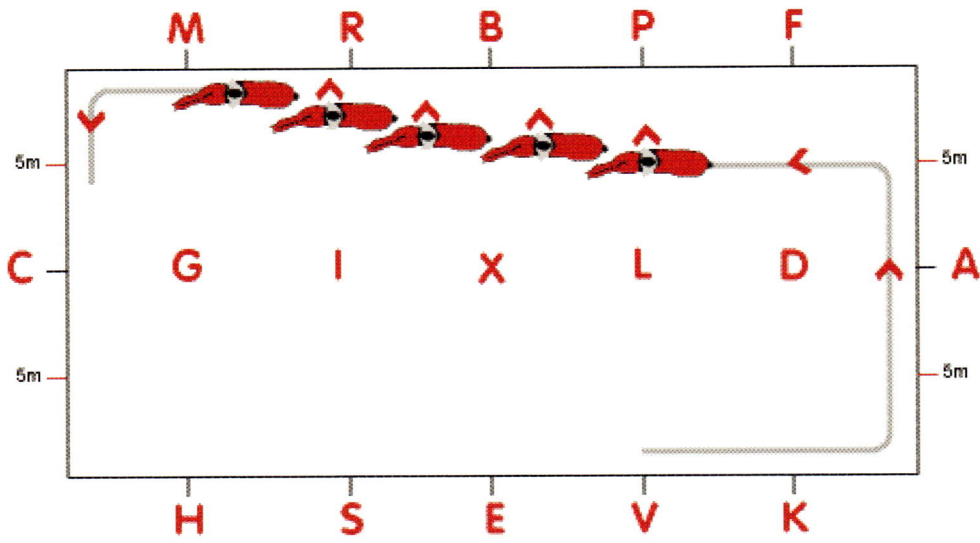

A diagram to show leg-yielding.

COMMON PROBLEMS

1. Horse is not straight.

2. Horse falls out through, or leads with, outside shoulder.

3. Rider not using outside aids to maintain straightness and forwardness.

4. Steps are not even.

5. Horse loses impulsion.

6. Too much neck bend.

7. Horse not responsive to rider's leg.

8. Rider loses position.

2. **Leg-yielding on a circle**

    AIMS AND BENEFITS

    - To increase the size of the circle by leg-yielding out.

- Increases coordination of the rider's aids.

- Improves suppleness of the horse.

- Teaches the horse to move away from rider's inside leg.

EQUIPMENT

Can use markers on the floor as a guide for circle size.

DESCRIPTION

- Rider rides a 20m circle from A or C and gradually decreases the size of the circle. To make the circle bigger, rider leg-yields back out on to the larger circle.

- Can be moved to any size of circle anywhere around the arena.

- Transitions to canter as the horse reaches the bigger circle can be added for more experienced riders.

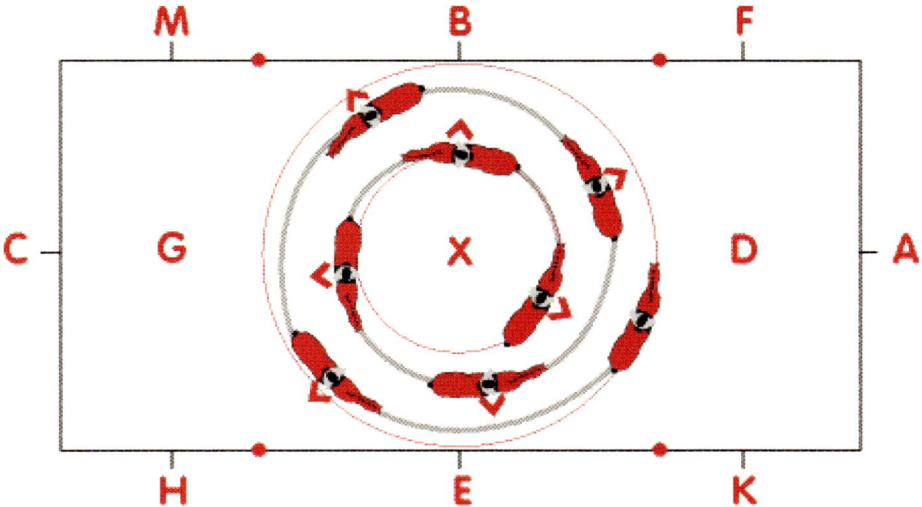

Leg-yielding in and out on a circle.

COMMON PROBLEMS

1. Horse falls out through shoulder.

2. Loss of forwardness so the steps sideways are larger than the steps forwards.

3. Rider not using outside aids to control sideways movement.

4. Too much neck bend.

5. Rider loses position.

3. **Turn about the forehand on a diamond**

    AIMS AND BENEFITS

    - Increases coordination of the riders aids.

    - Improves suppleness of the horse.

    - Teaches the horse to move away from rider's leg.

    DESCRIPTION

    Ask the rider to ride a diamond shape and, on each corner or point, ride a quarter turn using turn about the forehand to move the horse around the corner. It is important that the walk sequence is maintained and the horse does not pivot around the inside leg.

    COMMON PROBLEMS

    1. Horse has too much neck bend.

    2. Horse rushes through movement.

    3. Rider not using outside aids to control the amount of sideways movement.

    4. Hind legs not crossing.

    5. Lack of coordination of the aids from the rider.

    6. Lines not straight and diamond shape not regular.

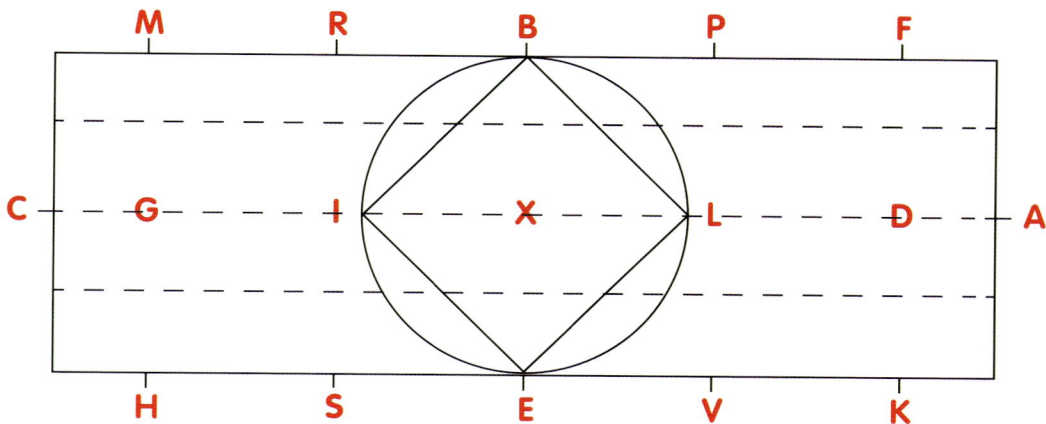

Turn about the forehand on a diamond.

4. **Lengthened trot strides**

   AIMS AND BENEFITS

   - Improves the horse's suppleness and engagement.
   - Teaches the rider to move the horse within a gait.
   - Teaches the rider to control impulsion.
   - The transitions into and out of lengthened (or medium) strides should be smooth and balanced; the circles are used to help the rider balance the horse.

   DESCRIPTION

   Ask the rider to ride a 10m circle in the corner and collect the trot slightly then, down the long side, ask the horse to lengthen then shorten and rebalance before the corner. The rider then makes another 10m circle at the end to help rebalance the horse. This can also be ridden across the diagonal using the same exercise. Encourage the rider to gradually increase the length of strides and to control the movement. The downward transition should be clear and balanced and the horse should not run around the corner.

   COMMON PROBLEMS

   1. Loss of rhythm and tempo.
   2. Horse losing balance.

3. Rider losing balance.

4. Uneven steps.

5. Rider dropping rein contact.

6. Rider asking for too much too quickly and unbalancing the horse.

7. Horse unbalanced in the downward transition and rushing.

8. Horse quickens instead of lengthening the stride.

9. Horse hollows and stiffens across the back.

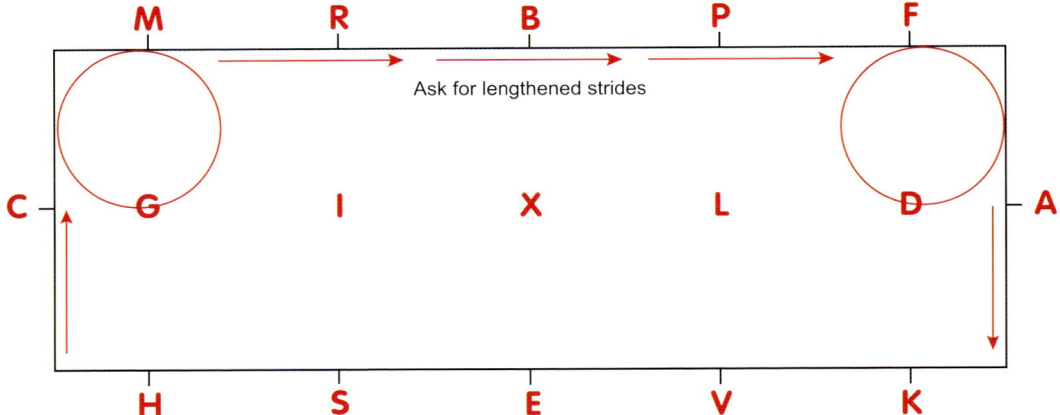

Where to ask for lengthened strides.

Coaching jumping

Progression after basic lessons

Once riders have mastered riding effectively over small, simple fences, there are many skills that they need to develop further. Repetition combined with effective correction is the key to establishing good long-term skills. As a coach part of your skill is to provide repetition without appearing to be asking for the same thing every session. Take time to watch other coaches for inspiration and you will find there are a multitude of exercises, which work towards the same outcome.

Positional corrections

Development of a good position over a fence can take a long time. Timing and suppleness are often key. It is so important to recognise positional faults early on and find a way to help the rider overcome them before they become an ingrained way of riding. Don't be afraid to go back to basics and spend time on the flat and over small fences to iron out issues. Try to evaluate why the position is poor; is it because of a lack of understanding, physical stiffness or asymmetry, incorrect length of stirrup leathers, or a lack of confidence? By identifying the cause you can begin to find a solution, such as further explanation and demonstration, recommending Pilates or a physiotherapist's assessment, altering stirrup leathers or slowing down the speed at which the rider is being challenged. It can be helpful to teach a rider who is normally in a group privately for a couple of sessions to allow you to focus fully on them and further progress to be made.

Improving the canter

Many poor jumping performances are linked to the absence of a good canter that is active, rhythmical and balanced. Spend time helping riders to recognise and feel the difference between good and bad for each of these elements. This can be done through a combination of flatwork, poles and fences. Riders need to be able to recognise and correct canter leads, which can be much more challenging during a jumping session than during flatwork because of the large number of extra things they have to think about. Likewise, by teaching them to adjust the length of the canter strides, they will be better able to feel and adjust the horse between linked fences. This does not need to be done in a technical way; at lower levels simply asking for small amounts of difference will start to increase rider awareness.

Improving timing

Often, as riders develop, they find it challenging to do everything quickly enough and they don't plan ahead enough. For example; after a jump the turn away is poor, they lose energy in the canter and so the next jump loses flow. This is often because the rider focuses on the first fence only and then has to correct each additional mistake rather than preventing them. By designing exercises that have changes of speed and direction in quick succession you can start to encourage them to think more quickly. Using gridwork can help a rider's timing greatly in relation to going with the horse's movement during a jump.

Riding different approaches

If your clients plan to work towards competitions they will need to be prepared to jump fences that are positioned in many different ways. This means that, through your sessions, you need to replicate as many different options as possible: short versus long approaches, fences coming away from the track at sharp angles, related fences on doglegs, limited turning space after fences. Provided you increase the difficulty of these elements progressively, the riders will be well prepared for riding courses successfully.

Some exercises to assist with jumping

1. **Canter leads**

   AIMS AND BENEFITS

   Encourages riders to think and react quickly and increase awareness of canter leads when jumping.

   EQUIPMENT

   Four fences — minimum of four pairs of wings, four pairs of cups and eight poles. (More can be used if you add spreads).

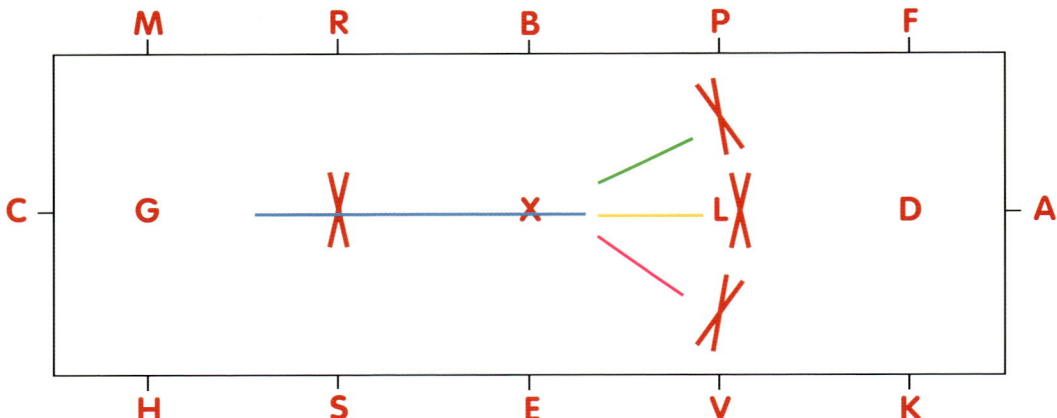

   DESCRIPTION

   Start the exercise on either the left or right rein in canter (use both directions through the session to keep work balanced). Once the rider has established a good jumping canter on the correct lead they can start the exercise turning down the centre of the school from C. They jump the first fence and try to identify which canter lead they have landed on. If they have left canter they then ride to the left-hand fence (green); if they have right canter they ride to the right-hand fence (pink); if unable to tell in time they ride straight to the middle fence (orange). If jumping the left- or right-lead options they should land after the second fence, check for the correct canter lead and correct it if necessary before cantering around the outside of the arena to finish. If jumping the middle fence they should identify their

13 | Towards More Advanced Coaching

canter lead on landing and turn at A according to which lead they are on.

By asking the riders to shout out which lead they are on you can check and verify that they are correct.

DIFFERENTIATION

For less experienced riders the distance between the first fence and the different second fence options needs to be sufficient for them to have time to think before changing direction. This can be shortened to increase difficulty as they improve. Small cross-poles or uprights may be used initially, particularly for the first fence, as you do not want the horses to jump in too big and cover the ground after it too quickly. Again, as experience develops, bigger fences can be used, and spreads or fillers incorporated. More experienced riders can be asked to choose a direction before the exercise starts and then ask the horse to land on the appropriate lead after each fence.

An example of a gridwork exercise in its initial stage where the rider is riding straight through the grid. The jumps at the side will be built up later in the session.

COMMON PROBLEMS

1. Riders can initially find that the time between the fences is not long enough for them to think, process and react. It is important to make things easy at the beginning and help them more at this point.

2. Because of the number of additional things for them to think about, the quality of the turns before and after the fences can deteriorate, so it is important to encourage riders to not forget the basic points.

3. An exercise like this will quickly flag up a rider who does not yet recognise canter leads consistently through their flatwork. You may find, if a rider is not improving through this lesson, taking a step back to work on recognition of canter leads without jumping is needed.

2. Adjusting the canter

AIMS AND BENEFITS

For the rider to be able to recognise consistency of rhythm and be able to adjust the canter to be longer or shorter. There are additional benefits of increasing awareness of distances between related fences and feeling/seeing a good take-off point.

EQUIPMENT

Two fences — minimum two pairs of wings and cups, four poles.

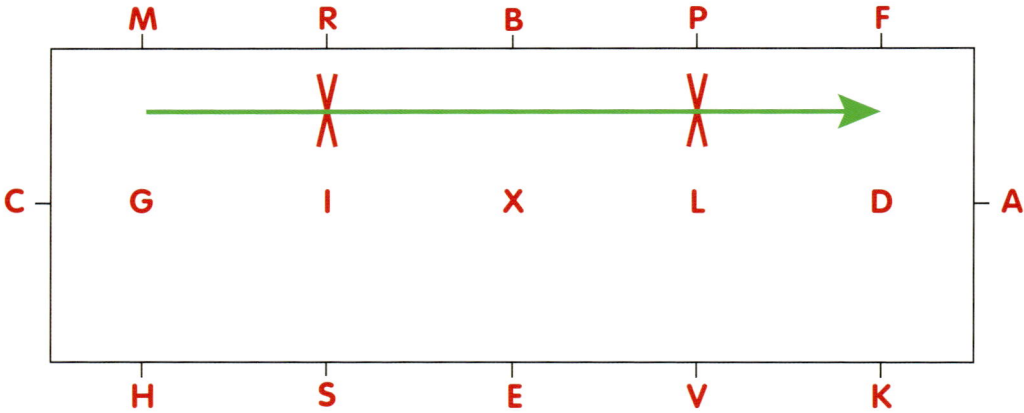

DESCRIPTION

Two related fences are set out on the three-quarter line (but could be other locations), around 6–8 non-jumping strides apart. The exercise can be alternated to jump from either direction provided that ground-lines are used correctly. The exercise can be built progressively starting with ground poles if required. Riders should establish a good working canter before riding down over the two fences. They should count the strides between the fences (can be out loud) to establish a regular number. They should then be asked to repeat this to check that they can maintain the rhythm consistently.

Moving on, they can be asked to ride a shorter (but still energised) canter and add an extra non-jumping stride between the fences. Similarly, to ride a longer (but not flat) canter and remove a non-jumping stride between the fences. Work away from the actual jumping needs to be completed to help riders develop the shorter and longer canter.

DIFFERENTIATION

For less experienced riders, ground-poles and low fences are most suitable. With more experienced riders, fences can be raised, spreads or fillers used and other tasks linked to the start and/or end of the exercise — for example, riding sections of smaller and bigger canter between specified markers round the arena before and after the exercise.

COMMON PROBLEMS

1. Riders losing the quality of the canter when trying for smaller or bigger strides. You need to be vigilant and may need to return to basic flatwork to help improve this before re-attempting the exercise.

2. Riders may struggle with the starting point of maintaining the same number of strides between the two fences each time. Ask them to practise by choosing two markers round the arena and concentrating on the non-jumping canter strides.

3. **Maintaining rhythm (clock)**

    AIMS AND BENEFITS

    Helps riders to establish and maintain rhythm combined with riding a correct circle.

    EQUIPMENT

    Four fences — minimum four pairs of wings and cups, eight poles.

    DESCRIPTION

    The exercise should be started with four ground poles at the quarter points of a circle. With less experienced riders the circle should be kept as large as possible; even with experienced riders the circle is best kept at a minimum of 20m. The work can begin in trot to allow riders to establish the shape of the circle and prepare themselves for what will come. Move them on to canter, establishing a good-quality canter outside of the exercise

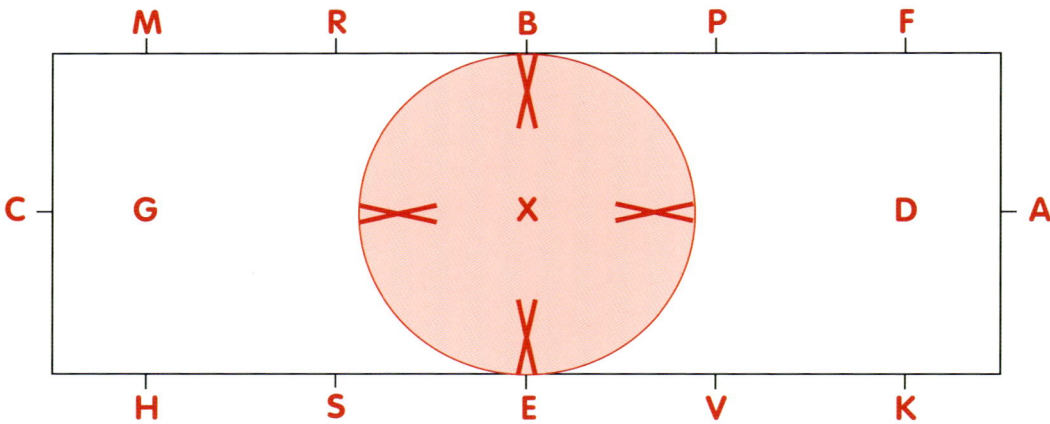

and then, when ready, a rider can turn on to the circle. The exercise can be developed progressively by building one fence initially, then building the opposite one, before adding the final two. The exercise should be completed in both directions to keep balance and you need to allow riders several circles to get into the flow before leaving the exercise.

DIFFERENTIATION

With less experienced riders you may not progress to four fences or, if you do, they should be very low ones. For more advanced riders, this exercise could be combined with concepts from the previous exercise where the canter is shortened and more strides are added, helping them to jump in a very controlled way. Also, in a way similar to previous exercises you can add difficulty by linking it with other school movements and transitions.

COMMON PROBLEMS

This is a deceptively challenging exercise as there are many factors for the rider to manage. Much can be gained by keeping it simple, so do not be tempted to make it too challenging too early.

1. Circle shape not being even, so the horse falls out or in, making it hard for the rider to maintain rhythm. Make sure enough time is spent establishing a good circle at the start. As fences are added it will become harder for the rider to maintain a good circle, as often the horse moves more energetically. Do not be afraid to be very slow in the progression of difficulty. Keep it interesting by alternating direction and adding work outside of the exercise.

2. Riders do not have a rhythm established before turning into the exercise. If they do not

get this right before starting then it will be extremely challenging for them. Ask them to count strides between pairs of markers round the outside of the school to check that they are maintaining a good rhythm.

3. Riders land after a fence and the curve to the next one bulges out because of them not thinking ahead. Make sure they are riding one fence ahead; looking to the next and planning the turn, using outside aids to guide the horse. They need to return to an upright position on landing to be able to influence the horse easily.

4. **Jumping on an angle**

   AIMS AND BENEFITS

   If riders plan to compete they will need to be able to jump on an angle during a showjumping jump-off or when riding cross-country courses. It teaches accuracy and ensures that they have the horse truly focused, between leg and hand.

   EQUIPMENT

   Two fences — minimum two pairs of wings and cups, four poles.

   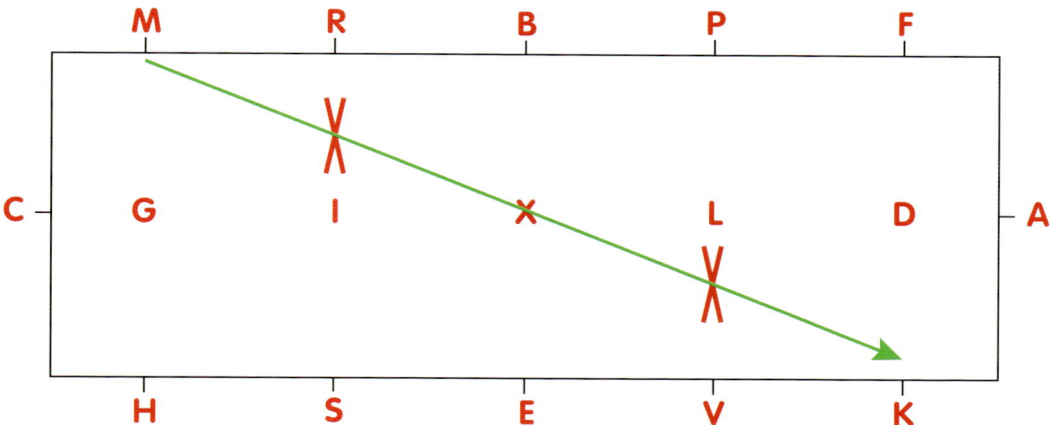

   DESCRIPTION

   The exercise builds up to jumping two related fences on a diagonal line where each one is jumped on an angle. To begin with, a single ground-pole can be used to introduce concepts. Ask the rider to ride a straight approach and then an angled approach from both left and right. They should still aim for the centre of the fence and ride straight and rhythmical approaches and get-aways. This can then be progressed from a ground-pole to a single fence, before adding the second one. When adding the second element start with a ground-pole so they are riding a fence to a ground-pole to allow them to understand progressively what they must do.

DIFFERENTIATION

When first using this type of work, keep the angles of approach gentle, as the steeper the angle the more chance there is of the horse misunderstanding and running out. As the rider develops confidence, the angles can be increased, the length of approach shortened and height/difficulty of the fences increased. A test for a more experienced rider is to have the two fences set up as a double.

COMMON PROBLEMS

1. Rider not having their horse between leg and hand, so the horse runs out rather than jumping. Make riders aware of this possibility (without making them feel negative), and discuss how they can prevent it.

2. It can feel quite alien for riders, as up to this point they will have been drilled to always ride straight to a fence. By taking things slowly and evaluating each rider's needs you can ensure that they can embrace this new challenge.

Gridwork

There are many reasons why grids may be used as part of training a rider to jump. The real benefit is that, through setting up a combination of fences and poles, a schooled horse should be helped to jump consistently and take off and land in a predictable way, provided they are ridden forward from the leg. This makes things somewhat easier for the rider, allowing the focus to be on them developing skills such as:

- Maintaining a good rhythm.

- Keeping sufficient energy in the gait.

- Feel for seeing a stride/recognising where the take-off point is.

- Timing and coordination.

- Fold and position during jumps (including suppleness).

- Confidence — often riders will happily jump a bigger fence at the end of a grid because it is being set up for them.

Aside from the rider, gridwork has many benefits when educating a less-experienced horse. It:

- Improves suppleness and athleticism.

- Improves reaction speed.

- Can help improve technique.

- Can help regulate the speed of a horse who rushes.

There are infinite combinations of poles and fence constructions with which to build a grid, and what you use depends on the desired outcome. Make sure you use a grid wisely and really consider how it will help (or not). Distances should be chosen in the same way as for building simple combinations and be appropriate for the horse's stride length (see table over the page).

Note that a grid built with poor distances may work against you and damage a rider's confidence and feel. It is not a good idea to try to use grids with groups of very different horses and ponies. In general, if using a trot approach or working with less experienced/less confident riders distances will need to be shortened slightly, as they are less likely to be

The different types of grid you could create are infinite; poles can also be used within grids.

travelling forwards well (evaluate each horse/rider individually). You must also be careful about the use of trot or canter poles on the way into the grid; if a horse trips or stumbles it can be almost impossible for them to complete the grid without further mishap. If you do wish to use poles at the front of the grid then leave a couple of non-jumping strides after them before the first element of the grid to allow recovery time if needed. In general with less experienced riders, less is more — remember if they lose balance early on then every subsequent jump may make the situation worse. Better that they have sufficient time between jumps to recover.

Some examples of grids to suit different riders

Novice rider who needs to develop feel for take-off spot and improve fold over fences.

You ideally want to keep the grid simple and make sure that the rider does not have to think about much other than moving with the horse and folding well. A grid that is progressively built to have three simple jumps with one or two strides between each would be sufficient. By coming from a trot approach with a placing pole before the first fence they should naturally meet it on a good stride, allowing them to think about moving with the horse as they take off. If they allow the horse to canter away from the first fence the second and then third should be jumped easily and in a predictable way. Add one element at a time once the first has been ridden well. You can progressively raise the height (within reason) and possibly add a spread pole to the last fence at the end of the session. Hopefully, the rider will leave the session feeling more confident and in better balance with the horse.

More experienced rider who needs to improve their reaction speed and suppleness.

In this case you can use a more complex grid (provided it is built progressively) in order to challenge the rider a little and encourage them to react faster. You may use a series of bounce fences followed by another one or two fences one non-jumping stride apart. The last elements could be a little bigger, and could include a spread. The bounces encourage quick reactions and, by following it with a larger or more challenging single fence, the rider is incentivised to keep their focus. The grid should still be built progressively to ensure confident development, but perhaps less time needs to be spent consolidating each new combination. A placing pole may still be useful on the way in to help the rider start in good form; either a trot or canter approach could be used depending on the individual horse/rider.

Table of distances and striding

Jump distances can be measured in feet or metres. An average human stride is approximately one yard (1yd) which is 3ft.

	Pony		Cob/small horse		Competition/large horse	
Trot poles	1.22m	4ft	1.37m	4ft 6in	1.52m	5ft
Trot place pole	2.44m	8ft	2.74m	9ft	3.05m	10ft
Canter place pole	2.44–2.74m	8–9ft	2.74–3.05m	9–10ft	3.05–3.66m	10–12ft
Bounce	2.74m	9ft	3.05–3.35m	10–11ft	3.66m	12ft
Upright to upright — one non-jumping stride.	6.40m	21ft	6.70–7.00m	22–23ft	7.32–8.08m	24–26½ft (max)
Spread to upright	6.10m	20ft	6.40–6.70m	21–22ft	7.00–7.32m	23–24ft
Upright to spread	As above					
Trot approach deduct 2–3ft (85–95cms) from all distances						
Upright to upright on two non-jumping strides	9.60m	10½yds	10.00m	11yds	11.00m	12yds
Spread to upright	9.14m	10yds	9.45–9.75m	10–10½yds	10.00–10.40m	11–11⅓yds
Upright to spread	As above					
Trot approach deduct 2–3ft (85–95cms) from all distances						
Related on three non-jumping	12.80m	14yd	13.76m	15yd	14.63m	16yd
Related on four non-jumping	16.46m	18yd	17.37m	19yd	18.29m	20yd
Related on five non-jumping	19.20m	21yd	20.57m	22½yd	21.95m	24yd

Related distances — walk total number of human strides (1yd each), deduct between 3 (pony) and 4 for landing and take-off combined, divide remainder by 4 for competition distance (for school ponies divide by 3), to get number of strides.

One human stride will measure about 1yd (3ft): 0.91m

Introducing cross-country

Cross-country is, for many riders, the most exciting part of riding and the temptation to get going can be huge. As a coach you have always to remember the risks associated with cross-country and never underestimate the importance of a rider being suitably prepared. Riders attempting more than they are ready for account for a large number of falls and accidents; it is your role to guide and help them be ready. Similarly, it is easy for a coach to get swept away in the excitement and push riders faster than is sensible. In order to be a good cross-country coach you can develop your own practice as follows:

1. Spend more time developing your own skills riding cross-country; the more first-hand experience you have, the more you can pass on to your clients. Try to ride many different horses and work with a variety of coaches to build up your own knowledge bank.

2. A fantastic way to develop is to shadow some experienced coaches; try to partner up with those who have ridden successfully at a high level and/or have high-level coaching qualifications/accreditation. It is ideal to shadow someone at least one or two levels higher than yourself. Go and watch them teach, make notes and ask questions. Think about what they do and what they don't do; why didn't they choose an exercise or obstacle that you would have chosen? It is important to spend time watching them teach the level of rider that you are planning to work with; this way you can gain valuable insight into the safest way to coach and how to help riders progress in the most effective way.

Safety

Make sure that any rider you coach has the correct PPE, including a current safety standard body protector. Take time to learn how these should fit and check them; a badly fitting body protector can actually do damage in the event of a fall. Poor fit of body protectors is common with children because of the expense of this equipment and parents trying to maximise their use with growing children. As for any riding session, the hat must be to current standards and fit correctly; for cross-country the hat should not have a fixed peak. Many riders now wear air jackets for cross-country; these do not replace the need for a body protector but if the client so wishes they can be worn over the top of one.

Horses may find it harder to balance under some conditions on grass, so evaluate the need for studs dependent on what the horse is used to wearing. If a horse does wear studs, they may benefit from a stud girth, depending on their action when jumping. Brushing or event boots are a sensible precaution to minimise injury to the lower limb from solid obstacles. They must fit well and any Velcro should be in good repair — a loose boot while galloping could be a serious hazard. Because of the extra movement the horse may make over different terrain and during jumping efforts, a breastplate or girth is a sensible addition. When teaching inexperienced

13 | Towards More Advanced Coaching

A horse and rider suitably prepared for cross-country.

riders, a neckstrap is a highly valuable piece of tack. A saddle that is a more forward-cut than normal will be very helpful for the rider, as will one with a lower cantle; both of these features allow the rider to move without hindrance.

Never teach cross-country over obstacles that are not in good repair, or are poorly designed. Make sure the course you are using has been professionally built, meets current safety recommendations, and that the venue has appropriate insurance. Any portable fences must have been secured correctly following current British Eventing guidelines. The ground conditions are so important, as changes can alter the question you are asking the horse and rider radically. Even if you have used a course regularly you should walk and visually inspect each obstacle and the take-off and landing areas around them, this allows you to report any problems if necessary and coach your clients effectively.

Introducing position and improving balance

Riders must learn to adapt their position to allow the horse to gallop underneath them efficiently, and be able to adjust it over different terrain and obstacles. This means adopting a light seat position where weight is taken through the lower legs and feet and the upper body stays up off the horse's back. The rider will need to be able to maintain this position for significant periods of time. This requires suppleness, balance and physical fitness. To be able to balance with ease, the stirrup leathers need to be shortened from a normal jumping length so that the angles at the knee and hip can become more acute, allowing the rider to keep their legs stable underneath them and use the joints as shock-absorbers. Although out of the saddle the rider must stay close to it and, in order to remain in balance with the horse's centre of gravity, lower their shoulders a little while simultaneously letting their seat move backwards.

Time spent on the flat helping the rider establish this position and getting used to controlling the horse's direction, speed and quality of gait are essential to success at cross-country. Not only does the rider need to be able to sustain this position; they also need to be able to quickly and easily switch from it, to a slightly more upright position (but still with the seat off the saddle) and back to an upright, sitting position, more like when approaching a showjump. To help the rider to develop this during flat lessons, include a variety of school movements and transitions alternating between each of these positions.

Once the basic position is established you will need to introduce transitions within the canter; the ability to lengthen and shorten the canter is essential in order to cope with different terrain and more technical obstacles. This initial positional work can be started in the arena but the rider then needs to be introduced to the adjustments required going up and down hill on grass, where their centre of gravity needs to move a little forward and backward respectively.

Introducing riding at a cross-country speed

If riders have only ridden and jumped in an arena until this point in their training, then it is likely that their understanding of riding at a more forward speed is limited. Most often they will feel they are moving faster than they actually are — however, there are some individuals who think that cross-country is meant to be ridden flat out! The coach's job is to help them find different 'gears' within the canter and gallop, while always aiming for rhythm and balance. During early sessions encourage them to increase or decrease the speed and maintain the new speed for long enough to establish a consistent rhythm, while remaining in the light seat position. When they are increasing speed, take care not to encourage sudden acceleration, but instead help them to keep the horse balanced and responsive to the aids. A great skill to develop, even during the early cross-country sessions, is for the rider to use their body position and weight to influence the horse's speed; if they can learn to slow the horse down with little effort it will build their confidence hugely.

Once the basic position and feel for adjusting speed are established it is time to start jumping.

Introducing simple simulated jumps in the arena

The arena is a great place to do the early preparatory work as described above and allows you to get riders going when you don't have access to an outdoor schooling area (although there will be limitations, depending on the size of the arena). Similarly, it is very useful to introduce both riders and horses to more technical obstacles in a situation where these can be built progressively and using collapsible equipment. There are many things that can be done in the arena; the following are some ideas of session topics that work well, and with a little imagination much can be achieved.

Simulated cross-country in an arena is useful for introducing riders to more technical types of cross-country fences. Introducing these in this way provides an opportunity to build up the fences progressively.

Introducing narrow/skinny fences

Narrow or 'skinny' fences are a common element in cross-country course. These are of varying widths and degree of technicality, dependent on slope and related obstacles. They can be introduced easily on the arena and the skills developed will enhance the general jumping ability of both riders and horses. As with any exercise, this should be done progressively, increasing in difficulty at a rate that suits the horse/rider in front of you.

Start by building a fence with shorter than normal poles, but still with full-size wings to give a frame and draw the horse towards it. Make sure it has a clear ground-line (a simple filler works well), to help the horse understand the question being asked. You can also add V-poles on either side of the fence to give some extra direction for the rider and horse at the beginning; these can be used with the pole end next to the fence at the same height as the fence itself. These extra guides will hopefully mean that there is little chance of a run-out or stop during the early attempts, allowing the rider to focus on their coordination and the quality of the horse's way of going.

When introducing narrow fences its best to start with full wings to provide a frame, so the horse is drawn to the centre of the fence.

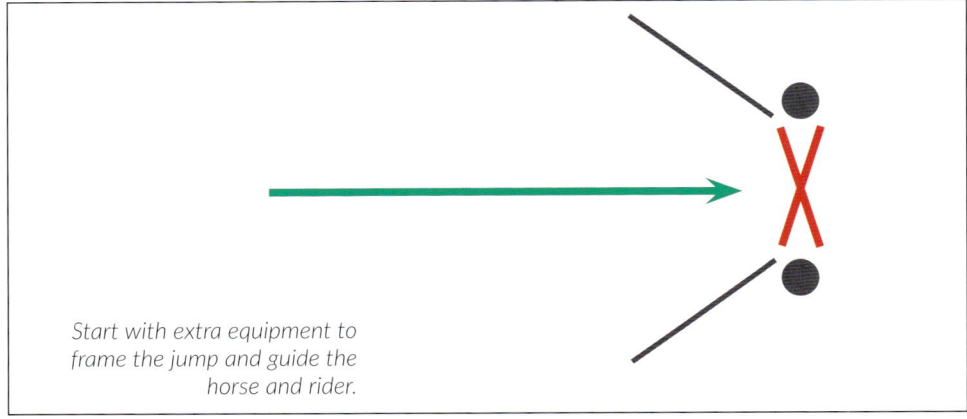

Start with extra equipment to frame the jump and guide the horse and rider.

If the fence is left low to start with, then an approach from trot can allow the rider a little more directional control immediately before the jump — speed can be the enemy with technical fences. Once the rider feels confident and is negotiating the fence in good form, replicate from canter. Next it is a case of progressively removing the guide poles (laying them on the floor first), one side at a time, raising the fence a little and jumping it from both directions. To increase the challenge build the jump up further (or add a second one) using low blocks to support the poles, so that the rider has to have the horse completely focused. Another way to develop this exercise would be to alter the length and angle of approach, and link it to other fences.

Introducing corners

Many of the skills learned in tackling narrow fences can also be applied to jumping a corner. Corners should be jumped by choosing a line of approach that means that the front and back edges are jumped on an angle, but the horse and rider are square on to the centre of the fence (see diagram below). Previous schooling over showjumps from angled approaches will be beneficial for helping the rider to approach a corner confidently. The rider should present the horse toward the narrower end of the corner to avoid an overly wide jumping effort; this means that precision and accuracy are necessary to prevent the horse from running out. If a rider can jump fences on the angle, and narrow ones, then riding a corner should be straightforward.

Plan your session progressively, starting with a low fence that is not very wide. Use a guide pole on the narrow side of the fence (in a similar way to a V-pole on a skinny), and a cone or block can be positioned in front of the wide end to give the rider some visual cues to find the right take-off spot. Once the rider has established confidence these props can be removed, the jump heightened and widened. You could consider using fillers on both sides to give a more solid appearance to the jump.

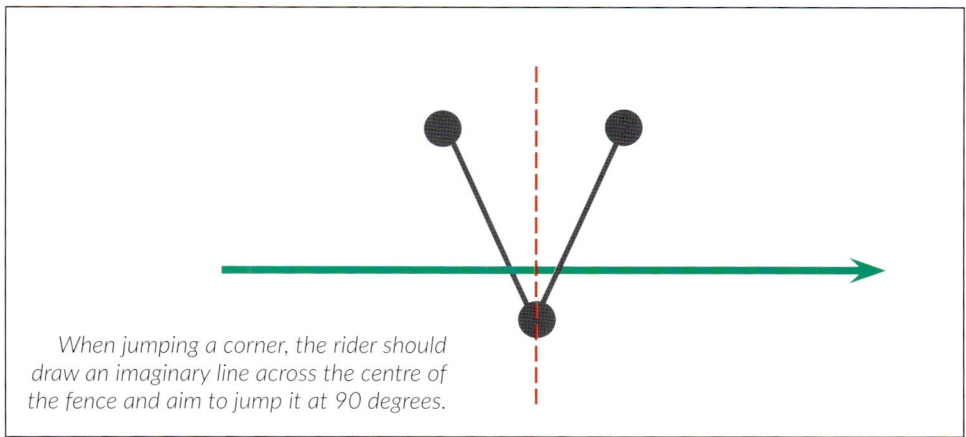

When jumping a corner, the rider should draw an imaginary line across the centre of the fence and aim to jump it at 90 degrees.

Introducing ditches (using water trays)

Clearly you can't dig a ditch in an arena in the middle of a session — however, you can use poles, planks or narrow water trays to replicate one. Whatever you use, make sure safety is considered — you must not use anything likely to be tripped over or stood on.

Water trays can be used in the school to simulate a ditch; this rider is jumping the water tray on its own before a pole is added.

When riders first learn to jump they are unlikely to be asked to jump anything that has no height above the ground surface. Over a ditch, a horse tends to jump forward and out rather than up as would be expected over a regular fence; also they may lower their head and neck to look at the ditch before take-off. These alterations to the horse's jumping technique mean that the rider's balance must be considered.

Once you have built a suitable simulated ditch, start the rider from a trot approach before progressing to canter. Focus should be on the rider giving the horse confidence through positive riding, combined with looking up and forward and keeping their upper body upright until the horse takes off. Often with ditches, on take-off the rider remains a little behind the movement with their upper body, but allows the horse to stretch in front by releasing their shoulders and hands. This position allows the rider to remain safe if the horse does stop or jumps hesitantly.

Once the ditch has been successfully mastered it can be combined with other obstacles, for example, upright fence, two non-jumping strides, ditch, two non-jumping strides, upright fence.

It is important when introducing ditches to the rider that the horse they are partnered with has some experience. For horses new to ditches it can be a confusing question and can take time and patience to instil confidence — clearly this will not help a novice rider. A lead horse can be a good way to help an inexperienced horse understand what is being asked of them.

This rider is walking her horse up to the ditch, so the horse can look at it before they attempt to jump it. It is often a good idea to use an experienced lead horse when introducing a less experienced horse to new types of obstacle.

Introducing simple obstacles outside

When you are able to take riders out to jump on grass, all the concepts described above should be remembered. Start off with simple obstacles such as roll tops or logs, helping riders to establish rhythm, balance and the ability to jump from a forward gait. The simulated fences discussed previously should be tackled in a similar way when encountered on grass. Be progressive in your approach, in order to build confidence and consolidate skills. There are some aspects which it is not possible to teach in a simulated fashion, so these will be new at this stage.

Steps. Provided the rider has sufficiently developed impulsion within the gait, steps up are fairly easy to introduce. However, drops or steps down require alteration of the rider's balance. Start with very small ones so you can allow the rider to feel what happens and adapt to remaining upright on take-off and letting their upper body move backwards and lower legs forwards as the horse steps down. They also will need to be taught to 'slip' their reins to allow the horse to balance on landing. This new position can be very alien for the rider, and it is easy for them to get thrown around if they do not maintain core stability and move athletically with the horse. Keep practising over small drops until they are really comfortable, so as to avoid denting their confidence.

Jumps uphill and downhill. The key is helping the rider to understand about impulsion and balance. Jumping uphill requires a lot of power and bounce in the canter; practising cantering up inclines will allow the rider to feel how the energy of the gait decreases naturally if efforts are not made to sustain it. Jumping downhill builds on the concepts learnt over drops; the rider needs to learn to stay with the horse and allow them to stretch in front, but keep their body position sufficiently upright so as not to unbalance the horse on landing.

When going down a drop the rider will need to alter their position. Encourage the rider to maintain an upright position and secure lower leg; they will also need to 'slip' the reins.

Start introducing riders and horses to water by asking them first to walk in and out of the water before trotting and then cantering.

Water. Provided the horse is comfortable with water obstacles then they should pose no great challenge to the rider. The main element riders need to learn to deal with is how water can slow the horse down on entry. Provided they keep the forward movement controlled between leg and hand and their body upright and close to the saddle they will remain secure. Start by introducing simply riding in and back out of water in walk, trot, then canter. Once the concept has been grasped small steps in and out can be introduced using the same techniques as for steps on dry land. For inexperienced horses, using a lead horse initially can be invaluable. When moving on to jumps into water, remember that the horse may be startled just before take-off when they see the water on landing. It is therefore important that the rider does not get in front of the movement, so is in a good position to give the horse confidence.

Summary — managing and developing your coaching practice

Developing your coaching philosophy

Your philosophy will have a direct impact on your behaviour as a coach. Every element of coaching is affected by our personal beliefs — they affect how we see the world, what actions we take and why we take them (the what, why and how of coaching). Your beliefs are your set of principles that guide your practice as a coach — why you coach as you do.

Developing a philosophy allows both coach and student to have a base from which to build and learn according to a consistent, coherent way of thinking. A philosophy provides boundaries within which the coach-participant relationship can be formed.

Remember that, as a coach, you are in a position of authority and, as such, your opinions will often be taken as fact by others around you.

You must be prepared to be flexible and adapt to changing circumstances. Your coaching philosophy should be a guiding tool to your actions as a coach, but you should see these as principles rather than rules, so you can manage any dilemmas that may arise between philosophy and practice.

Your responsibilities as a coach

Riding contributes to people's development, not only physically, but also socially and emotionally. To ensure that this is a positive experience for your students, you must operate within accepted ethical frameworks.

You are responsible for conducting yourself and any services you provide according to professional and ethical standards. You will also be responsible for promoting the interests and protecting the rights of your students, the equine industry and the British Horse Society.

You need to consider:

- Risk assessing.

- Strategies and coaching methods to prevent injury.

- Child protection procedures.

- Ethical and legal guidelines regarding the use (and misuse) of drugs.

- You need to be aware of the legal responsibilities you hold as a coach, especially concerning the advice you give to your participants and the way you organise and supervise your coaching sessions.

- As a coach you should give advice and guidance to your participants, but you should not offer advice beyond your level of qualification. If things go wrong (for example an accident or injury occurs) you may find yourself being blamed and your coaching practice will be scrutinised.

- You should also ensure that you have adequate insurance cover.

The British Horse Society Accredited Professional Community incorporates all of the above requirements and is recommended for anyone coaching in the equestrian industry.

What is an Accredited Professional?

An Accredited Professional meets the highest professional standards within the industry and is approved and accredited by the British Horse Society. As the largest professional body representing equestrian coaches globally, Accredited Professionals set the benchmark for the equine industry.

The Accredited Professional Community membership promotes a professional coaching and grooms community by connecting people, ideas and resources to embed world-class standards, drive continual professional development and promote innovation in equestrian coaching.

Benefits from being an Accredited Professional include:

- Exclusive access to the online professional community where you can network, share ideas, discuss and gain access to the latest information and guidance.

- Access to an online business toolkit.

- Accredited Professional marketing toolkit including business cards and advertising materials.

- Discounts on Accredited Professional branded clothing.

- Option to deliver BHS recreational courses such as Pony Stars, Ride Safe, Horse Explorers and the Challenge Awards.

- Insurance cover. If you have taken the Accredited Professional Coach Plus package, your membership will include insurance covering you for:

  » £10,000,000 public liability insurance.

  » £100,000 personal accident cover.

  » Grooms' insurance.

  » Care, custody and control.

- Inclusive BHS Safeguarding and First Aid courses.

- Discounts on BHS assessments.

- Entry to BHS accredited CPD events.

- Support available from Accredited Professional Mentors.

- Opportunity to advertise on the BHS website.

TRAINING TIPS

1. Make a habit of asking your students for feedback after each session.

2. Ask other coaches to observe your sessions.

3. Try recording your coaching sessions on video — it can be very revealing!

Remember — 'If you can't explain it simply, you don't understand it well enough.' — Albert Einstein

What's Next?

What's Next?

Thank you for exploring *Complete Equestrian Volume 3*. We anticipate that any reader completing this volume will now be fully committed to providing the very best for any horse they come across — we wish you good luck on your journey!

This volume is perfect for those seeking to progress their groom and professional rider pathways. If you are seeking to work as an independent groom, it will provide you with the knowledge to care for a number of horses to the highest industry standards. For those looking for a role as a professional rider it provides you with the skills and knowledge to ride and train horses across all three disciplines at a basic level.

Most readers completing this volume will be dedicated to finding a career in the equestrian industry, so we encourage all readers to consider our Career Pathways. The qualifications are structured for the beginner through to the expert and supports you to become a highly-accredited equestrian coach, with the all-round knowledge and skills to empower your clients and the next generation to reach their goals and ambitions.

Becoming a coach with the BHS offers a progressive career, encompassing all elements of equestrianism. It will empower you to stand above the crowd and utilise the widest remit of knowledge and expertise to coach our current and future generations.

You are halfway through your journey and we invite you to continue to develop and progress to Stage 4 and BHSI qualifications to be in reach of the internationally recognised status of Fellow of The British Horse Society. An expert in equitation, horse care and welfare, training and coaching, a Fellow of the BHS is renowned throughout the global equine industry as an ambassador for the equestrian profession and a thought-leader in our sector.

All of our qualifications are reviewed regularly to provide the most up-to-date, robust and high-quality method of exploring candidates' knowledge of riding, horse care and coaching skills, catering for every level from novice owners and beginners through to international experts.

Assessments are available at BHS Approved Centres throughout the majority of the year and are a friendly, supportive introduction to the equestrian industry.

The BHS Education team will be happy to guide you through the assessment structure. Browse our site www.bhs.org.uk/pathways, email education@bhs.org.uk or give the team a call on 02476 840508. Advice, guidelines and a syllabus are available for every level, so you can be confident in what you will be asked to do, and these resources will help you to be sure you are making the right choices — whatever they are!

Good luck!